Socialism

EMILE DURKHEIM

Translated by
CHARLOTTE SATTLER

SOCIALISM

(*Le Socialisme*)

Edited and with an Introduction by
ALVIN W. GOULDNER
Department of Sociology, University of Illinois

From the edition originally edited, and with a
Preface by,
MARCEL MAUSS

COLLIER BOOKS, New York, N.Y.
Collier–Macmillan Ltd., London

Socialism was originally published in English under the title *Socialism and Saint-Simon*

This Collier Books edition is published by arrangement with The Antioch Press

Published simultaneously by Collier-Macmillan Limited, London

Collier Books is a division of The Crowell-Collier Publishing Company

First Collier Books Edition 1962

To the memory of my friend
NATHANIEL CANTOR

Introduction

DURKHEIM'S STUDY OF socialism is a document of exceptional intellectual interest for several reasons. Not the least of these is that it presents us with the now somewhat unusual case of a truly first-rate thinker who had the inclination to contribute to the history of sociological theory and to comment extensively on the work of a key figure in that history, Henri Saint-Simon. The core of this volume contains Durkheim's presentation of Saint-Simon's ideas, their sources and their development.

Indeed, Durkheim so subordinates himself in these pages that we might well wish that he had developed his own critical reactions to Saint-Simon at greater length. This is somewhat unusual in the annals of current sociological scholarship in America, which has tended to leave "mere" exegesis and historical commentary to text book writers, and which sometimes unwittingly fosters the barbaric assumption that books and ideas more than twenty years old are beyond scientific salvation. In contrast to such current preoccupations with the modern, it is noteworthy that at the time Durkheim (1858-1917) wrote these lectures on socialism and Saint-Simon (1760-1825), the latter was dead some seventy years.

In some quarters a concern for the history of sociological theory is now regarded as misguided. Of course, it is easy to understand how the usual trite chronicle of thinkers and ideas could foster such a disillusioned appraisal. Yet this dim view of the history of sociological theory may be prematurely pessimistic about earlier theory and unduly optimistic about the state of current theory.

Though current theoretical accomplishments in sociology are frequently substantial and occasionally brilliant, nothing is to be gained by short-circuiting this discipline's sense of historical continuity. We may, of course, burnish our generation's attainments by neglecting the earlier sources from which they derive. But such a rupture of historical continuity may well undermine even our own generation's accomplishments. For it may set a precedent, disposing later scholars to turn their back on our work.

There is, it would seem, some inconsistency between the sociologist's growing recognition of the importance of deliberately cultivated theoretical continuity—as a methodological imperative—and a growing tendency to neglect the earlier contributors to sociological theory. An awareness of the historical development of sociology, of its past as well as its present state, is the only firm basis for evaluating whether we have "progressed," and, if so, how much and in what ways. Alfred North Whitehead has said that "a science which hesitates to forget its founders is lost." But to forget something, one must have known it in the first place. A science *ignorant* of its founders does not know how far it has travelled nor in what direction; it, too, is lost.

There is one basic justification for a social scientist's neglect of the history of his discipline: he must demonstrate that current theory and research have substantially assimilated the problems and perspectives formulated by the earlier thinkers. Failing in this, he must demonstrate that these earlier problems and perspectives are no longer to be regarded as a proper concern of his discipline.[1]

[1] To obviate possible misunderstandings, let me stress that I am in no way suggesting that a distinction between the history of sociological theory and current theory be obliterated. I concur entirely in Robert Merton's judgement that "although the history and the systematics of sociological theory should both be of concern in training sociologists, this is no reason for merging and confusing the two." R. K. Merton, *Social Theory and Social Structure,* Free Press, rev. ed., 1957, p. 5. I believe, too, that I am also cognizant of the extent to which earlier theories are larded with false starts, archaic doctrines, and fruitless errors. I more than doubt, however, that present systematic sociological theory has come anywhere near assimilating the still viable parts of early theory. Moreover, I am not confident that *current* theory has a smaller proportion of false starts, archaic doctrines, and fruitless errors. If this is true, then these same deficiencies in earlier theories cannot justify their neglect. The decisive question

Since Durkheim's time, however, academic sociologists have increasingly neglected some of the central social problems of our time. (Your editor is no exception to this statement.) For example, there are few sociological researches into the sources, growth, and diffusion of modern socialism, however numerous studies of the Soviet Union have become. While there have been careful studies of various marginal sects and cults, there are few detailed sociological analyses of a socialist or communist party.

Related to this lacuna, is the common neglect of property institutions by sociologists, apparently on the assumption that this is the economist's job alone. If this is reasonable, however, one wonders why sociologists have not also left studies of industrial relations to economists, and studies of political parties and elections to political scientists. Furthermore, since the decline of the "culture lag" school, which for a period flourished at the University of Chicago, there has been little systematic analysis of the role of modern science and technology,[2] and these institutions now find

is, of course, whether there is reason to believe that there is still something scientifically promising in the early work. By far the best indication that there is, can be found in the work of two of the most creative of contemporary sociological theorists, Robert Merton and Talcott Parsons. In the case of Parsons there can be little doubt that his immersal in the earlier theorists, as evidenced by his *Structure of Social Action*, provided an indispensable basis for his own systematic theory. More specifically, as Parsons himself has explicitly acknowledged, his "pattern variables" schema is a direct outgrowth of his work on Ferdinand Tonnies' theory of Gemeinschaft and Gesellschaft. See T. Parsons and N. J. Smelser, *Economy and Society*, Free Press, 1956, p. 33. One may similarly note the extremely fruitful uses to which Robert K. Merton has put such classic theorists as C. H. Cooley, H. Spencer, W. G. Sumner, and, above all, G. Simmel, in his recent essay on "Continuities in the Theory of Reference Groups and Social Structure," *Ibid.*, pp. 281-386.

[2] That the exceptions to be found in the work of Bernard Barber, W. F. Cottrell, Gerard de Gré, and Robert Merton are notable, does not make them any the less exceptions. Note the similar discussion by Robert Merton concerning current deficiencies in the sociological study of science in his "Priorities in Scientific Discovery," *American Sociological Review*, Dec. 1957, p. 635.

only a peripheral place in the sociological theories current today. Finally, although there are numerous sociological studies of family discord and even some of industrial tensions, there are few sociological studies of international relations, of war and peace.[3]

Durkheim's study of socialism and Saint-Simon assumes importance today precisely because, at various points, it considers all of these major questions and, in some measure, does so in their interrelationship to each other. Because it has something to say about these problems, it may be expected that educated laymen as well as professional sociologists will find much of interest in these pages.

One way in which this study is of peculiar value to sociologists, and others interested in the development of sociological theory, is that it provides us with a basis for a fuller understanding of Durkheim's own contribution as a sociologist, producing greater clarity concerning some of the intellectual forces which shaped it, and, in particular, of its links to Saint-Simon, to the latter's disciple, Auguste Comte, and to Karl Marx. Some recent analyses of Durkheim's work have viewed it too much in terms of what it presumably became, and too little in terms of what it came from. There has also been a tendency to over-emphasize Durkheim's Comteian heritage and the influence which this had upon him,[4] to the neglect of other influences.

[3] I have, previously, had occasion to examine a set of twenty-five text books in introductory sociology, published between 1945-1954, to determine what they had to say about the causes and effects of war. I found that in the 17,000 pages which these volumes contained, there were only some 275 pages which dealt with war in any of its manifestations. More than half of the texts dealt with this single most important problem of the modern world in less than 10 pages.

[4] Such an overemphasis is to be found, I believe, in Parsons' interpretation of Durkheim. For example, "Insofar as any influence is needed to account for his [Durkheim's] ideas, the most important one is certainly to be found in a source which is both authentically French and authentically positivistic—Auguste Comte, who was Durkheim's acknowledged master. Durkheim is the spiritual heir of Comte and all the principal elements of his earlier thought are to be found fore-shadowed in Comte's writ-

Without doubt Durkheim's theory and research was much influenced by Comte's. But if Durkheim's work comes out of Comte's, it does not come *only* from this source; if there was continuity between Durkheim and Comte, there was also discontinuity. In Durkheim, we see a man who sometimes found himself constrained to oppose his own intellectual mentor. Durkheim, we may say, was an uneasy Comteian.

One striking demonstration that Durkheim was not simply the devoted disciple of Comte can be seen in this study of socialism. Here, Durkheim firmly denies to Comte, and bestows on Saint-Simon, the "honor" of having founded both positivist philosophy and sociology.[5] It should be clear

---

ings. . . . Every element in his thinking is rooted deeply in the problems immanent in the system of thought of which Comte was so eminent an exponent." Talcott Parsons, *The Structure of Social Action,* McGraw-Hill Co., 1937, p. 307. One might say exactly the same thing about the relationship between Durkheim's and Saint-Simon's thought, and, quite understandably so, since Comte derived practically all of his main ideas from Saint-Simon. (But more on this later.) It is therefore extremely difficult to distinguish between the Saint-Simonian and the Comteian influence on Durkheim.

[5] Despite Durkheim's yeoman-like efforts to dispel the conception that Comte was the "father" of sociology, the belief in "Comte the father" persists, even among sociologists, as an almost indestructible myth. Contemporary sociologists, of course, no longer lend credence to such ebullient fantasies as Chugerman's who held that, ". . . shutting himself in his room for a day and a night, he [Comte] evolved the general conception of social science and the project of the positive philosophy . . ." S. Chugerman, *Lester F. Ward,* Duke University Press, 1939, p. 174. Nonetheless, one still finds fundamentally erroneous statements concerning Comte's significance in relation to Saint-Simon's. N. S. Timasheff, for example, has recently reaffirmed this myth in maintaining that "Auguste Comte . . . was the first major figure to assert and then prove by deed that a science of society, both empiric and theoretical, was possible and desirable." N. S. Timasheff, *Sociological Theory: Its Nature and Growth,* Doubleday and Co., 1955, p. 15. Similarly erroneous judgements are to be found in Jacques Barzun and Henry Graff, *The Modern Researcher,* Harcourt, Brace and Co., 1957, p. 203. Such judgements might have been understandable had they been made prior to 1859,

from this alone that references to Comte as Durkheim's "acknowledged master" are misleadingly simple; they do not portray their relationship in anything like its true complexity. Above all, the usual formula fails to indicate that, in certain pivotal ways, Durkheim's work constituted a deepgoing polemic against Comte. Durkheim's study of *The Division of Labor* has been interpreted as an expression of his opposition to the utilitarian individualists, and particularly Herbert Spencer.[6] In actuality, this volume has an-

---

when Saint-Simon's *Mémoire sur la Science de l'homme*, originally written in 1813, was first published. This essay definitely establishes that Saint-Simon's formulation of positivist philosophy, and of sociology, clearly preceded his association with Comte. This is also borne out by Durkheim, Halévy, Bury and Saint-Simon's recent biographers, Frank Manuel, Mathurin Dondo, and F. M. H. Markham. If the myth of "Comte the founder of sociology" still persists in American sociology, despite long-standing evidence to the contrary, this suggests that it performs certain ongoing social functions for those holding it. There is an interesting problem here for a study in the sociology of knowledge. One hypothesis for such a study might be that acknowledgement of Comte as the putative father of sociology is less professionally damaging than acknowledgement of Saint-Simon who, as Durkheim points out, was also one of the founders of modern socialism. If sociologists acknowledge descent from Saint-Simon rather than Comte they are not only acquiring a father, but a blacksheep brother, socialism, thus reinforcing lay opinions to the effect that socialism and sociology must be similar because they have the same prefix. Needless to say, such an hypothesis would not premise that there is a "plot" afoot to do Saint-Simon out of his rightful heritage! While it may make no difference to the substance of a science concerning who, in fact, its "founding father" was, nonetheless, shared professional *beliefs* concerning this may be significant for a discipline's professional organization and its practitioners' self-images. A "founding father" is a professional symbol which can be treated as a trivial detail by no one who wishes to understand the profession as a social organization. Where there are conflicts, by later generations, concerning who their "founding father" was, we suspect that this may be a serious question essentially reflecting a dispute over the character of the profession.

[6] Parsons notes that Durkheim "directs attention immediately to the moral elements in social life," and that this is indicative of his polemic against Herbert Spencer, the utilitarian individualists,

other polemical target, namely, Comte himself, a fact which comes out forcefully in its culminating chapters.

The Polemic Against Conte

In Comte's view, the increasing division of labor in modern society threatened its social cohesion. For it brought with it "a fatal disposition towards a fundamental dispersion of ideas, sentiments, and interests. . . ."[7] The increasing division of labor was, in this analysis, subversive of social stability because it undermined the fundamental requisite of order, namely, the consensus of moral beliefs. It was one of the basic aims of Durkheim's *Division of Labor* to refute this Comteian view. Durkheim flatly rejected Comte's analysis, holding that it was not the division of labor as such which "normally" induced social disorder.

Durkheim's argument, in effect, hinges on a Saint-Simonian assumption: namely, that with the emergence of the new industrial order new social needs arose and new ways of satisfying old needs were required. Like Saint-Simon's, Durkheim's position was relativistic. The growing division of labor is "natural" in modern society, Durkheim maintains; it normally produces social solidarity. Indeed it produces what he seems to have regarded as a "higher" type of solidarity, an "organic" solidarity. This he contrasted with

---

and the Manchester school of economists. Parsons, *Ibid.*, p. 310. Not only does this neglect consideration of the implications of Durkheim's polemic against Comte, but it also omits consideration of the manner in which Durkheim's stress on the "moral" elements in society is related to his polemic against the socialists. In a review of Durkheim's study of *Suicide*, one of Durkheim's contemporaries, Gaston Richard, makes this clear. See *L'année Sociologique*, 1897, p. 404. Durkheim was engaged on several fronts simultaneously: On the one hand, opposing the socialists and the utilitarian individualist's neglect of moral elements and, on the other, opposing Comte's overstatement of the contemporary significance of moral norms in a society with an advanced division of labor.

[7] As quoted in Durkheim's *The Division of Labor in Society*, tr. G. Simpson, Free Press, 1947, p. 358.

the "mechanical" solidarity of earlier societies which had rested upon shared moral beliefs, or on uniformity in their "collective conscience." Comte, he says, failed to see that the social solidarity produced by the division of labor with its web of interdependence, was gradually being substituted for the earlier solidarity which had rested mainly on shared moral beliefs.

Of course, says Durkheim, modern society requires consensus in moral beliefs. Shared moral beliefs as well as the division of labor, both, contribute to the maintenance of social solidarity. But modern society no longer requires the *same degree* of moral consensus, nor does this consensus entail the same items of belief, necessary for earlier periods. In Durkheim's view, the respective roles of mechanical and organic solidarity were changing. "What is necessary is to give each, at each moment in history, the place that is fitting to it. . . ."[8] The division of labor "more and more tends to become the essential condition of social solidarity."[9] Indeed, "the ideal of human fraternity can be realized only in proportion to the progress of the division of labor."[10] We cannot look to the past as a guide, says Durkheim. In a manner reminiscent of Saint-Simon, who had also held that the division of labor must become the basis of a new morality, Durkheim indicates[11] that contemporary society must develop a new moral code corresponding to changed modern conditions.

It is sometimes suggested that there was an important change in focus in Durkheim's later work, and that he gradually reemphasized and saw new importance in the role of

---

[8] *Ibid.*, p. 398, see also pp. 364 et seq.

[9] *Ibid.*, p. 400.

[10] *Ibid.*, p. 406.

[11] *Ibid.*, p. 401. The role of both the division of labor and of shared moral beliefs as bases of social solidarity are also to be found in Saint-Simon. With respect to the latter, note, as one of many instances cited by Durkheim in the following volume, Saint-Simon's comment in a letter to Chateaubriand: "The similarity of positive moral ideas is the single bond which can unite men into society."

shared beliefs.[12] Whatever the validity of this observation, here, in *The Division of Labor*, his first great work, Durkheim is unmistakably conducting a polemic against Comte *for having overstressed the need for moral consensus in maintaining social stability*. It is certainly not the case that Durkheim neglects the role of shared beliefs in the *Division of Labor*; it is not that he is then unaware of their significance and only later works through to an understanding of them. From the beginning, he was fully aware of the significance which had long since been imputed to shared beliefs by Comte, but he deliberately chose to oppose Comte's estimate of their role in modern society.

Durkheim readily admits that the division of labor presently engenders social tensions. These arise, however, "because all the conditions of organic solidarity [i.e., social solidarity deriving from increased occupational specialization] have not been realized."[13] His position is again fundamentally Saint-Simonian. Saint-Simon had held that social patterns engendering tension do so, either because they are the archaic survivals of earlier conditions which no longer obtain, or are the first growths of a new social system which has not yet matured.[14] It is in both of these ways that Durkheim explains the tensions associated with the increasing division of labor.

He holds, for example, that the new moral rules appropriate to the new division of labor have not yet developed. Because of this, class war and crises of over-production result, for the relations between specialized functions are not yet properly integrated and regulated. Or, again, Durkheim states that the division of labor engenders tensions because people have been forced into occupations at variance with their natural talents. It is not the division of

[12] *Cf.* Parsons' comment that ". . . reversion to mechanical solidarity represents the authentic line of Durkheim's development." *Ibid.*, p. 321.
[13] Durkheim, *Ibid.*, p. 365.
[14] *Cf.* Frank E. Manuel, *The New World of Henri Saint-Simon*, Harvard University Press, 1956, p. 232.

labor as such, but an archaic "forced division of labor" that generates social tensions.

Occupational specializations must be assigned, says Durkheim, in keeping with the natural distribution of talents and not on the basis of hereditary wealth or birth. He does not, however, develop this into a critique of private property, as had the Saint-Simonians, Bazard and Enfantin, in which it was indicated that private ownership of industrial property can inhibit its rational administration and productivity, since those owning factories may not be those who can best administer them.

In his *Division of Labor*, at any rate, Durkheim was not gropingly moving toward an appreciation of shared moral norms; he was, in fact, moving away from Comte's emphasis on their significance in modern society. Durkheim was, also, much more self-consciously aware than Comte of the ways in which *commitment* to certain types of norms might yield forms of social disorganization. For example, in the *Division of Labor* he notes that it is because people in modern society *share* certain conceptions of "justice" that they object to the "forced" division of labor, and to the assignment of roles on the basis of inherited wealth or birth. In his later work on *Suicide*,[15] Durkheim stresses that Protestant norms actually induce a higher rate of suicide. He stresses that normlessness (or anomie) is not the only source of social disorganization or the only stimulant to a high suicide rate. A commitment to Protestant beliefs may also induce a disorganizing "egoism," Durkheim argues. And he regards anomie and egoism as having a close connection, a "peculiar affinity" for each other.

Durkheim makes an interesting point in his discussion of "acute anomie." This, he says, arises during periods of sudden prosperity or depression which rapidly change people's class position. People exposed to such sudden class shifts are prone to suicide, he says, because they are normless. But here "normless" is used in a peculiar sense. It does not mean that people lack norms, but rather that the norms

[15] Emile Durkheim, *Suicide,* tr. J. A. Spaulding and G. Simpson, Free Press, 1951, esp. ch. 2.

which they *do have* no longer correspond to the new class position in which they suddenly find themselves. It is this disparity between their old norms and their new circumstances which induces tension. Thus moral norms play a positive role in *generating* disorganization; they can disrupt social order rather than strengthen it, unless they are in keeping with the changing circumstances of life.[16] Social order does not rest on norms alone, Durkheim is saying here; it depends on the way in which norms are integrated with other conditions.

Similarly, Durkheim maintains that to the extent that people believe in "progress" there will always be a strain toward anomie, involving a perpetually restless dissatisfaction with the *status quo*.[17] A certain amount of anomie is therefore a normal condition in modern society. The "enfeeblement" of the "collective conscience" is an inevitable and normal development in a modern industrial society with an increasing division of labor.

Comte had stressed the need for social consensus, regarding its decline as the principal peril to modern society. Durkheim, however, maintained that *too high* a degree of social cohesion could also induce disorganization. This is clearly expressed in his *Suicide* where he remarks, "If, as we have seen, excessive individuation leads to suicide, insufficient individuation has the same results. When a man has become detached from society, he encounters less resistance to suicide in himself, and he does so likewise when social integration is too strong."[18] Thus a collective conscience which was either too weak *or too strong* could induce social disorganization.

In contrast again with Comte, Durkheim held that a cer-

---

[16] Comte's bitter polemic against the "dogma of unlimited Liberty of Conscience" because it "tends to hinder the uniform establishment of any system of social ideas," apparently misses the point that this "dogma" was, in fact, a *shared moral belief*. Auguste Comte, *System of Positive Polity*, Vol. 4, tr. Richard Congreve, Longmans, Green and Co., 1877, p. 531.

[17] "The entire morality of progress and perfection is thus inseparable from a certain amount of anomy." *Suicide, Ibid.*, p. 364.

[18] *Ibid.*, p. 217.

tain amount of social conflict was normal and natural in modern society. In part, he sees it as the price of modern freedom. In the *Division of Labor,* for example, he makes the point that conflict and competition among individuals was natural. It was the prevention of such conflicts, by the imposition of outmoded arrangements based on inherited wealth and position, that was abnormal. Let natural talents rather than artificial institutions decide the issue, he says.[19]

The contrast of Durkheim's position with Comte's also comes out forcefully in respect to their differing strategies for controlling the divisive effects of the increasing division of labor. Interestingly enough, Comte had held that the dispersing effects of occupational differentiation should be checked by government regulation. This is at variance with Comte's tendency to minimize the role of political intervention and his usual reliance on the "spontaneous" sources of social solidarity. Durkheim takes issue with this proposal and is, in this respect, a more consistent Comteian than Comte himself. The central difficulty of modern society, Durkheim insists, is the lack of social structures mediating between the individual and the state. Comte's solution, he holds, would only compound the atomizing heritage of the French Revolution.

Project for a Corporative Society

In the *Division of Labor,* he never proposes a clear-cut alternative solution to the problem, although the direction which his solution is to take is already manifest there. It is only in the *Suicide* that he proposes a specific remedy for the dispersing effects of the division of labor which he later expands upon in the preface to the second edition of the *Division of Labor.* In this he takes a step beyond and against Comte in maintaining that not only was the state incompetent to control this problem, but so too were the family and religious organizations. None of these could supply the necessary connective tissue in modern society.

What is needed, holds Durkheim, are new kinds of inter-

19 *Division of Labor,* see especially pp. 374, *et seq.*

mediary groups which can regulate the specialized occupational life of modern men. He advances a plan for the development of communal or corporative organization among people working in the same occupations and industries. Men in the same segment of the economy will understand each other's problems well enough to respond to them flexibly. They can establish a viable group life which can exercise effective moral control over all the participants on the basis of intimate knowledge.

These occupational corporations were to be represented in a national assembly, with employers and employees each having separate representation. The number of representatives for each was to be determined by the importance that public opinion assigns to their group. The corporations are to be organized on a national basis, coextensive with the national development of the modern economy. They are to maintain carefully their independence of the state.

Ultimately, however, they will become the basis of political organization and the fundamental political entity. This is notably convergent with Saint-Simon's conception of government in the new positivist-industrial order. In a formula later adopted by Marx, Saint-Simon had expected that government would cease being political in any special sense, and would not involve the coercion of men but the rational administration of things. Territorial and geographic bases of social and political organization will not disappear, claims Durkheim, but will play a less important role in the corporatively organized society. This, too, converges with Saint-Simon's prediction that in modern industrial society loyalties will be less localistic and more cosmopolitan.

Durkheim's rationale for introducing this plan is noteworthy. In a manner at variance with Saint-Simon's, Comte's, and Marx's evolutionism, Durkheim does not claim that the corporative organization of society is already embedded in the evolutionary drift, or that it is inevitably predestined by evolutionary design. Nor does he merely justify his proposal on the grounds that it conforms with certain values which he takes for granted. His position is that historical analysis shows that such corporative organization has been functional in the past and that there are current social needs for which such groups could again be useful. In short, he does not simply describe what it is, nor does he hold that corporative organization "must be"; he maintains that it *can be* instituted, and that if it were it would prove useful in reducing current social disorganization.

The plan is an interesting synthesis of diverse intellectual streams. It is a blend of the Comteian concern for small groups, with their complex and spontaneous bonds of social interaction, together with the Saint-Simonian emphasis on planned associations. It is a "utopian" plan in the sense that no plausible mechanisms are suggested for instituting it. Significantly enough, however, it is presented in a deliberately anti-utopian framework, in that it explicitly eschews any effort to specify particulars. Durkheim's formulations here bear the impress of the Marxian polemic against utopianism; indeed, it seems that Durkheim knew Marx well enough to quote the latter's metaphors freely.[20]

What Durkheim seems to have been attempting was a synthesis of Marxist and Comteian views, a compromise which leads him back to Saint-Simonian formulations which had influenced both Marx and Comte. Above all, Durkheim was here seeking to combine the Comteian focus on regulating moral norms with the Marxian focus on economic institutions. The decisive need today, suggests Durkheim, is to provide a moral regulation not merely of society in general but of the economy in particular. What is needed is a regulation that will correspond to the characteristics of the new *industrialism* which, as Saint-Simon had also forcefully emphasized, Durkheim holds to be the distinctive feature of modern society.

What brings about the exceptional gravity of this state [of anomic normlessness], is the heretofore unknown development that economic functions have experienced for about two centuries. Whereas formerly they played only a secondary role,

20 *Ibid.*, p. 393.

they are now of the first importance. We are far from the time when they were disdainfully abandoned to the inferior classes. In the face of the economic, administrative, military, and religious functions become steadily less important. Only the scientific functions seem to dispute their place, and even science has scarcely any prestige save to the extent that it can serve practical occupations, which are largely economic. That is why it can be said, with some justice, that society is or tends to be essentially industrial.[21]

Durkheim also seems to have regarded his proposal for occupational corporations as consistent with socialist proposals. For even a socialist society, he insists, will require means of morally regulating interpersonal relations and adjusting the activities of different groups to each other. If socialist society is to be stable, it will have to do more than increase productivity and living standards; even elimination of the "forced division of labor" will not suffice; socialism, too, requires a set of regulating moral norms, capable of daily implementation.

To reiterate the main line of Durkheim's argument in *The Division of Labor*: The increasing division of labor is a normal development in modern industrial society. It does not naturally produce social disorganization, but does so only under certain conditions. The two most important of these are, first, where anomie prevails in the economy, that is, where there is a lack of moral norms governing industrial activities or relations. The second is where there is a "forced division of labor," that is, where people are constrained to take up positions in the division of labor at variance with their natural talents.

At this point, Durkheim could have pursued two different directions: He could have focused either on the problem of anomie or on the study of the forced division of labor. If he had pursued the latter he could, for example, have examined the reasons why the hereditary transmission of wealth or position does not disappear and give way to new social arrangements more in keeping with the modern division of labor.

21 *Ibid.*, p. 3.

He does not take this direction at all. This cannot be explained by stating that Durkheim believed that the forced division of labor would naturally wither away in the course of time, and that it therefore required no planned remedy. For he clearly rejects this tack with respect to normlessness or anomie in the economic sphere. In the latter case, he does not count on the "natural" or spontaneous development of new ethical beliefs to provide the required regulation of economic activities; he deliberately proposes a planned solution to the problem, the occupational corporation.

Attention is focused on the problem of anomie, rather than the forced division of labor, because Durkheim was still deeply committed to Comteian assumptions. He still believes that *some* degree of moral consensus is indispensable to social solidarity, either in a capitalist or a socialist society. If, however, he had further developed the problem of the forced division of labor this could only have obscured his differences with the socialists (as well as the utilitarian individualists) whose basic weakness, he maintained, was their neglect of the role of moral norms.

This tack would also, at some point, have constrained Durkheim into a concern with systems of stratification and power relations, in short into a greater convergence with Marxism. This would have made it difficult, if not impossible, for him to continue using the Comteian model of modern society which saw it as basically tending toward order and stability. Unlike Saint-Simon, who had stressed the role of social classes and of class conflict in providing an impetus or resistance to change, Comte had minimized the role of internal class conflicts.

To Durkheim, as to Comte, the basic features of the new society were already in existence—that is, modern industrialism with its rational methods and its increasing division of labor. Consequently, their problem was to develop a new moral order consistent with it, so that it might remain stable and develop in an orderly manner. Their central task was not defined as producing social change so much as facilitating a natural tendency toward social order. Their problem was, in short, that of "fine-tuning" the new industrial regime rather than basically reorganizing it. They saw modern society as young and immature, as an insufficiently developed industrialism. One merely needed to stimulate and gently guide the natural processes of its maturation. In contrast, of course, Marx—who had retained the Saint-Simonian emphasis on social classes and class conflict—did not regard modern society as an adolescent *industrialism* but as a senile *capitalism* which, containing the ripe "seeds of its own destruction," needed to be readied for burial. Expecting that the capitalist would resist his own dismissal, Marx believed that change would not be smooth and orderly, and that therefore modern society possessed deep instabilities.

It is in part because he views modern society in the Comteian manner, as requiring moral rearmament rather than economic reconstruction, that Durkheim focuses on the problem of anomie and proposes the development of occupational corporations to control it. This is partly a supplement to and partly a polemic against the socialist's neglect of the role of moral norms.[22] But even in this, Durkheim's attitude is no longer that of Comte's; he does not seem to view moral reform as necessarily prior to political or economic reform, as Comte had, but rather as corollary or coincident with it.

The question for Durkheim was *how* the needed moral reform was to be obtained. How could the new morality be developed? Saint-Simon and Comte had in part supposed that the new morality would not be developed but would be (indeed, had been) discovered by positive science and sociology. Durkheim, however, is not sanguine about this solution on several grounds. While he continues to believe that social science can ultimately provide a basis for values, and that a scientific ethic will someday be possible, he nonetheless argues that, at this time, science is not suffi-

---

[22] *Cf.* especially Ch. X of this volume. Here the nub of Durkheim's critique of Saint-Simon and socialism is that it provides for no moral restraints on economic aspirations. Durkheim, however, is hard put to cope with Saint-Simon's final work on

ciently advanced to do so. Science could not yet discern the content or the particulars of the new morality. ". . . it is vain to delay by seeking precisely what this law must be, for in the present state of knowledge, our approximation will be clumsy and always open to doubt."[23] The problem is too pressing to wait for the development of a positive or scientific ethic.

The Development of Moral Beliefs

How then could a new morality appropriate to modern circumstances be secured? It would have to be naturally or spontaneously developed, if it could not now be scientifically discovered. But this raises the question as to how, in general, systems of moral beliefs normally and spontaneously arise. For there is no reason to suppose that the spontaneous development of a new morality will differ from the spontaneous development of earlier moralities. The question of values then becomes a thoroughly empirical one. In short, Durkheim is led to a consistently positivistic position about moral beliefs, becoming concerned with the study of the ways in which they actually evolve and devel-

the "New Christianity" in which a morality transcending economic interests is proposed. While Saint-Simon's approach to morality occasionally bears vestiges of Voltaire's "Footman's God," it is clear in this final work that Saint-Simon had emphasized a need for a morality transcending economic objectives. Durkheim's subsequent effort to maintain his original position concerning Saint-Simon's neglect of moral factors is, to my mind, not entirely successful, though it remains a telling criticism of contemporary communism. In the end, it seems as if Durkheim's criticism is not so much directed against Saint-Simon's neglect of moral elements, but, rather, at the latter's failure to spell out the mechanisms by means of which these were to be built into modern group life. In effect, then, his criticism of Saint-Simon is that he was a "utopian," precisely in the Marxist sense, in that he had not worked out mechanisms adequate to the realization of his moral objectives. Marx had held that Saint-Simon was a utopian in that he had not conceived mechanisms to implement socialism's economic objectives. For Durkheim, the problem in part became one of the mechanics of producing a moral change.

[23] *Division of Labor*, p. 31.

op. This knowledge about the *spontaneous* development of values could then be used to further the *planned* development of a morality suitable for modern times.

It is in some part because he becomes growingly interested in the spontaneous development of social norms, the ways in which they emerge and become internalized in the individual, that he comes to focus on the role of educational institutions and of the family. This is also one of the reasons for his study of religion, which is essentially a study of the development of moral beliefs in their most dramatic expression. A central point in most of these studies is his concern with the factors that shape and sustain moral beliefs, and not merely in what *they* sustain. In this, again, Durkheim differs importantly from Comte who was basically concerned about the *consequences* of moral beliefs for social consensus and who had contributed little to an empirical understanding of the social forces fostering their development.

The problem was far from definitively resolved in Durkheim's work. Nonetheless, there is one theme which recurs in his studies. It is, above all, that moral norms grow up around sustained patterns of social interaction. It is clear, even in *The Division of Labor*, that he was beginning to focus on patterns of social interaction, as providing the focus around which moral beliefs emerge and develop.

The trouble was that Durkheim never clearly worked out an explicit analytic distinction between patterns of social interaction, or social structures, and patterns of moral beliefs or sentiments, the "collective conscience." This confusion is especially discernible in his *Suicide*, and particularly in his discussion of types of suicide. For example, the "anomic suicide" is characterized as being both normless and socially detached, that is, he is described in terms of both his moral beliefs (or absence of them) and his social relations. The "egoistic suicide" is held to be burdened by norms calling upon him to take individual responsibility for his own decisions and, also, by being socially isolated from others. Despite this theoretical failure to clearly distinguish between patterns of moral belief and social interaction, Durkheim does break through to a clear solution in his *practical* proposals.

In the final chapter of *Suicide*, for example, he says that the problem of suicide "bears witness . . . to an alarming poverty of morality."[24] We cannot simply "will" the problem out of existence in a utopian way. A people's morality "depends on the grouping and organization of social elements," on the social arrangements which exist. Ways of thinking and acting cannot be changed without "changing the collective existence itself and this cannot be done without modifying its anatomical constitution. By calling the evil of which the abnormal increase in suicide is symptomatic a moral evil, we are far from thinking to reduce it to some superficial ill which may be conjured away by soft words. On the contrary, the change in moral temperament thus betrayed bears witness to a profound change in our social structure. To cure one, therefore, the other must be reformed."[25]

Since the older forms of social organization, the family, the guild, the church, have been weakened or eliminated, new forms of social organization must be erected in their place to stem the tide of anomie. What Durkheim seems to have been assuming, is that patterns of social interaction form the basis upon which moral beliefs spontaneously develop. It is precisely for this reason that he advances as his remedy for moral anarchy in industry the establishment of new modes of social interaction, the occupational corporation. If science cannot yet invent or discover a new morality, then we must use what we know about the spontaneous development of moral beliefs to planfully foster their natural emergence.

Convergences with Marx

In many ways this is a significant convergence with Marx, at least on the level of the working assumptions which they

---

24 *Suicide*, p. 387.
25 *Ibid.*

used in their roles as applied social scientists.[26] For Durkheim was here saying something quite consistent with the
Marxian formula that "social being determines social consciousness."[27] What Durkheim did, however, was to general-
ize the Marxian formula. Instead of focusing mainly, as
Marx usually did, on the manner in which class or economic relations shape patterns of belief, Durkheim holds
that social (not merely economic) relations influence the
development of beliefs.

Durkheim's analysis of religion and religious beliefs[28] also
has important convergences with Marx's, although it is much
more acute and sophisticated than the latter's, particularly
in its analysis of symbolism. For example, Durkheim notes
that in certain primitive societies the totem is the symbol
of the god or godhead; but it is also a symbol or flag of
the particular clan which worships it. The godhead and
the clan are thus symbolically equal to each other. Consequently, concludes Durkheim, religious ideas emerge out of
society.

In contrast with Marx, Durkheim does not deal solely
with the relation between religion and class or work relations in a society. When Durkheim holds society to be the
basis from which religion emerges, he conceives of society
as containing a richer variety of relevant elements: power
relations and economic conditions are included to be sure,
but so, too, are kin and clan groupings as well as ecological
factors. Here, too, he can be regarded as having relativized
Marx's approach to the development of moral beliefs. Durkheim, then, was beginning to bridge the gap between Marxism and Comteianism.

What Durkheim began to see was that moral beliefs had

---

[26] With reference to Durkheim and Marx as applied social sci-
entists, see Alvin W. Gouldner, "Theoretical Requirements of
Applied Social Science," *American Sociological Review*, Vol. 22,
No. 1 Feb., 1957, pp. 92-102.
[27] For a classically Marxian statement of this, see K. Marx and
F. Engels, *The German Ideology*, International Publishers, n.d.
[28] E. Durkheim, *The Elementary Forms of the Religious Life*, tr.
J. W. Swain, Free Press, 1941.

to be treated in a systematically scientific manner, that their emergence and development as well as their contribution to society needed empirical study. He began to see that the problem of values could not be handled in the manner of radical positivism, that is, by postulating that science could, or would ultimately, formulate and validate moral beliefs. Nor could values be coped with in a theological way, by regarding them as divinely given and thus without a developmental history. Both of these positions had placed values beyond scientific study.

But once existent moral beliefs are no longer taken as given, and once they come to be viewed as problems for empirical investigation, then they must inevitably be seen as interconnected with many other elements of social life. Not only are many things contingent upon them, but they are reciprocally contingent upon many other things. Values then come to be regarded as one constituent of society, an important one to be sure, but still only one. Values and moral beliefs are no longer viewed as the sole or key constituent of society.

As Durkheim puts it, in the *Division of Labor*, society is the necessary condition of the moral world. This is almost a complete reversal of the Comteian position that moral consensus is *the* necessary condition of social order. Moreover, Durkheim adds, "society cannot exist if its parts are not solidary, but solidarity is only *one* of the conditions of its existence. There are many others which are no less necessary and *which are not moral.*"[29] (Our emphases.)

The systematic exploitation of these early insights could have only been fatal to the Comteian position. For Comte had assumed that social solidarity was the prime condition for social survival, and he had further assumed that moral consensus was the basis of social solidarity. Durkheim's critique of Comte's stress on moral norms is inhibited, in part, by his simultaneous polemic against the socialists and individualist utilitarians for their neglect of moral norms. But though the critique of Comte is inhibited, it is, nonetheless,

[29] *Division of Labor*, p. 399.

present and important to understand for a proper perspective on Durkheim.

To understand Durkheim's critical orientation to Comte, what needs to be remembered is that, unlike Comte, Durkheim was exposed to the full force of Marxism and to the growing challenge of European socialism. By 1870, the first French labor party had been formed. There was increasing class and industrial conflict in France, culminating in the great Décazeville strike of 1886, the year that Durkheim was drafting *The Division of Labor*. (One year later Durkheim gave the first French university course in sociology.) Durkheim's concern with "solidarity" is probably related in part to the growing cleavages in French society which are reflected in the growth of socialism.

As a matter of fact, Durkheim began his sociological studies by focusing on the question of the relationship between individualism and *socialism*. These studies were interrupted and it was not until 1895, a decade later, that he returns to the study of socialism. Marcel Mauss, one of the intimate group of collaborators that Durkheim gathered around himself, relates in the introduction to this volume that some of Durkheim's students had been converted to socialism. There also seems to have been some mutual esteem between Durkheim and some of the leading socialists of the time, particularly Guesde and Juarès. Mauss further indicates that, although Durkheim always remained uncommitted to socialism, "he 'sympathized' (as it is now called) with the socialists, with Juarès, with socialism." The picture that emerges of Durkheim, supported in part by Mauss' introduction, is that Durkheim was under pressure to adjust Comteianism to Marxism, That there was somewhere a bridge between these two traditions was suggested by their possession of a common ancestor, Saint-Simon. Durkheim's sympathetic revisitation of Saint-Simon, the man most detested by Comte, may be understandable as an incompleted effort to find a passage and to mend the rift between two of the major theoretical systems of his time, Marxism and Comteianism.

This perspective on Durkheim's work finds further confirmation in his little known lectures on *Professional Ethics and Civic Morals*.[30] In these, many of which consist of an examination of the evolution of certain western values, Durkheim stresses the following points of relevance to our own analysis:

1. He holds that it is the existence of social classes, characterized by significant economic inequalities, that makes it in principle impossible for "just" contracts to be negotiated. It is this system of stratification which, he argues here, offends the moral expectations of people in contemporary cultures, because it constrains to an unequal exchange of goods and services. The exploitation thus rendered possible by notable power disparities among the contracting parties conduces to a sense of injustice which has socially unstabilizing consequences. Thus, almost surprisingly, both Durkheim and Marx converge on a concept of "exploitation" as a contributant to current social instabilities.[31]

2. These power disparities derive largely, says Durkheim, from retention of the institution of inheritance. Inheritance *ab intestat*, Durkheim firmly insists, "is today an archaic survival and without justification";[32] it is in conflict with modern contractual ethics and practices. Testamentary dispositions, in his view, are also likely to be outmoded. Durkheim anticipates their ultimate elimination in modern society and looks forward to a time when property will no longer be transmitted through the family.

3. But if inheritance is eliminated, asks Durkheim, what institution would become the repository of private wealth, upon the death of its original owner? In his answer, we see a totally different and neglected aspect of Durkheim's project for the corporative reorganization of modern society. The corporative organization of people in the same industry or profession was not seen by Durkheim as having only a mo-

---

[30] These have recently been translated and published in the United States and Great Britain. See Emile Durkheim, *Professional Ethics and Civic Morals*, tr., C. Brookfield, Free Press, 1958.
[31] *Ibid.*, p. 213 *et seq.* This convergence, and its implications, are discussed somewhat more fully in Alvin W. Gouldner, "Reciprocity and Autonomy in Functional Theory," in L. Z. Gross (ed.), *Symposium on Social Theory*, Row, Peterson, 1958.
[32] *Ibid.*, p. 216.

rality-building function. The occupational corporation was also expected to have important *economic* functions, inheriting and managing private property following the demise of its original owners. The occupational corporations were Durkheim's "moral equivalent" for the Marxian nationalization of industry by the state, and were expected to "satisfy all the conditions for becoming . . . in the economic sphere, the heirs of the family."[33]

That Durkheim never succeeded in integrating the Marxian and Comteian traditions is evident; but he approached the foothills to an intellectual confrontation which challenges theorists to this very day.

ALVIN W. GOULDNER
May 10, 1958
Urbana, Illinois

About the Translation

This volume was translated by Charlotte Sattler. The editor served as a consultant, particularly in matters concerning Durkheim's sociological vocabulary, but did not generally supervise the translation. The translator's intention was neither to render Durkheim as a twentieth century stylist nor as an "up-to-date" sociologist but, rather, to present him as he was, a turn of the century French academician. As will be obvious to those who know the original, or who read M. Mauss' occasional footnotes throughout the volume, Durkheim's original manuscript was frequently incomplete and sometimes illegible. Under these conditions, the main objective was to rescue the fruit of Durkheim's thought, not the flower of his style.

The reader will notice three types of footnotes: Those which are unsigned were written by Durkheim himself; those which are signed M.M. were added by Mauss; those signed A.W.G. were added by the editor of this volume.

[33] *Ibid.*, p. 218.

Introduction to the First Edition

This book is the beginning of a work which was never finished. It is the first part of a History of Socialism drafted in the form of lectures. The course was given at Bordeaux, at the Faculty of Letters, from November 1895 to May 1896.

This is the place the study occupies in the work and thought of Durkheim:

We know the problems from which it emerged. As early as his years at normal school, through personal inclination and in an atmosphere animated by political and moral interests, and together with Jaurès and his other friend, Hommay, (who died in 1886), he dedicated himself to the study of society. He then put the question quite abstractly and philosophically, under the title: "The Relationship of Individualism and Socialism." In 1883 he had fixed upon the relations between the individual and society as his subject. Through a continuing analysis of his theory and of the facts, between the first plan of his *Division of Social Labor* (1884) and the first draft (in 1886), he came to see that the solution of the problem belonged to a new science, sociology. This was in small favor at the time, especially in France where the intemperance of the last Comtistes had brought it into ridicule. Further, sociology was far from well established. For Comte, Spencer, and even Espinas and the Germans, Schaeffle and Wundt, had only indicated their philosophies of it. Durkheim undertook the task of giving sociology a method and a body. The study of socialism was consequently interrupted.

This theoretical and scholarly task led to the definitive drafting (1888 to 1893) of the *Division of Labor*, to the course on *Suicide* (1889-90), *The Family* (1888-89), (1891-93), and to that on *Religion* (1894-95). This was the range of sociology that Durkheim taught including the *Rules of Method* (1896), and *Suicide* (1897). Durkheim's thinking had taken definitive form. Creating the foundations of a science had of course absorbed his energies. But he did not lose sight of his point of departure.

Social problems remained at the bottom of his interests. *The Division of Labor, Suicide,* have moral, political, and economic implications for the professional group. The course on *The Family* terminated with a lecture (published in *la Revue Philosophique* of 1920), in which he shows that it is necessary to grant the professional group a portion of the ancient political and property rights which domestic groups had, if the individual is not to be alone in the face of the State and live in a kind of alternation between anarchy and servitude. The present course, the course on *Moral Education* (published in 1925) returns to this central idea in Durkheim's clearly moral and political work. He again took up this question in his *Civic and Professional Morality* (part of the course on the *Physiology of Right and Customs*) which we are planning to publish after this work.

Moreover the idea was so important that it impressed great minds. Thus Georges Sorel, penetrating if not scholarly or precise, whom we knew since 1893, did not fail to use it in several articles in *Devenir Social.* Later revolutionary syndicalism was in part affected by it. This should be noted in passing to make a simple historical point. We could have a great deal to say on this subject. For in this affair, we were—at least a certain number among us—more than mere witnesses, from 1893 to 1906.

However, until 1895 Durkheim could not spare a moment from his work to return to the study of socialism. And even when he did go back to it, as we will see in this book, he did not depart from his customary point of view. He considered this doctrine from a purely scientific point of view, as a fact which the scholar should look upon coldly, without prejudice, and without taking sides. He treats it as a problem in sociology; for him, it is a question of explaining an ideology—the socialist ideology—and to explain it one must analyze the social pressures which constrained a few men such as Saint-Simon and Fourier, Owen and Marx, to advance new principles of morality and of political and economic action. In addition, this course, we believe, is a model of the application of sociological and historic method to the analysis of the causes of an idea.

Indeed, through this unbiased form of research, Durkheim satisfied at once the needs of both his moral and scientific thought. He sought to take a stand and to justify it. He was inclined toward this by a series of events—some small and personal, others more serious. He clashed with touchy moralists and classic or Christian economists for their objections to collectivism, which they struck at through his *Division of Labor*. Due to conflicts of this kind, he was excluded from professorships in Paris. Some of the most brilliant among his own students were converted to socialism, especially Marxist, and even Guesdist. In one "Social Study" circle some examined *Capital* as they elsewhere considered Spinoza. Durkheim sensed this opposition to liberalism and bourgeois individualism. In a conference organized by this circle and the Workers' Party at Bordeaux, Juarès in 1893 extolled Durkheim's work. However, if it was Lucien Herr who in 1886-88 converted Juarès to socialism, it was Durkheim who in 1889-96 had turned him away from political formalism and the shallow philosophy of the radicals.

Durkheim was quite familiar with socialism at its very sources, through Saint-Simon, Schaeffle, and Karl Marx, whom a Finnish friend, Neiglick, had advised him to study during his stay in Leipzig. All his life he was reluctant to adhere to socialism (properly so-called), because of certain features of this movement: its violent nature, its class character—more or less purely workingmen's—and therefore its political and even politician-like tone. Durkheim was profoundly opposed to all wars of class or nation. He desired change only for the benefit of the whole of society and not of one of its parts—even if the latter had numbers and force. He considered political revolutions and parliamentary evolution as superficial, costly, and more dramatic than serious. He therefore always resisted the idea of submitting himself to a party of political discipline, especially an international one. Even the social and moral crisis of the Dreyfuss Affair, in which he played a large part, did not change his opinion. He therefore remained uncommitted—he "sympathized" (as it is now called) with the socialists, with Juarès, with socialism. But he never gave himself to it.

To justify himself in his own eyes, in those of his students, and one day in the eyes of the world, he began these studies. The public course enjoyed great success. The definition of socialism which was published in resumé impressed Guesde and Juarès who declared themselves in agreement with Durkheim. Durkheim prepared for 1896-97 a course on Proudhon whose works he owned and had studied, as he had done with Saint-Simon and his followers. He intended to devote a third year to Lassalle about whom he then knew little, to Marx and to German socialism, which he knew well already. He intended to confine himself to the works of the masters, to their thought, rather than to their personal lives or to works of second rank.

But in 1896 Durkheim, undertaking the *L'Année Sociologique*, returned to pure science, and the *History of Socialism* remained incomplete. He always regretted his inability to continue or resume it.

This book therefore contains only the first part: Definition, Beginnings of Socialism, Saint-Simon. It comes a little late. But at the time Durkheim taught it, the history of socialist doctrines was hardly appreciated, nor was it much developed. Things have changed. Bourguin, MM. Gide and Rist have produced their work. Socialism is here—a workers' and political force which evaluates itself. Saint-Simon is popular; indeed, since the war, nearly everyone calls himself a Saint-Simonian. The centenary of the first socialist messiah has been properly celebrated.

A number of works have clarified questions that Durkheim did not pretend to resolve and did not even raise. M. Charlety's book on Saint-Simon and the Saint-Simonians is written with all the resources of modern history. And the fine introduction that MM. C. Bouglé and Elie Halévy contributed to the *Exposition de la Doctrine de Saint-Simon*, by Bazard and others, very adequately furnishes sources and details. The biographical work of M. Georges Dumas and M. Maxime Leroy is not even surmised in this course.

However, we are publishing it. First, it states a careful and classic definition of socialism. Also—unless we are greatly mistaken—no other comprehensive statement on the beginnings of socialism can compare in clarity and force. Finally, Durkheim's critical and historical opinions (for example, with regard to the origins of socialism) have in themselves without doubt philosophical interest and perhaps even empirical truth.

Some of these lectures have appeared in *la Revue de métaphysique et de morale,* and in *la Revue philosophique.* We thank the editors for permitting us to reproduce them here.

The manuscript is carefully executed and very few of the passages are illegible. We have not attempted to fill gaps. Every alteration is noted between brackets. We have verified the quotations, and have made no changes in the text except to mark chapter titles. We were obliged to cut out a few lectures. The repetitions in the course have not been touched.

The manuscript is divided into lectures. We occasionally cut them up and set up chapters and books—with no difficulty. All the titles are Durkheim's

Madame Louise Durkheim had copied the manuscript almost entirely. I had only to assist her in passages difficult to read. Illness and then death stopped her at the eleventh lecture. Lectures XII and XIV had been ready.[1]

MARCEL MAUSS

[1] Presumably, Mauss meant to say that lectures XII *through XIV* had been ready. In what follows lecture numbers have been eliminated.—(A.W.G.)

Contents

Chapter 1

Definition of Socialism

WE CAN CONCEIVE of two different ways of studying socialism. We can see it as a scientific doctrine on the nature and evolution of societies in general and, more specially, of the most civilized contemporary societies. In this case, the analysis does not differ from that to which scholars submit the theories and hypotheses of their respective sciences. They are considered abstractly, outside of time, space, and of future history, not as something whose genesis one attempts to find, but as a system of propositions which express or are deemed to express facts. We then ask what is its truth or falsity, whether or not it corresponds to social reality, in what measure it is consistent with itself and with things as they are. This is the method, for example, that M. Leroy-Beaulieu followed in his book on *Collectivisme*. This will not be our point of view. The reason for it is that, without diminishing the importance of our interest in socialism, we would not know how to perceive in it a clearly scientific character. In fact, research can only be so-called if it has a definite object, which it aims to translate into intelligible language. Science is a study bearing on a delimited portion of reality which it aims at knowing and, if possible understanding. To describe and explain what is and what has been—this is its only job. Speculation about the future is not its affair, although it may seek as its final objective to render this possible.

Socialism, on the contrary, is entirely oriented toward the future. It is above all a plan for the reconstruction of societies, a program for a collective life which does not exist as yet or in the way it is dreamed of, and which is proposed to men as worthy of their preference. It is an ideal. It concerns itself much less with what is or was than what ought to be. Undoubtedly, even under its most utopian forms it never disdained the support of facts, and has even, in more recent times, increasingly affected a certain scientific turn of phrase. It is indisputable that it has thus rendered social science more services perhaps than it received from it. For it has aroused reflection, it has stimulated scientific activity, it has instigated research, posed problems, so that in more than one way its history blends with the very history of sociology. Yet, how can one fail to note the enormous disparity between the rare and meager data it borrows from science and the extent of the practical conclusions that it draws, and which are, nevertheless, the heart of the system? It aspires to a complete remolding of the social order. But in order to know what the family, property, political, moral, juridical, and economic organization of the European peoples can and ought to be, even in the near future, it is indispensable to have studied this multitude of institutions and practices in the past, to have searched for the ways in which they varied in history, and for the principal conditions which have determined these variations. And only then will it be possible to ask oneself rationally what they ought to be now —under the present conditions of our collective existence. But all this research is still in its infancy. Several are hardly going enterprises; the most advanced have not yet passed beyond a very rudimentary phase. Since each of these problems is a world in itself, the solution cannot be found in an instant, merely because the need is felt. The bases for a rigorous prediction about the future, especially one of such breadth, are not established. It is necessary that the theoretician himself construct them. Socialism has not taken the time; perhaps one could even say, it did not have the time.

That is why, to speak precisely, there cannot be a scientific socialism. Because, were such a socialism even possible, sciences would be necessary that are not yet developed and which cannot be improvised. The only attitude that science permits in the face of these problems is reservation and circumspection, and socialism can hardly maintain this without lying to itself. And, in fact, socialism has not maintained this attitude. Note even the strongest work—the most systematic, the richest in ideas—that this school has produced:

Marx's *Capital*. What statistical data, what historical comparisons, what studies would be indispensable to solve any one of the innumerable questions that are dealt with there! Need we be reminded that an entire theory of value is established in a few lines? The truth is that the facts and observations assembled by theoreticians anxious to document their affirmations are hardly there except to give form to the arguments. The research studies they made were undertaken to establish a doctrine that they had previously conceived, rather than the doctrine being a result of the research. Almost all had developed before asking science for the help it could lend them. It is fervor that has been the inspiration of all these systems; what gave them life and strength is a thirst for a more perfect justice, pity for the misery of the working classes, a vague sympathy for the travail of contemporary societies, etc. Socialism is not a science, a sociology in miniature—it is a cry of grief, sometimes of anger, uttered by men who feel most keenly our collective *malaise*. Socialism is to the facts which produce it what the groans of a sick man are to the illness with which he is afflicted, to the needs that torment him. But what would one say of a doctor who accepted the replies or desires of his patient as scientific truths? Moreover, the theories ordinarily offered in opposition to socialism are no different in nature and they no more merit the title we refuse the latter. When economists call for *laissez faire*, demanding that the influence of the state be reduced to nothing, that competition be freed of every restraint, they are not basing their claims on laws scientifically developed. The social sciences are still much too young to be able to serve as bases for practical doctrines, which are so vast and of such breadth. Such policies are maintained by needs of another kind—a jealousy of individual autonomy, a love of order, a fear of novelty, misoneism as it is called today. Individualism, like socialism, is above all a ferment which affirms itself, although it may eventually ask Reason for reasons with which to justify itself.

If this is so, then to study socialism as a system of abstract propositions, as a body of scientific theories and to discuss it formally, is to see and show a side of it which is of minor interest. Those aware of what social science must be, of the slow pace of its processes, of the laborious investigations it implies to resolve even the narrowest questions, cannot be fond of these premature solutions, these vast systems so summarily sketched out. One is too aware of the discrepancy that exists between its simple methods and its elaborate conclusions, and one is consequently prompted to scorn the latter. But socialism can be examined in an entirely different light. If it is not a scientific formulation of social facts, it is itself a social fact of the highest importance. If it is not a product of science, it is an object of science. As such, we do not have to borrow from socialism such and such a proposition ready made; but we do have to know socialism, and to understand what it is, where it comes from, and where it is going.

It is interesting to study socialism from this point of view, for two reasons. First, one can hope that it will aid us in understanding the social conditions which gave rise to it. For precisely because it derives from certain conditions, socialism manifests and expresses them in its own way, and thereby gives us another means of viewing them. It is certainly not that socialism reflects these conditions accurately. On the contrary, for the reasons mentioned above, we can be certain that it refracts them involuntarily and gives us only an unfaithful impression, just as a sick man faultily interprets the feelings that he experiences and most often attributes them to a cause which is not the true one. But these feelings, such as they are, have their interest, and the clinician notes them with great care and takes them seriously. They are an element in the diagnosis, and an important one. For example, he is not indifferent as to where they are felt, when they began. In the same way, it is highly material to determine the epoch when socialism began to appear. It is a cry of collective anguish, let us say. Well then, it is essential to fix the moment when this cry was uttered for the first time. For if we see it as a recent fact related to entirely new social conditions, or, on the contrary, as a simple recurrence—at the most a variant of the lamentations that the wretched of all epochs and societies have made heard (eternal claims of the poor against the rich), we will judge its tendencies quite differently. In the second case, we will be led to believe that these grievances can no more be terminated than human misery can end. They will be thought of as a kind of chronic illness of humanity which, from time to time in the course of history and under the influence of transitory circumstances, seems to become more acute and grievous, but which always ends by at last abating; then one will strive only to discover some anodyne to lull it into security again. If, on the contrary, we find that it is of recent date, that it is related to a situation without analogy in history, we can no longer assume it is a chronic condition and are less ready to take such a view.

But it is not only to diagnose the nature of the illness that this study of socialism promises to be instructive; it is, also, in order to find appropriate remedies. To be sure, we can be certain in advance that the remedies are not precisely those sought by the systems, just as the drink demanded by a feverish patient is not necessarily what he needs. Still, the needs that he does feel do not cease to serve as some guide in the treatment. They are never without some cause, and sometimes it is best to satisfy them. For the same reason, it is important to know what social rearrangements, that is, what remedies, the suffering masses of society have spontaneously and instinctively conceived of, however unscientific their elaboration might have been. This is what socialist theories express. The material that one can gather on this subject will be especially useful if, instead of confining ourselves to one system, we make a comparative study of all doctrines. For then we have greater opportunity to eliminate from all these aspirations what is necessarily individual, subjective, contingent, in order to extract and retain only their most general, most impersonal, and therefore most objective characteristics.

Not only does such an investigation have its usefulness, but it should prove in other respects more fruitful than the usual examinations to which socialism is subjected. When studied only in order to discuss it from a doctrinaire point of view, since it is based only on a very imperfect science, it is easy to show how far it goes beyond the very facts on which it leans, or to oppose contrary facts to it, in a word to criticize all its theoretic imperfections. One can, without much difficulty, review all the systems; there is none whose refutation is not relatively simple, because none are scientifically established. But as scholarly and as well-conducted as it may be, such a critique remains superficial, for it avoids what is essential. It concerns itself only with exterior and superficial form of socialism and so does not perceive what gives it depth and substance, namely collective diathesis, the profound uneasiness of which the particular theories are merely the symptoms and episodic superficialities. When one has sharply disputed the theories of Saint-Simon, Fourier, or Karl Marx, one is not, for that, especially informed on the social conditions which created them, which have been and still are their *raison d'être*, and which tomorrow will produce other doctrines if these fall into discredit. All these fine refutations are a veritable work of Penelope, endlessly beginning again, because they touch socialism from without, and because what is within escapes them. They blame the effects, not the causes. But it is the causes that must be attacked, if only to understand the effects. For this, socialism must not be considered in the abstract, outside of every condition of time and place. On the contrary, it is necessary to relate it to the social setting in which it was born. It is essential not merely to subject it to dialectic discussion, but rather to fathom its history.

This is the standpoint we will take. We will regard socialism as a thing, as a reality, and try to understand it. We will attempt to determine what it consists of, when it began, through what transformations it passed, and what determined those transformations. A research of this kind does not differ markedly from those we carried on in previous years. We are going to study socialism as we did suicide, the family, marriage, crime, punishment, responsibility, and religion. The difference is that we are going to find ourselves in the presence of a social fact which, being very recent, has only had a short development. The result is that the field of possible comparisons is very limited, which renders the phenomenon more difficult to understand, all the more because it is very complex. Therefore, in order to have fuller understanding, it will not be useless to coordinate it with certain information which we owe to other research. For the social conditions to which socialism corresponds are not presented to us for the first time. We met them, on the contrary, in every one of our previous studies every time we were able to trace the social phenomena we were concerned with to the contemporary era. It is true we were able to examine these social conditions in only a fragmentary way; but may not socialism permit us to grasp them in their entirety, because it represents them in a block, so to speak? We cannot make any less use—if need be—of the fragmentary results we obtained.

But in order to undertake this study, it is necessary to determine the object on which it will bear. It is not enough to say we are going to consider socialism as a thing. We must indicate the signs by which one recognizes it, that is, to give a definition of it which permits us to perceive it everywhere it is met, and not to confuse it with what it is not.

In what manner should we proceed to this definition?

Is it enough to reflect deeply on the idea we have of socialism, to analyze it, and to express the results of this analysis in the clearest language possible? It is certain that, to attach a meaning to this commonly used word, we have not waited for sociology to raise the question systematically. Would it not then be necessary only to answer ourselves, to examine ourselves carefully, to seize upon the conception we have and develop it into a definite formula? Proceeding so, we could indeed arrive at what we personally understand socialism to be, not what it actually is. And as each one comprehends it in his own way, according to his temperament, his turn of mind, his prejudices, we would obtain only a subjective, individual notion, which could not serve as the substance for any scientific examination. What right would I have to impose on others my own personal way of seeing socialism, and what right have the others to foist theirs on me? Will we better succeed by eliminating from these concepts, varying with individuals, what they possess of individuality, in order to retain only what they have in common? Put another way, to define socialism, would it not be proper to express not the idea I have of it, but the commonly accepted notion of it held by men of my time? Thus, shall we call it, not what I hold it to be, but what is generally designated by the word? But we very well know the indeterminacy and inconsistency of these common average conceptions! They are made from day to day, empirically, devoid of all logic and method. The result is that at times they are applied equally to very different things, or else exclude from it, on the contrary, what is very closely related to the things to which they are applied. The common run, in constructing its concepts, sometimes permits itself to be guided by exterior and fallacious resemblances, sometimes allows itself to be deceived by apparent differences. Accordingly, if we follow this path, we run a serious risk of calling by the name of "socialist" every type of contrary doctrine, and inversely, to exclude doctrines which possess all of its essential characteristics but which the mass has not been in the habit of calling "socialist." In one case, our study would focus on a confused mass of heterogeneous and disunited facts; in the other, it would not embrace all the facts which are comparable and of a sort to mutually clarify each other. In both cases it would end up in a bad state.

Furthermore, to evaluate the worth of this method, it suffices to see its results, that is to examine the definitions most commonly given to socialism. This examination is all the more useful as, since these definitions express the most widespread ideas on socialism, the most common ways of conceiving it, it is important to rid ourselves at once of those prejudices which otherwise could only stop us from understanding one another and obstruct our research. If we do not free ourselves of them before proceeding further, they will wedge themselves between us and things and have us see the latter other than as they are.

Of all definitions, the one which is perhaps most consistently and generally brought to mind whenever there is a question of socialism, is that which has it consist of a pure and simple negation of private property. I do not know, it is true, of a passage by an authoritative writer where this formula is expressly proposed, but it is found implicitly at the base of more than one of the discussions that socialism has occasioned. For example, M. Janet believes, in his book on *les Origines de Socialisme* (page 2), that, to firmly establish that the French Revolution had no socialist character, it is sufficient to have it understood that "it has not violated the principle of property." And yet one can say that there is not a single socialist doctrine to which such a definition applies. Let us consider, for example, the one which most limits private property—the collectivist doctrine of Karl Marx. It indeed withdraws from individuals the right to possess the means of production, but not to every form of wealth. They retain an absolute right over the products of their work. Can this limited restriction of the principle of private property be considered as characteristic of socialism? But our economic organization now presents restrictions of the same kind, and in this regard is distinguished from Marxism only by a difference in degree. Is not everything which is directly or indirectly a monopoly of the state taken from the private domain? Railways, post office, tobacco, manufacture of money, powders, etc. cannot be carried on by individuals, or can be only by virtue of an express concession of the state. Will we say then that in reality socialism starts where the practice of monopoly begins? If so, then it is everywhere; it is of all times and countries, for there never has been a society without monopoly. This definition is far too broad.

But further: far from denying the principle of individual property, socialism, not without reason, can claim that it is the most complete, the most radical, affirmation of it that has ever been made. In fact, the opposite of private property is communism; but there still is in our present institutions a vestige of old familial communism— that is, inheritance. The right of relatives to succeed each other in the ownership of their goods is but the last vestige of the ancient right of co-ownership, which at one time all members of a family held collectively over the total household. But, one of the propositions which appears most often in a socialist theories is the abolition of inheritance. Such a reform would therefore have the effect of freeing the institution of private property of all communist alloy, as a consequence rendering it more truly itself. In other words, one can reason thus: in order that property may be said to be truly individual, it is necessary that it be the work of the individual himself and of him alone. But, patrimony transmitted by inheritance does not have this character; it is only a collective work appropriated by an individual. Private property, one can say, is that which begins with individual and ends with him; but what he receives by virtue of the right of succession existed before him and was made without him. In presenting this reasoning, I do not intend to defend the socialist thesis, but to show that there are some communist doctrines among its adversaries, and consequently it is not through this that it is possible to define socialism.

We will say as much of the concept—no less widespread—according to which socialism consists of a narrow subordination of the individual to the collectivity. "We can define as socialist," says Adolphe Held, "every tendency which demands the subordination of individual welfare to the community." In like manner, Roscher, mixing judgment and criticism with his definition, calls socialist those tendencies "which claim a consideration of the common good above what human nature permits." But there has never been a society in which private interests have not been subordinated to social ends; for this subordination is the very condition of all community life. Can one say, with Roscher, that the sacrifice which socialism demands of us has this characteristic, namely, that it exceeds our capacities? This is to appraise the doctrine, and not to define it, and such an appraisal cannot serve as a criterion to distinguish it from what it is not, for it leaves too much to discretion. The extreme limit of sacrifice that individual egoism tolerates cannot be determined objectively. Each person advances or withdraws from it according to his disposition. Each one, as a consequence, would be free to understand socialism in his own way. Further, this submission of the individual to the group is so little in the spirit of certain socialist schools, and of the most important of them, that they have instead a tendency toward anarchy. This is the case notably with Fourierism and the Mutualism of Proudhon, where individualism is systematically pushed to its most paradoxical consequences. Does not Marxism itself propose, according to a celebrated comment by Engels, the destruction of the state as a state? Wrongly or rightly, Marx and his disciples believe that from the time that socialist organization is established, it can function by itself, automatically, without any constraint, and we will have already found this idea in Saint-Simon. In a word, if there is an authoritarian socialism, there is also one which is essentially democratic. How, in fact, could it be otherwise? As we will see, it sprang from revolutionary individualism, just as the ideas of the nineteenth century issued from those of the eighteenth, and as a result it cannot do other than to bear the stamp of its origin. There remains, it is true, the question of knowing if these different tendencies are susceptible of logical reconciliation. But we do not for the moment have to consider the logical worth of socialism. We seek only to know of what it consists.

But there is a last definition which seems more suited to the object described. Very often, if not always, socialism has had as its principal aim the amelioration of the condition of the working classes, by introducing greater equality into economic relations. This is why it is called the economic philosophy of the suffering classes. But this tendency, of itself, is not sufficient to characterize it, for it is not peculiar to it. Economists also aspire to lessen inequality in social conditions; they believe, however, that this progress ought to be made by the natural play of supply and demand and that every legislative intervention is useless. Shall we then say that what distinguished socialism is that it wishes to obtain this same result by other means, namely by legal action? This was the definition of Laveleye. "Every socialist doctrine," he says, "aims to introduce more equality into social conditions and, secondly, to realize these reforms by action of the law or the state." But, on the one hand, if this objective is distinctively one which these doctrines pursue, it is necessary that it be theirs alone. The connection between the state and large industries, great economic undertakings, which by their importance embrace all of society, mines, railways, banks, etc. has as its aim the protection of collective interests against certain private influences, not the improvement of the lot of workers.

Socialism goes beyond the workingman's problem. In certain of the systems it occupies only a secondary place. This is the case with Saint-Simon, who is regarded as the founder of socialism. It is the case also with the academic socialists, who are much more concerned with safeguarding the interests of the state than with protecting the disinherited. On the other hand, there is a doctrine which aims to realize this equality much more radically than socialism; it is communism, which denies all private property and by that, all economic inequality. But, although there has often been this confusion, it is impossible to regard communism as a simple variant of socialism. We will return shortly to this question. Plato and More, on one hand, and Marx, on the other, are not disciples of the same school. *A priori*, it is not possible that a social organization, conceived in contemplation of the industrial societies we actually have under our eyes, could have been imagined when these societies had not yet been born. Finally, there are many legislative measures which one could not regard as exclusively socialist and which nonetheless have the effect of diminishing the inequality of social conditions. The progressive tax on inheritance and on income necessarily has this result, and nevertheless is not a concomitant of socialism. What should one say of the foundations granted by the state, of the public welfare and loan institutions, etc? If one labels them as socialist, as sometimes happens in the course of running discussions, the word loses every kind of sense, so broad and indefinite a connotation does it take.

It can be seen what one is exposed to when, in order to find a definition of socialism, one is satisfied to express with some precision the idea he holds of it. He confuses it with this or that particular aspect, this or that special tendency of certain systems, simply because—for whatever reason— he is more struck with one particularity than another. The only way to escape these errors is to practice the method we have always followed in similar circumstances. Let us forget for the moment the idea that we have of the object to be defined. Instead of looking within ourselves, let us look outside; instead of questioning ourselves, we will question things. There exist a certain number of doctrines which concern social matters. Let us observe and compare them. Let us group together those which present common characteristics. If, among the groups of theories thus formed, there is one which by its distinctive characteristics reminds us sufficiently of what is ordinarily meant by the word socialism, we will apply that word to it without changing the denomination. In other words, we will call socialist all systems which present these traits, and we will thus have the sought-after definition. Undoubtedly, it is very possible that it may not include all the doctrines that commonly are so-called; or, on the contrary, may embrace those which in ordinary speech are called otherwise. But it does not matter. These discrepancies will only prove once again the looseness of the classifications which are at the base of everyday terminology. The essential thing is that we have before us a succession of facts, unified and clearly circumscribed, to which one may give the name of socialism without doing violence to the language. Under these conditions our study will be possible, since we will have for our material a determinate kind of thing; and on the other hand, it will elucidate the common belief as much as it can be clarified, which is to say, to the degree it is consistent and expresses something definite. Thus conducted, the research will indeed answer well all that one can logically ask oneself when we pose the question: What is socialism?

Let us apply this method.

*   *   *

Social theories separate themselves at once into two large categories. One seeks only to express what is or what has been; it is purely speculative and scientific. Others, on the contrary, aim to modify what exists; they propose, not laws, but reforms. They are practical doctrines. What has preceded is sufficient to warn us that if the word socialism corresponds to something definable, it is to the second group that it should be applied.

Now this genus comprises species. The reforms thus proposed sometimes concern politics, sometimes education, administration, or economic life. Let us stop at this last kind. Everything allows us to assume that socialism is a part of it. Without doubt, in a broad sense, one can say that there is a political socialism, a pedagogic socialism, etc.; we will even see that perforce, it extends to these different realms. It is certain, however, that the word was created to designate theories which refer above all to the economic state and which demand its transformation. It is necessary, however, to keep from believing that this feature is sufficient to characterize it. For individualist economists also protest against the present structure, claiming it must be freed from every social restraint. The reforms which M. de Molinari demands in his *Évolution économique* are no less subversive of the present social order than those to which the most intemperate socialism aspires. We must therefore refine our classification and see if, among the economic transformations called for by the different reformist sects, there are those which are distinctive of socialism.

In order to properly understand what is to follow, some definitions are necessary.

It is usually said that the functions exercised by the members of the same society are of two kinds: some are social, others are individual. The builders of the state, the administrator, deputy, priest, etc. deal with the first sort; commerce and industry, that is to say, the economic functions (monopolies excepted) belong to the second. To tell the truth, the terms used are not faultless; for in one sense all the functions of a society are social—economic functions like the others. In fact, if they are not in normal operation, all of society feels it, and inversely, the general state of social health affects the functioning of the economic organs. However, this very distinction, made up only of the words that express it, does not permit itself to be established. In fact, economic activities have this particularity: they are not in definite and regulated relationships with the organ which is charged with representing and directing the social body in its entirety, namely, what is commonly called the state. This absence of connection can be ascertained both in the way that industrial and commercial life acts on it, as in the manner it acts on the latter. On the one hand, what goes on in factories, in mills, and in private stores, in principle escapes the awareness of the state. It is not directly and specifically informed of what is produced there. The state can indeed, in certain cases, feel its reverberations; but it is not advised in a different way nor in different circumstances than are other branches of society. For that to happen, it is necessary that the economic situation be seriously disturbed and the general state of society noticeably modified. In this case, the state is being injured, and so, vaguely takes notice of it, as do other parts of the organization, but not differently. In other words, there exists no special communication between it and this sphere of collective life. In principle, economic activity is outside of collective consciousness. It functions silently and the conscious centers do not feel it while it is normal. Likewise it is not activated in a specialized and regular way. There is no system of determinate and organized channels by which the influence of the state makes itself felt upon economic organs. In other words, there is no system of functions charged with imposing on it the action coming from the superior centers. It is altogether different in other activities. Everything that occurs in the various administrations, in local deliberating assemblies, in public education, in the army, etc., is susceptible of reaching the "social brain," by paths specially destined to assure these communications, so that the state is kept up to date without the surrounding portions of society being notified. Further, there are other paths of the same kind, by which the state sends back its action to the secondary centers. Between them there are continuing and diversified exchanges. We can say then that these latter functions are organized; for what constitutes the organization of a living body is the institution of a central organ and the connection with this organ of secondary organs. In contrast, we say of present economic functions that they are diffused, the diffusion consisting in the absence of organization.

This granted, it is easy to establish that among economic doctrines, there are some which demand the linking of commercial and industrial activities to the directing and conscious agencies of society, and that these doctrines are opposed to others which, on the contrary, call for a greater diffusion. It seems incontestable that in giving to the first of these doctrines the name socialist, we do not violate the customary meaning of the word. For all the doctrines ordinarily called socialist agree on this claim. Assuredly, the connection is conceived of in different ways, in accordance with various schools. According to some, all the economic functions should be connected with the superior centers; according to others, it is enough that some are. For the latter, the attachment is to be made by means of intermediaries, that is, by secondary elements, endowed with a certain autonomy —professional groups, corporations, etc.; for the former, it must be immediate. But all these differences are secondary, and consequently we can stop at the following definition which expresses the characteristics common to all these theories:

We denote as socialist every doctrine which demands the connection of all economic functions, or of certain among them, which are at the present time diffuse, to the directing and conscious centers of society. It is important to note at once that we say connection, not subordination. In fact this bond between the economic life and the state does not imply, according to our belief, that every *action* should come from the latter. On the contrary, it is natural that it receive from it as much as it gives it. One can foresee that the industrial and commercial life, once put in *permanent* contact with it, will affect its functioning, will contribute to determining the manifestations of its activity much more than today, will play in the life of government a much more important role; and this explains how, while complying with the definition we have just obtained, there are socialist systems which tend to anarchy. It is because, for them, this transformation must result in making the state subordinate to economic functions, rather than putting them in its hands.

* * *

Although socialism is a common issue, we have been able to see by the definitions usually given of it how inconsistent and even contradictory is the notion commonly held of it. The adversaries of the doctrine are not the only ones to speak of it without having a clearcut idea. Socialists themselves often prove—by the way they understand the word—that they only imperfectly know their own theories. It constantly occurs that they take this or that particular tendency for the whole of the system, for the simple reason that they are personally impressed with one detail over others. Thus it is that one generally ends by almost reducing the social problem to the question of the worker. One could hardly involve himself in these innumerable confusions if one wishes to put himself in the state of mind necessary to approach the study we are going to undertake from a scientific point of view. An evaluation of the current notions on socialism warns us that we must make a clean slate of what we believe we know of it, if we are to expect the research we are beginning, to provide something more than a pure and simple confirmation of our prejudices. We must face socialism as we do a thing we do not know, as a type of unexplored phenomenon, and we must hold ourselves ready to see it from a perspective more or less different than we ordinarily do. Besides, from a point of view no longer theoretical, but practical, such a method if generally practiced would have the advantage of bringing at least a truce to the warring passions this problem arouses, since it checks disagreements and keeps all at a distance. Instead of requiring minds to choose forthwith a solution and label, and in consequence dividing them instantly, it unites them, at least for a while, in a common feeling of ignorance and reservation. By making them understand that before judging socialism, before making an apologia or a criticism of it, it is necessary to comprehend it (and that by means of patient research), it offers them a common terrain where they can meet and work together, and so prepares them to consider even irritating problems with greater calm, serenity and impartiality. For, in this kind of thing, once one is obliged to challenge his own point of view, and depart from it—if only provisionally and in method—one is much less inclined toward exclusive and oversimplified solutions and can possibly take count of the whole complexity of things.

After having discussed the definitions at hand and noted their inadequacy, we ourselves searched for the signs by which one could recognize socialism and distinguish it from what it was not, and by an objective comparison of the different doctrines concerned with social problems, we came to the following formula: one calls socialist those theories which demand a more or less complete connection of all economic functions or of certain of them, though diffused, with the directing and knowing organs of society.

This definition calls for a few comments.

We have already observed that we were saying "connection" and not "subordination," and one cannot too strongly stress this difference, which is essential. Socialists do not demand that the economic life be put into the hands of the state, but into contact with it. On the contrary, they declare that it should react on the state at least as much as—if not more than—the latter acts on it. In their thinking, this rapport should have the effect, not of subordinating industrial and commercial interests to "political" interests, but rather of elevating the former to the rank of the latter. For, once this constant communication is assured, these economic interests would effect the functioning of the government organ much more profoundly than today and contribute in much larger measure to determining its course. Very far from relegating economic interests to second place, it would much rather be a question of calling upon them to play, in the whole of social life, a considerably more important role than is permitted today, when precisely because of their distance from the directing centers of society, they can activate the latter only feebly and intermittently.

Even according to the most celebrated theoreticians of socialism, the state as we know it would disappear and no longer be the central point of economic life—rather than economic life being absorbed by the state. For this reason, in the definition, we have not used the term "state," but the expression—expanded and somewhat figurative—"the knowing and managing organs of society." In the doctrine of Marx, for example, the state such as it is—that is to say, insofar as it has a specific role, and represents interests which are superior, *sui generis,* to those of commerce and industry, historic traditions, common beliefs and a religious or other nature, etc.—would no longer exist. Purely political functions, which today are its special sphere, would no longer have a *raison d'être,* and there would be only economic functions. It would no longer be called by the same name, which is why we have had to resort to a more general term. One last observation which should be made apropos of the proposed formula, is that one word is employed in its common usage, without having been carefully defined —contrary to the very principle we established. We speak of "economic" things or functions, without having previously said what they consist of, or by what external sign one may recognize them. The fault is due to the science of economics, which has not clarified its own fundamental concepts better, so that we must borrow it in the same condition in which it is presented to us. However, this is no great inconvenience, for if one does not know the precise limits of the economic domain, one understands generally the nature of the essential things it embraces—and that suffices for the moment.

Comparing this definition of the concept with those generally held of socialism, we can now ascertain the differences. Thus, according to the terms of our formula the theories which recommend, as a remedy for the evils suffered by present societies, a greater development of charitable and provident institutions (not only private, but public), would not be called socialist, although very often one does call them this—either to attack or to defend them. But it is not that our definition is in error; it is that by so calling them one gives them an unfitting name. For, however generous they may be, however useful it may be to put them into practice—which is not under discussion—they do not correspond at all to the needs and thoughts socialism has awakened and expresses. By characterizing them as socialist one mingles, within a single category and identical name, very different things. To establish welfare projects alongside of economic life, is not to bind the latter to public life. The diffuse state in which industrial and commercial functions are found does not diminish because one creates welfare funds to ameliorate the fortunes of those who, temporarily or forever, have ceased to fulfill these functions. Socialism is essentially a movement to organize, but charity organizes nothing. It maintains the *status quo;* it can only attenuate the individual suffering that this lack of organization engenders. By this new example, we can see how important it is to ascertain carefully the meaning of the word if one does not wish to be mistaken about the nature of the thing, or the significance of the practical measures taken or recommended.

Another important remark our definition gives rise to is that neither class war, nor concern about rendering economic relations more equitable and even more favorable for workers, figures in it. Far from being the whole of socialism, these characteristics do not even represent an essential element of it, nor are they *sui generis,* part of it. We are, it is true, so accustomed to an entirely different conception that at first such a statement is rather surprising and could arouse doubts as to the exactness of our definition. Do not both partisans and adversaries constantly present socialism to us as the philosophy of the working classes? But it is now easy to see that this tendency is far from the only one which inspires it but is actually only a particular, and is a derived form of the more general tendency (in the service of which we have expressed it). In reality, amelioration of the workers' fate is only one goal that socialism desires from the economic organization it demands, just as class war is only one of the means by which this reorganization could result, one aspect of the historic development producing it.

And in fact, what is it, according to socialists that causes the inferiority of the working classes and the injustice whose victims it declares them to be? It is that they are placed in direct dependence, not on society in general, but on a particular class powerful enough to impose its own wishes on them. That is, the "capitalists." The workers do not do business directly with society; it is not the latter which directly remunerates them—it is the capitalist. But the last is a mere individual who as such concerns himself—and that legitimately—not with social interest but with his own. Thus, the services he buys he seeks to pay for not according to what they are worth socially—that is to say, according to the exact degree of usefulness they have for society —but at the least possible price. But in his hands he has a weapon that permits him to force those who live only by their labor to sell him the product for less than it is really worth. This is his capital. He can live, if not indefinitely, at least for a long while, on his accumulated wealth, which he consumes instead of using to give work to the laborers. He purchases their help only if he wishes and when he wishes, whereas they, on the contrary, cannot wait. They must sell without delay the only thing they have to sell, since, by definition, they have no other means of subsistence. So they are obliged to yield in some degree to the demands of him who pays them, to reduce their own demands below what they should be if public interest alone served as the measure of value, and consequently are forced to allow themselves to be hurt. I do not have to evaluate here whether this preponderance of capital is real or if, as orthodox economists say, the competition capitalists create among themselves eliminates it. It is enough to present the socialist argument without judging it.

These premises posed, it is clear that the only means of at least tempering this subjection and ameliorating this state of affairs, is to moderate the power of capital by another [force] which at first may be of equal or superior strength but which [in addition] can make its action felt in conformity with the general interests of society. For it would be altogether useless to have another individual and private force intervene in the economic mechanism. This would be to replace with another kind—and not to suppress—the slavery from which the proletariat suffers. Therefore, only the state is capable of playing the role of moderator. But for that it is essential that the economic media cease to operate outside of it, without the state being aware of them. On the contrary, by means of a continuing communication the state must know what is happening, and in turn make its own action known. If one wishes to go still further, if one intends not only to attenuate but put a radical stop to this situation, it is necessary to completely suppress the medium of the capitalist who, by wedging himself between worker and society, prevents labor from being properly appreciated and rewarded according to its social value. This last must be directly evaluated and recompensed—if not by the community (which is practically impossible), then at least by the social agency which normally represents it. This is to say that the capitalist class under these conditions must disappear, that the state fulfill these functions at the same time as it is placed in direct relation with the working class, and in consequence, must become the center of economic life. The improvement of the workers' lot is thus not a special objective; it is but one of the consequences that the attachment of economic activities to the managing agents of society must produce. And in socialist thought, this improvement will be all the more complete as the connection itself is stronger. In this there are not two paths: one, which would aim at the organization of economic life, and the other, which would strive to make the situation of the great majority less noxious. The second is but an outcome of the first. In other words, according to socialism there is presently an entire segment of the economic world which is not truly and directly integrated into society. This is the working class, not the capitalists. They are not full-fledged members of society, since they participate in the community's life only through an imposed medium which, having its own nature, prevents them from acting upon society and receiving benefits from it in a measure and manner consistent with the social value of their services. It is this which creates the situation they are said to suffer from. What they desire, consequently, when they demand better treatment, is to be no longer kept at a distance from the centers presiding over collective life but be bound to them more or less intimately. The material changes they hope for are only one form and result of this more complete integration.

Thus our definition actually takes into account these special concerns which at first did not seem to enter; only, they are now in their proper place—which is a secondary one. Socialism does not reduce itself to a question of wages, or—as they say—the stomach. It is above all an aspiration for a rearrangement of the social structure, by relocating the industrial set-up in the totality of the social organism, drawing it out of the shadow where it was functioning automatically, summoning it to the light and to the control of the conscience. One can see that this aspiration is not felt uniquely by the lower classes but by the state itself which, as economic activity becomes a more important factor in the general life, is led by force of circumstances, by vital needs of the greatest importance, to increasingly supervise and regulate these economic manifestations. Just as the working masses tend to approach the state, the state also tends to be drawn towards them, for the single reason that it is always further extending its ramifications and its sphere of influence. Socialism is far from being an exclusively workingman's affair! Actually there are two movements under whose influence the doctrine of socialism is formed: one which comes from below and directs itself toward the higher regions of society, and the other which comes from the latter and follows a reverse direction. But since at root each is only an extension of the other, as they mutually imply each other, as they are merely different aspects of the same need of organization, one cannot define socialism by one rather than the other. Without doubt these two currents do not inspire entirely distinct systems; according to the place occupied by the theoretician, according to whether he is in closer contact with workers, or more attentive to the general interest of society, it will be one rather than the other which will have more influence on his thinking. The result is two different kinds of socialism: a worker's socialism or a state socialism, but the separation is a simple difference of degree. There is no workers' socialism which does not demand a greater development of the state; there is no state socialism disinterested in workers. They are just varieties of the same genus; but it is the genus we are defining.

However, if economic problems are posed by every socialist doctrine, most of the systems do not limit themselves to it. Almost all have more or less extended their claims to other spheres of social activity: to politics, to the family, marriage, morality, to art and literature, etc. There is even one school which has made it a rule to apply the principle of socialism to the whole of collective living. It is what Benoît Malon[1] called "integral socialism." Is it then necessary in order to remain consistent with our definition, to exclude from socialism these differing theories, and to regard them as inspired by another spirit, as springing from an altogether different origin, simply because they are not directly concerned with economic functions? Such an exclusion would be arbitrary, for if there are doctrines in which these sorts of speculation are not found, if so-called "realistic" socialism precludes them, they are nevertheless common to a fairly large number of schools. Furthermore, since they are found in all the variations of socialism, where one observes them, one can be sure they are placed in the service of socialist thought. For example, they are understood generally—at least today—to demand a more democratic organization of society, more liberty in marriage relations, juridical equality of the sexes, a more altruistic morality, a simplification of legal processes, etc. Thus they have a family likeness which indicates that though not essential to socialism, they are not without connections with it. And, in fact, it is easy to understand that such a transformation necessarily entails other rearrangements throughout the entire extent of the social structure. The relationships that an organ as complex as industry maintains

[1] See Benoît Malon, *Le Socialisme integral*, Paris, 1882.

with the others, especially with the most important of all, cannot be modified at this point without everything being affected. Imagine in the individual organism that one of our vegetative functions—until then located outside consciousness—has just been bound to it by direct paths of communication. The result would be that the very depths of our psychic life would be profoundly changed by this onset of new sensations. Even more, when one understands what socialism is, it becomes clear that it can hardly be circumscribed within a limited region of society, but that theoreticians, zealous in pursuing the consequences of their thinking to their limits, have been led to go beyond the purely economic domain. Those schemes of individual reforms then are not neatly joined within a system but are due to the same inspiration and consequently must be given a place in our definition. This is why, after having defined socialist theories as we did in the first place, we add: "Secondly, one also calls socialist those theories which, though not directly related to the economic order, nevertheless have a connection with it." Thus socialism will be defined essentially by its economic concepts, while being able to extend beyond them.

Chapter 2

Socialism and Communism

HAVING DEFINED SOCIALISM it is necessary, in order to obtain a clearer picture of it, that we distinguish it from another group of theories with which it is often confused. These are the communist theories, of which Plato first gave in antiquity a systematic formula, and which were again treated in modern times in Thomas More's *Utopia* and Campanella's *City of the Sun*—to cite only the most famous.

Confusion has often been created by the friends as well as the enemies of socialism. "From the time," says Laveleye, "that man had enough culture to be struck by social inequities . . . dreams of reform germinated in his mind. Therefore in all eras and all countries, after primitive equality disappeared, socialist aspirations are everywhere noted— sometimes in the form of protests against existing evil, sometimes in the form of utopian plans of social reconstruction. The most perfect model of these utopias is . . . Plato's *Republic*." (*Socialisme contemporain;* pref., p. v.) In his *Socialisme intégral* Benoît Malon expresses the same idea, and going beyond Plato, presents the communism of the Pythagorians as the precursor of contemporary socialism. In his *Étude sur les réformateurs contemporains*, Louis Reybaud, in 1840, had proceeded by an analogous method. For him the problem Plato posed does not differ from that raised by Saint-Simon and Fourier. The solution alone is different. Occasionally, the two words, socialism and communism, are taken for each other. In his book on *Socialisme au VXIIIe siècle*, M. Lichtenberger, wishing to give a definition of socialism, expresses himself thus: "One calls socialist the writers who, in the name of the power of the state and in an equalitarian and communist sense, have undertaken to modify the traditional organization of property." (Preface, p. 1). Others, while recognizing that one had to distinguish between communism and socialism, between Thomas More and Karl Marx, saw in the two only simple differences of degree and nuance. This is what Wolesley did in his book *Communism and Socialism*; for him socialism is a genus, communism a species, and at the end he claimed the right to use the two expressions almost interchangeably. Finally, in the workers' program of Marseilles, MM. Guesde and Lafargue, to clearly indicate that Marxist collectivism had nothing unrealizable about it, presented it as a simple extension of ancient communism.

Is there actually an identity or, at the least, a close relation between these two kinds of systems? The question is very important, for, according to the answer one gives, socialism would appear under an entirely different aspect. If it is merely a form of communism, or blends with it, one must see it as an old concept more or less rejuvenated, and is led to judge it like communist utopias of the past. If on the contrary it is distinct from it, it constitutes a manifestation *sui generis* which demands special examination.

One primary fact which, without being proof, should put us on guard against the confusion, is that the world socialism is quite new. It was coined in England in 1835. In that year a group which took the somewhat emphatic name of "Association of All Classes of All Nations" was founded under the auspices of Robert Owen and the words "socialist" and "socialism" were used for the first time in the course of the discussions that took place on that occasion. In 1839, Reybaud used it in his book on *Réformateurs modernes,* in which the theories of Saint-Simon, Fourier, and Owen are studied. Reybaud even claims authorship of the word, which in any event is no older than fifty (sic) years. But let us pass on from the word to the thing.

A first difference, superficial but striking nonetheless, is that communist theory appears in history only sporadically. The manifestations of it are usually isolated from each other by long intervals of time. From Plato to Thomas More almost ten centuries elapsed, and the communist tendencies that one notes in certain Fathers of the Church are not enough to supply continuity. From *Utopia* (1518) to the *City of the Sun* (1623) there is a separation of over a century, and after Campanella one must wait until the eighteenth century to see communism reborn. In other words, expressions of communism are not abundant. The thinkers it inspires are secluded individuals who rise up at long intervals but do not comprise a school. Their theories seem to express the personality of each theoretician rather than the general and usual state of society. They are dreams in which generous spirits take delight, which draw attention and maintain interest because of their nobility and dignity, but which, not answering the real needs felt by the social organism, exist in the imagination and remain practically unproductive. Moreover, it is in this way that those who have conceived them, present them. They themselves see in them hardly more than likely fictions which from time to time it is good to place before men's eyes, but which are not destined to become realities. "If," says Sir Thomas More, in ending his book, "I cannot adhere to all that has just been reported from the island of Utopia, I recognize that many things are happening there which I wish— much more than I hope—to see imitated by our societies." In addition, the very method of exposition followed by these authors clearly indicates the character of their thinking. Almost all take for their framework a completely imaginary country, placed outside of every historic situation. This plainly shows that their systems resemble social reality only slightly and aim but feebly to modify it. The way in which socialism has developed is quite different. Since the beginning of the century, theories which bear this name follow one another without interruption. It is a continuous current which, in spite of a certain diminution towards 1850, becomes more and more intense. And further, not only do schools follow schools, but they appear simultaneously —aside from any preliminary understanding or reciprocal influence—by a kind of pressure which is strong evidence that they respond to a collective need. Thus at the same time one sees Saint-Simon and Fourier in France, Owen in England—to recall only the most important names. So the success they aspire to is never purely sentimental and artistic; it does not satisfy them to elevate the soul while lulling it with fine dreams—they expect to have a practical result. There is none among them who does not view his concepts as easily realizable; as utopian as they may seem to us, they are not that to their authors. They think not with the drive of private feelings but of social yearnings, which they demand be so efficaciously satisfied that mere fictions could not suffice. Such a contrast in the manner in which these two kinds of doctrines manifest themselves can be due only to a difference in their nature.

In fact, in certain essential ways they are poles apart. Socialism, as we have said, consists of linking industrial activities to the state (we use this last word as a kind of abbreviation in spite of its lack of exactness). Communism tends instead to put industrial life outside the state.

This is particularly noticeable in Platonic communism. The city, as he conceives it, is formed of two very distinct parts; on the one side, the class of laborers and artisans; on the other, magistrates and warriors. It is to the latter two groups that specifically political activities fall. To the one belongs the military defense of the general interests of the community, should they be menaced within or without; to the other, regulation of its inner activities. Together they constitute the state, since they alone are capable of acting in the name of the community. It is the laborers and artisans, on the other hand, to whom economic functions are assigned; it is this group which, according to Plato, must provide the sustenance of society. But the fundamental principle of Platonic politics is that this inferior class must be radically separated from the other two; in other words, the economic organ is placed outside the state, far from having connection with it. Artisans and laborers participate neither in administration nor legislation and are excluded from military service. Thus they have no path of communication which connects them to the controlling centers of society. Inversely, these last must be strangers to everything that relates to economic life. Not only must they take no active part in it, but they are made indifferent to all that happens in it. They are forbidden to personally possess anything; private property is denied them, and allowed only to the workers. Under these conditions, lawmakers and warriors have no reason to interest themselves in whether commerce and agriculture prosper more or less, since nothing comes to them from these activities. All they ask is that the sustenance which is absolutely indispensable to them be furnished. And since they are trained from infancy to abhor the easy life of luxury, as they need almost nothing, they are always assured of having what is essential, without being conscious of it. Thus, just as access to political life is closed to laborers and mechanics, so the guardians of the state are not to intervene in the economic life. Between these two elements in the life of the city, Plato creates a break in contact. To make it as complete as possible he requires that the former live apart from the latter. The entire personnel of public service (civil or military) will have to live at a site from which one can easily supervise what is going on within and without the state. Thus, while socialist reform seeks to locate the economic organism at the very center of the social organism, Platonic communism assigns it the outermost position possible. The reason for this separation, according to Plato, is that wealth and all that relates to it is the primary source of public corruption. It is the thing that, stimulating individual selfishness, sets citizens to struggling and unleashes the internal conflicts which ruin states. It is the thing, also, which by creating personal interests alongside the general welfare removes from the latter the weight it must have in a well-regulated society. It is necessary therefore to place it outside of public life, as far as possible from the state which it could pervert.

All communist theories formulated later derive from Platonic communism, of which they are hardly more than variations. Even without examining them all in detail, one can be sure that they display the same characteristic, in opposition to socialism, and are far indeed from blending with it. Note for example, the Utopia of Thomas More. On one point it deviates from Plato's system—More does not admit of classes in his ideal society. All citizens participate in public life; all elect the law makers and all can be elected. Likewise all must work, must contribute to the material livelihood of the community as farmers or mechanics. It seems therefore that this double diffusion of political and economic functions must have the effect of uniting them closely. How could they be separated since each serves the other equally? Still, if the separation is obtained by other means than in the Republic of Plato, it is no less complete. It does not occur in space, it is true, but in time. There are no longer two orders of citizens, between which there is a break of continuity. But in the life of each citizen, More makes two parts; one which is dedicated to farm and industrial labor, the other to public matters, and between the two he sets a barrier so that the first cannot have an effect on the other. The process which he employs for this is borrowed from Plato. In order to separate the managers of the state from economic affairs, Plato prohibits them the right of possession. More extends this prohibition to all citizens, since in his system they all share in the management of the state. They are forbidden to appropriate for themselves the product of their work but must have and consume everything in common. Even meals will be communal. Under these conditions economic interests will not be able to affect the decisions inhabitants make when they deliberate on public affairs, since they will no longer have economic interests of their own. Unable to enrich themselves, they will henceforth be indifferent to whether much or little is produced. All that is required is that their subsistence be assured. And since in the manner of the lawgivers and warriors they are trained to have very few needs —as their life must be very simple—very little is essential to them and thus they have very little concern on this score. The manner in which they direct society, whether it be in choosing magistrates, or in training the elected judges, is thus completely removed from economic influences. Still more: not only does More arrange affairs so that the functions of supply do not act in any way on public matters, but he also attempts to reduce the importance of the former so that it does not occupy too vital a place in life. The extreme frugality which is obligatory in a utopian society allows him to reduce to six hours a day the work each must furnish to assure material existence. Later, Campanella would even go as far as demanding only four hours. As for the reason which determines these differing provisions, it is the same one which had earlier motivated Plato: namely, the anti-social influence which is attributed to wealth.

So to equate socialism and communism is to equate contrary things. For the first, the economic organ must almost become the controlling branch of society; for the second, one could not be far enough removed from the other. Between these two manifestations of collective activity, some see a close affinity—almost an identity in character; others, on the contrary, perceive only antagonism and repulsion. For communists, the state can fulfill its role only if it is completely insulated from industrial life; for socialists, this role is essentially industrial and the connection could not be too complete. To the former, wealth is malevolent and must be put away from society; to the latter, on the contrary, it is bad only if it is not socialized. Without doubt—and this is deceiving—in both there is to be regulation, but it must be noted that it operates in opposing ways. Here, it aims to elevate industry by binding it to the state; there, to elevate the state by excluding it from industry.

It is true that both systems allocate types of activity to the collective sphere which according to individualist concepts would belong in the private domain, and undoubtedly this has contributed most to the confusion. But here again they are sharply contrasted. According to socialism, strictly economic functions, that is to say, activities productive of services (commercial and industrial), must be socially organized, but consumption is to remain private. There is, we have seen, no socialist doctrine which refuses the individual the right of possession and use (in his own way) of what he has legitimately acquired.

Quite to the contrary, in communism, there it is consumption that is communal and production which remains private. In Utopia each works in his own way, as he thinks proper, and is simply obliged not to be idle. He cultivates his garden, occupies himself with his trade, just as he would in the most individualistic society. There is no common rule which determines relationships among the different workers, or the manner in which all these diverse activities should cooperate for collective goals. As each one does the same thing—or almost the same—there is no cooperation to regulate. Only, what each has produced does not belong to him. He cannot dispose of it at will. He brings it to the community and consumes it only when society itself makes use of it collectively.

The difference between these two types of social arrangements is as great as that which separates the organization of certain colonies of polyps from that of superior animals. In the first, each of the associated individuals hunts on his own count, in his own right; but what he catches is deposited in a common store, and he cannot have his share of the community wealth, that is to say he cannot eat without all society eating at the same time. On the contrary, among vertebrates each organ is obliged in its functioning to conform to rules designed to put it in harmony with the others; the nervous system assures this conformity. But each organ, and in every organ each tissue, and in every tissue each cell, maintain themselves apart, freely, without being dependent on the others. Each major part of the organism even has its special food. The distance is no less considerable between the two societal concepts which have been so frequently likened.

*　　　　*　　　　*

To explore the history of socialism it was necessary first to ascertain what we designate by this word. We therefore have given a definition which, while expressing the external characteristics common to all the doctrines we agree to so label, permits us to recognize them wherever we encounter them. That done, there was nothing further but to investigate in what epoch the thing thus defined begins to appear in history and to follow its development. We found ourselves then in the presence of a confusion which, when it occurs, results in pushing back the origins of socialism to the very beginnings of historic development and to view it as a system almost as old as humanity. If, as has been said, ancient communism is merely a form—either more general or more particular—of socialism, in order to understand this last, in order to be able to retrace the complete evolution, we would have to go back as far as Plato, and even beyond, to the Pythagorean doctrines, to the communist practices of the lower societies which are only the application of them. But we have seen that, in reality, far from being able to contain the two kinds of doctrines in one definition, they contradict each other in essential characteristics. Whereas communism consists of an excommunication of economic activities, socialism, on the contrary, tends to integrate them more or less tightly into the community, and it is by this tendency that it is defined. For one, they could not be relegated far enough from the essential branches of public life; for the other, they had to be its center of gravity, For the first, the job of the state is specific, primarily moral, and it can acquit itself only if withdrawn from economic influences. For the second, it must before all serve as a unifying bond between the various industrial and commercial relations, for which it would act like a communal sensorium.

But it is not only in the conclusions they reach that these two schools oppose one another; it is also in their points of departure. Although at the beginning of this course we were able only in anticipation to speak of what follows from the socialist method, nevertheless one can easily agree—and the lessons to come will establish it further—that socialism has as its basis observations (whether exact or not is irrelevant) which all refer to the economic state of certain societies. It is because, in the most civilized societies of modern Europe, production appears unable to regulate itself to consumption requirements, or because industrial centralization seems to have given birth to enterprises too large for society to be disinterested in, or because the unceasing transformations of machines—with resultant social instability—rob the worker of all security and place him in a state of inferiority which prevents him from concluding equitable contracts—it is on this and other similar evidence that socialism bases its demand for reform of the existing order. In short, it is only countries with developed industry that it impugnes; and in these it is exclusively the conditions of exchange and production of value that it attacks. All else is communist principle. The fundamental communist idea—everywhere the same under scarcely different forms—is that private property is the source of selfishness and that from selfishness springs immorality. But such a proposition does not strike at any social organization in particular. It is true, it applies to all times and all countries; it fits equally the system of large and of small industry. It does not aim at any economic fact, for the institution of property is a juridical and moral affair which affects economic life without being part of it. Finally, communism holds to a common authority of abstract morality, which is of no one time nor of any one country. What it questions are the moral consequences of private property in general and not—as does socialism—the expediency of a specific economic organization appearing at a particular time in history. The two problems are entirely different. On one side, you set out to judge the moral value of wealth in the abstract, and deny it; on the other, one asks whether a kind of commerce and industry harmonizes with the conditions of existence of the peoples practicing it, and if it is normal or unhealthy. Thus, while communism concerns itself only accessorily with so-called economic arrangements and modifies them only to the degree necessary to place them in keeping with its principle (the abolition of individual ownership), socialism, inversely, touches private property only indirectly, to the degree required to change it so that it may harmonize with the economic arrangements—the essential object of its demands.

It is this, however, which explains the great difference we noted in the way both systems manifest themselves historically. Theoreticians of communism, we said, are secluded men who appear at long intervals and whose word seems only to awaken feeble echoes among the masses surrounding them. They are in fact philosophers, who deal with problems of general morality while enclosed in study rooms, rather than men of action who speculate only to ease the actual suffering felt around them. What are the sources of selfishness and immorality? This is what they ask, and the question is eternal. But it can be posed only by thinkers and for them. Well, it is a peculiarity of philosophic thinking to develop itself only in a discontinuous manner. Before communist theory can arise, a mind must be found which through its native inclination and the nature of the times can raise the problem and resolve it in an ethical sense. One then sees it grow into a system, but the contingent combination of circumstances likely to create it can occur only rarely. In the intervals it slumbers without attracting attention; even during the moments when it burns with most vivid brilliance it is too speculative to exert much influence. The same reason accounts for the sentimental and artistic quality of all these theories. The very people who raise the problem feel keenly that it does not allow for practical solutions. Egoism is too essential to human nature to be uprooted from it—as desirable as that might be. But in the measure that one sees it as an evil, one knows it is a chronic illness of humanity. When, therefore, one inquires under what circumstances it could be extirpated, one cannot but be aware that he places himself outside reality, and that he can produce only an idyll whose poetry can be pleasing to the imagination, but which cannot pretend to be in the realm of fact. One experiences delight in representing the world thus regenerated—while knowing that this regeneration is impossible. The only useful effect one may expect from these fictions is that they instruct, as does a good novel. On the contrary, because socialism is bound to a socially concrete setting, it reveals itself at once as a social and enduring tendency. For the sentiments it expresses—being general—manifest themselves simultaneously at different points in society and assert themselves with persistence so long as the conditions which created them have not disappeared. And this is also what gives socialism a practical orientation. The situation to which it corresponds, being recent, is too harsh to tolerate or to be declared incurable. It is not an inveterate disease, like human immorality in general, which through long experience has rendered us almost insensate. Right or wrong, men have not yet had time to accustom and resign themselves to modern conditions. And, in fact, even were no remedies possible, they demand them insistently, and almost without interruption produce men who strive to find them.

Thus, in whatever way we view communism and socialism, we perceive contrast rather than identity. The problem they pose is not the same; the reforms demanded by them contradict, more than they resemble, each other. There is however one point at which they seem to approach one another: it is that the two fear, for society, what one might call economic particularism. Both are concerned with the dangers that private interest can present to the general interest. Both are impelled by this double feeling that the free play of egoism is not enough to automatically produce social order and that, on the other hand, collective needs must outweigh individual convenience. This is what gives them a certain family resemblance and which explains the confusion so often created. But in reality, the particularism which these two schools oppose is not the same. One school labels as antisocial everything which is private property, in a general way, while the other considers dangerous only the individual appropriation of the large economic enterprises which are established at a specific moment in history. Therefore, their significant motives are not at all the same. Communism is prompted by moral and timeless reasons; socialism by considerations of an economic sort. For the former, private property must be abolished because it is the source of all immorality; for the latter, the vast industrial and commercial enterprises cannot be left to themselves, as they affect too profoundly the entire economic life of society. Their conclusions are so different because one sees the remedy only in a suppression, as complete as possible, of economic interests; the other, in their socialization. They only resemble each other, therefore, in a vague tendency to attribute to society a certain predominance over the individual; but there is nothing in common in their reasons for asserting this predominance—nor about the situations producing these assertions, nor in the ways it is expected that such predominance will manifest itself. If it were correct to view these systems as two aspects of the same doctrine and to place them under one label, it would be necessary to extend the meaning of this label to every moral, political, pedagogic, economic and juridical theory which holds that the interests of society must more or less take precedence over any private interest—and the term would lose all precise meaning. In short, communism and socialism have this similarity: they both oppose radical and intransigent individualism. But this is no reason to confuse them, for they are no less opposed to each other.

So, to explain socialism and give its history, we do not have to go back to communist origins. These are two orders of historic fact which must be studied separately. Besides, if we return to our definition of socialism, we will see that far from being able to establish itself, even in embryonic form, as early as the ancient city, it was able to appear only at a very advanced moment in social evolution. In fact, the essential elements by which we defined it depend on several conditions which were not produced until later.

In the first place, in order to reach the point of attaching commerce and industry to the state, the value attributed to these two types of social organs by the public conscience had to be perceptibly equal—had to be conceived by all as of the same order and rank. But for a long period of time, a veritable chasm existed between the two. On the one hand commercial and industrial life was only slightly developed, whereas political life had already become relatively very active; the fluctuations through which the first passed affect the second but little. In order to be strong and powerful, nations did not then have the need of being very rich. Indeed, wealth seemed scarcely of interest except to individuals. But at that moment the individual and all that concerned him counted little. On the contrary, society was the single thing to which morality attached any worth.

Whether society was conceived by the multitude with the aid of religious symbols, or by philosophers—such as Plato—under the most rational forms, it appeared to men's minds to be marked with a sacrosanct character (which placed it far above the inferior world of individual interests) and consequently the state, which was its highest incarnation, shared in this same characteristic. Since society was charged above all with pursuing social ends, and as these were considered as rising to ideal spheres, superior to human goals, it was itself invested with religious dignity. Since the economic structure had in this philosophy been deprived of all social value (because it concerned only personal egoism) it could not be a question of binding one to the other—still less of mingling them. The very idea of such fusion was revolting—like sacrilege.

Thus, between these two types of interest a great incompatibility existed. They were situated at the two poles of moral life. Between them was the same distance as between the sacred and the profane. So one could not dream of burdening the same organ with the administration of both. This is why, in the communist solution everything which is of an economic order is removed as far as possible from the state and, so to speak, put under the ban of society. Before such a state of affairs could be ended and the socialist idea awaken, it was necessary, on the one hand, that economic activities assume more social importance, and on the other, that social activities assume a more human character. It was necessary that commerce and industry become more vital wheels of the collective machine and that society cease being regarded as a transcendant being, towering high above men, so that the state, without lowering itself, without condescending, could approach people more closely and concern itself with their interests. It was necessary that the state strip itself of its mystic quality, that it become a secular force, in order to be able to involve itself in ordinary affairs without inconsistency. Only to the extent that the distance between the two poles diminished —and in both directions—could the idea of binding and uniting them finally makes its appearance.

But this first condition is not enough. It is not sufficient that public opinion see nothing contradictory in the state's assigning itself such a role. It is also necessary that it appear able to assume it in order to generate a feeling of confidence. For this two additional conditions are required. First, the state must have developed sufficiently so that such an undertaking does not seem to exceed its abilities. Its sphere of influence must already be extensive enough so that one might conceive of extending it further—and especially in this direction. It is a question, really, of having the state intervene in an order of social phenomena whose complexity and fluctuation are too great for simple, inflexible regulation. So long as one has not seen the state acquit itself of tasks almost equally complex, one will hardly summon it to do others. In the second place, as developed as the state might be, it can do nothing if economic enterprises, by the nature of their organization, do not expose themselves to its influence. As a consequence of their small size, such enterprises are multiplied infinitely, and as almost every citizen has his own, this dispersion makes all common direction impossible. Each takes refuge within its household walls and they escape all social control. The state cannot penetrate each dwelling to regulate the conditions under which exchange and production should be made. It is therefore necessary that commerce and industry must already have attained, by spontaneous development, some beginning of centralization, in order that certain of the directing centers of society could have touched them and made their action routinely felt. In short, it is essential that the regime of big industry have been established. Such are the three conditions that socialism, as we have defined it, presupposes. But, they are all three of recent date.

Big industry dates only from yesterday—and it is only in this form that it acquired a truly social importance. As long as it was spread over a multitude of small independent enterprises, and as each of them could have no influence beyond a very limited circle, the manner in which they functioned could not profoundly affect—at least in principle—the general interests of society. Besides, until recent times the religious and public order took precedence over the temporal and economic order to such a point that the latter were relegated to the bottom of the social hierarchy. Finally, the development of the state is itself a new phenomenon. In the City it is still very rudimentary. Without doubt its power is absolute, but its functions are very simple. They are almost reduced to administering justice and making or preparing wars. And here it is the least essential.

Its action, when it exercises it, is violent and irresistable because it is without balance, but it is neither varied nor complex. It tends to be a heavy and repressive machine, whose rude wheels produce movements of only very general and elementary force. But given the complexity of economic life, in order that one could summon the state to become its pivot, it was necessary that it show itself capable of action which was consistent and varied, flexible and extensive. And what it needed for that was not an enormous coercive power, but a vast and conscious organization. It is only when the great European peoples were formed and centralized that one saw the state simultaneously administer multitudes of peoples and diverse services, the army, merchant marine, navy, arsenals, means of communication and transportation, hospitals, institutions of education, fine arts, etc.; that one saw it produce, in a word, a spectacle of infinitely diversified activity. Here—added to those preceding —is a new reason for not allowing us to view communism as an early form of socialism. It is because the essential conditions of socialism were not present when the great communist theories were formulated. It is true that one could suppose that the thinkers of this school anticipated in imagination the future results of historical development; that through their thinking they conceived a state of affairs altogether different from that they beheld before their eyes (and which was to realize itself only later in history). But not only is it less than scientific to admit the possibility of such anticipations, which are veritable creations *exnihilo*, it happens that the theoreticians of communism have their entire thinking oriented not toward the future, but toward the past. They are retrogressive. What they demand is not that one hasten the revolution and go beyond it in some way, but that one turn back. It is behind them that they seek their models. Thus the Platonic city does nothing but openly reproduce the ancient organization of Sparta, that is to say, what was most archaic in the constitutional forms of Greece. And on this point as on others, the successors of Plato have merely repeated the master. It is the primitive peoples whom they offer us as an example.

Chapter 3

Socialism in the Eighteenth Century[1]

IT FOLLOWS FROM all this that before the eighteenth century there could be no question of socialism. But at that period—at least in France—the three conditions we enumerated are indisputably present. Big industry is in process of development; the importance attributed to economic life is sufficiently established by the fact that economics began to be considered a science; the state is secularized and the centralization of French society is accomplished. One might therefore expect that, as early as this epoch, we will encounter doctrines which exhibit the distinctive characteristics of socialism. In fact, this has been maintained. And lately this has been again suggested, in a very conscientiously prepared book, a history of socialism in the eighteenth century.[2] But actually, if the theories to which this name has been given do in fact contain germs of what later will be socialism, they do not go beyond the communist conception.

Two doctrines in particular have been presented as converging closely with the history of socialism: those of Morelly and Mably. The first sets forth his ideas in the *Basiliade* (1753) and the *Code de la Nature* (1755); the other, in a rather large number of works of which the principal are: *Les doutes proposés aux philosophes économiques sur l'ordre naturel et essentiel des sociétés politiques* (Paris, 1768); *De la législation ou principes des lois* (Amsterdam,

[1] We do not deny that this chapter takes on more of the character of notes than those preceding. In fact, in one portion it closely follows the conscientious and intelligent book of M. André Lichtenberger, whom Durkheim cites elsewhere. In another part, for example, Durkheim passes a little quickly over Baboeuf and Baboeuvism, which are almost as little known today as at the time Durkheim taught (Bordeaux, 1895-1896).—(M.M.)
[2] Lichtenberger, A., *Le Socialisme au XVIIIe siècle*, 1895.

1776); *Les Entretiens de Phocion sur les rapports de la morale et de la politique; Des Droits et des Devoirs du citoyen* (1758). But considering only their external organization, both systems display the characteristic mark of communism, which is that the framework of explanation is purely imaginary. The social organization described for us in the *Basiliade* is attributed to a fictitious people whom Morelly locates on an island lost in the midst of a vast sea, far from any land. His book is an allegoric and utopian poem which he presents as a translation from the Indian. Likewise, in the *Droits et les Devoirs du citoyen,* (*Oeuvres,* XI, 383)[3] when Mably expounds his model state through the mouth of Stanhope, he takes himself in imagination to a deserted island and there founds his republic.

In both, the problem is posed in the same terms as those of Plato, More and Campanella. It has to do with determining the causes of vice and the means of overcoming it. "The moralists," says Morelly, "have always supposed that man was born evil and wicked, without presuming that one could pose and resolve this fine problem: to find a situation in which it might be almost impossible for man to be depraved and bad." (*Code de la Nature,* 14). And it is this problem he undertakes to resolve. Mably expresses himself no differently. Men cannot be happy except through virtue. The point then is to know what the obstacles are which prevent virtue from reigning, in order to overcome them. That is the objective the theoretician of politics aims at. "Is it not certain," asks Mably, "that politics should make us love virtue and that this is the one goal which lawmakers, laws and judges should propose?" (*Conversations de Phocion. Oeuvres,* X, 54.) We are thus in the presence of a problem, not of political economy, but of morality, and of abstract morality, independent of every condition of time and place.

The remedy is one communists of all times have proposed. The cause of evil is selfishness and what keeps it alive is individual interest. Individual interest can disappear only along with private property so it is the latter that should be

[3] Durkheim had to use the same edition as M. Lichtenberger, that of the year 1895.—(M.M.)

abolished. In ideal society economic equality among citizens must be complete. "The only evil I perceive in the universe," says Morelly, "is avarice. All others—whatever name they are given—are only shades, degrees of that. . . . But could this universal plague, individual interest, have taken hold if it had never found, not only food, but some dangerous leavening? I believe that one will not contest the evidence of this proposition; where no private property existed, none of these pernicious consequences could exist." (*Code de la Nature*, 29 and 30.)[4] And further: "Remove property, the blind and pitiless interest which accompanies it . . ., and there are no longer furious passions, savage behavior, ideas of evil." (*ibid.*, 132) The distinction of yours and mine is called the "fatal knife to the bonds of all society, which, when they have experienced the deadly edge, can hardly join together again." (*Basiliade*, I, 189)[5] Mably speaks the same language; the terms are almost identical. The mother of all vices is cupidity or avarice. "Passions are always disposed to march under the banners of greed. . . . To the miser there is no need for country, relative or friend. Wealth produces need, the basest of vices, or luxury, which gives the rich all the vices of poverty and the poor an envy they can satisfy only through crime or the most degrading baseness." (*Oeuvres*, XIV, 342-343.) The only means of rendering cupidity impossible is to suppress the ownership of goods. "Do you want to know," says Stanhope to Mably in their imaginary conversation, "what is the principal source of all the misfortunes which afflict humanity? It is the ownership of wealth." (*Droits et Devoirs. Oeuvres*, XI, 378.) The ideal, therefore, is "this community of possessions, so often praised, as often lamented by poets, which Lycurgus had established at Lacedaemon, which Plato wished to have revived in his Republic, and which—thanks to the depravity of customs—could be only an idle fancy in the world." (XI,379.) Plato's only error had been to permit agriculturists and artisans to hold possessions; this fault would have disturbed his state. (*Législation. Oeuvres*, I, 106.) Therefore

4 Durkheim had to use the second edition 1760.—(M.M.)
5 The edition cited is that of 1750.—(M.M.)

in both doctrines it is a question, not of organizing and centralizing economic life—which is the characteristic of socialism—but on the contrary, of divesting it, for moral reasons, of all social importance by suppressing private property. The solution is therefore (as are all communist solutions) essentially retrogressive. By their own acknowledgment it is from inferior societies, from primitive forms of civilization that the two authors borrow their program. It is there that they find their ideal realized as completely as possible. Morelly endlessly exalts those colonies in America where families live together in tranquility, supplying their needs by hunting. He equally extols the legislation of Lycurgus and ancient Egypt.

The name of Lycurgus returns again under the pen of Mably. "Lycurgus knew best the designs of nature and took most efficient steps so that citizens would not deviate from them." (*Observations sur l'histoire de Grèce. Oeuvres*, IV, 22.) Thus, far from believing that the reform they seek should consist of the establishment of new social forms, in harmony with the new conditions of collective existence, it is the most distant past from which such thinkers wholly borrow their idea. Like Plato, More and Campanella, they themselves consider the idea hardly susceptible of realization. They keenly feel unable to remake humanity at this point. "It is unfortunately only too true," says Morelly, "that it would be quite impossible to form a like republic in our day." (*Code de la Nature*, 189.) Therefore his aim, finally, is more speculative than practical. He proposes above all to clarify "the error of ordinary practice based on common morality" (*Basiliade*, I, 109)—more than he hopes to put an end to it. Mably is still more sceptical. "Men," he says, "are too depraved for there to be a sound politic." (*Oeuvres*, XIV, 46.) In a passage cited above one could see that he himself termed the ideal he recommended a chimera.

That granted, it does not need debating to determine whether Rousseau should or should not be regarded as a socialist. For his doctrine is merely a limited and attenuated form of the preceding ones. He likewise takes his models from ancient republics, whose organization seems to him the most perfect that ever existed. In his *Lettre à d'Alembert* he speaks with enthusiasm of this Sparta which cannot be cited "enough for the example we should draw from it." (*Oeuvres*, III, p. 175.)[6] He quotes Mably with respect although he had never been on very cordial terms with him and is interested in More's Utopia and in the *Basiliade* of Morelly.[7] The entire difference is that he does not go as far. Although a communist regime has his complete preference he does not consider it practicable outside a state of nature. He is therefore content to approach it as closely as possible. "My thought," says he, "is not to destroy absolutely private property—because that is impossible—but to enclose it within the narrowest boundaries, give it a bridle which curbs it, directs it, which subjugates it and keeps it always subordinate to the public good." (*Oeuvres inédites*, p. 100.)[8] Absolute economic equality is at the present unrealizable, but it is the ideal one must always have in sight and which should be realized as far as possible. "The fundamental law of your institution must be equality." (*Ibid.*, 72.) It is known, further, what he thinks of commerce and industry, as of arts. He judges them no differently than does Plato. Therefore like the latter, far from wishing to organize and socialize them, he seeks instead to remove them from society, or at least to give them as restricted a place as possible. Once these terms are defined, such a theory can only be called modern communism.

Still, if the eighteenth century knew communism, we cannot fail to notice that communism there presents some very specific characteristics which distinguish it from earlier theories of the same name and serve to forewarn that something new is in the process of being produced.

First, these theories are no longer sporadic. While, up until then they appeared at long intervals, separated from one another by rather considerable periods, in the eighteenth century we are in the presence of a veritable efflorescence

---

[6] Durkheim refers to the edition of 1854.—(M.M.)

[7] Lichtenberger, *Le Socialisme au XVIIIᵉ siècle*, 1895. p. 154.

[8] Durkheim uses the edition of Streckeisen-Moulton 1861 *Oeuvres et Correspondance inédites.*—(M.M.)

of communist systems. The two or three we just spoke of are the most famous and important, but they are far from being the only ones. From the beginning of the century, in Fénelon and the abbot St. Pierre, one finds numerous expressions of sympathy—though still vague—for a more or less communal regime. They are very clear in the curate Meslier, whose work, entitled *Le Testament de Jean Meslier*, is a violent critique of the effects of private property. Two disciples of Jean-Jacques, Mercier and Restif de la Bretonne, produced a Utopia containing more or less modified ideas of the master. Mercier's is entitled *L'An* 2440, and Restif's, *Le Paysan perverti*. More's *Utopia* is translated, and all the ancient and foreign works which express similar thoughts. And Fréon was able to write: "We have almost as many novels on morality, philosophy and politics as we have in the light vein." (*Lettres sur quelques écrits de ce temps*, XIII, 21.) And even where the communist idea does not take on systematic form one often finds isolated views and fragmentary theories which it obviously inspired. Though Montesquieu prefers monarchy to democracy, there is no doubt that he has an affection for the primitive rule of the city—and in particular the Lacedaemonian city—that he does not disguise. A certain amount of communism seems to him inseparable from a truly democratic organization, and on the other hand he considers the latter more suited than monarchy to small states. Finally, outside the writers whose specialty is to reflect on social matters, there is not a branch of literature in which these same leanings are not re-echoed. Novels, the theatre, and tales of imaginary voyages continually extol the virtues of savages and their superiority over the civilized. Everywhere it is a question of the state of nature, the dangers of luxury and of civilization, the advantages of equality.

There we already note a first peculiarity which warns us that we are in the presence of communism of a new type. But it is not the only one. Until now communist solutions had an entirely hypothetical character. All could express themselves in the following form: if one wishes to suppress egoism and have virtue reign successfully it is necessary to abolish private property. But this abolition was presented only as an effective means to that end, and not as being right in itself. It was not said that private property was destitute of every rational basis, that it did not conform to the nature of things, but simply that it had the regrettable consequence of detaching the individual from the group, and that it was necessary to suppress or reduce it if one wished to reduce or suppress its anti-social effects. Societies which practice inequality were not described as necessarily unjust, as morally intolerable, but simply as condemned to discord, as incapable of any cohesion. The communists of the eighteenth century go further. It is no longer merely the injurious results of property and inequality that they attack—it is property itself. "The eternal laws of the universe," says Morelly, "are that nothing belongs privately to man except what his actual needs require, or for his daily requirements for the gratification and comfort of his existence. The field is not his who works it, nor the tree his who gathers its fruits. Even the product of his own labors does not belong to him except for the portion which he is to consume; the balance, like his person, belongs to the whole of society." (*Basiliade*, I, 204.) Equality is not an artificial means recommended to the legislature in the interest of man; it is in nature, and the lawmaker in establishing it merely has or would have the way of nature followed. It exists by right, and its opposite is contrary to the right. It is in violation of what ought to be that conditions have become unequal. Of course, all these authors do not fail to develop the many disastrous consequences for society which result from inequality. But these consequences are put before our eyes only to prove—almost by their absurdity—the truth of the principle that inequality has been able to introduce itself only by a perversion of humanity, that it constitutes a moral scandal, that it is the negation of justice. In short, until then communists had scarcely suggested that things would be much better if they were as they had dreamed them, but the writers of the eighteenth century assert categorically that things must be as they expound them. The nuance is important. Therefore, although both, as we have noted, feel their ideal is not realizable, their renunciation does not have quite the same characteristics. In the resignation of the thinkers of the eighteenth century, there is something sadder, more distressed, more discouraged. This is the impression that a reading of Rousseau gives to a high degree. In fact, what they abandon—or believe they abandon—is not simply a fine dream from which nothing more can be expected than to uplift the heart, without reality having to conform to it exactly, but rather it is what they regard as the very law of reality and the normal basis of existence. In such an attitude there is a contradiction from which they cannot escape, and they therefore feel badly.

These are two great novelties in the history of communism. What is their meaning? They warn us that this time these particular theories are not individual constructions, but correspond to some new aspiration which has found its way to the soul of society. If inequality is now condemned, it is evidently because it offends some very deep sentiment; and since the disapproval is general, it must be that this sentiment has the same generality. If inequality is thought of as unnatural, it is because men's consciences have rejected the idea of it. If equality is no longer conceived as a simple ingenious means—concocted in the silence of the study—to hold together these systems of concepts whose objective value is more than doubtful, if one sees in it the natural state of man as opposed to the present state (which is regarded as abnormal), it is because it answers some need of the public conscience. This new inclination is the feeling —stronger and more generalized—of social justice; it is the belief that the position of citizens in societies and the remuneration of their services should vary exactly with their social value. But we see that this feeling—already sharpened by struggle and resistance—from then on acquired an abnormal intensity and sensitivity, since it went so far as to deny any type of inequality. There is no doubt that it is one of the elements of socialism. It is what characterizes all "socialism from below," which we will consider later. We must next inquire why, if it existed as early as the eighteenth century, this feeling for social justice did not then produce its later results; why did not the socialist idea follow from it in more clearcut fashion? It is because, as we will see, it was not provoked by the spectacle of the economic order, but concerned itself with this only indirectly.

*   *   *

When one compares the general orientation of communism with that of socialism, they appear so different that one wonders how it has been possible to see one only as a form of the other. To so regulate the productive operations that they cooperate harmoniously—that is the formula of socialism. To regulate individual consumption in such a way that it is everywhere equal and everywhere moderate—that is the formula communism. On the one side, one wishes to establish regular cooperation of economic functions with each other and also with other social functions, so as to lessen friction, to avoid loss of energy and to obtain the maximum return. On the other side, one seeks only to prevent some from consuming more than others. In the one case, individual interests are organized; in the other they are suppressed. What is there in common between these two programs? One could suppose, it is true, that the confusion is accounted for by the common factor that communism, though it levels consumption, also proposes to assure to each the strict necessities, and through that to improve the fortune of the wretched, and that, on the other side, socialism is in part also actuated by an analogous concern. Considering that out of this single tendency an entire system has been made, it indeed seems that from this point of view the two doctrines become indistinguishable. But aside from the fact that socialism actually reaches far beyond this single question, it poses it in an altogether different way and in entirely different terms than does communism. Communism views the respective situations of poor and rich in general, independent of any consideration about the state of commerce and industry, and in the way in which each contributes to it. So its demands, assuming they are legitimate, apply to all societies where inequalities exist, whatever the economic regime. Socialists, on the contrary, are concerned only with the particular part of the economic machine that we call the workers, and with the relationships they maintain with the rest of the structure. Communists treat poverty and wealth *in abstracto*, on logical and moral grounds; socialists examine the conditions in which the non-capitalist workingman exchanges his services, in a determinate social organization. We thus have a criterion which allows us to distinguish the two systems rather easily, even from the aspect in which they seem to resemble each other. When a writer compares the poor with the rich in a general and philosophic manner in order to have us see that this contradistinction is dangerous, or even that it is not founded in the nature of things, we can be certain that we confront a communist theory. But we use the name socialism only apropos doctrines in which it is not a matter of unfortunates, pure and simple, but of workers and of their situation *vis-à-vis* those who employ them. In short, communism is nothing other than charity raised to a fundamental principle of all social legislation; it is compulsory fraternity, since it implies that each is obliged to share with all. But we already know that to multiply projects of assistance and welfare is not to create socialism. To ameliorate misery is not to organize economic life, and communism does naught but push charity to the point of suppressing all property. It arises from a double feeling: pity for the wretched, and fear of the antisocial greed and hate which the spectacle of wealth can rouse in their hearts. Under its most noble form, it expresses a movement of love and sympathy. Socialism is essentially a process of economic concentration and centralization. It indirectly draws a whole section of society, i.e. the workers—because they are a part of it—into the orbit of the directing centers of the social body.

And still we know that in spite of everything some relationship does exist between these two doctrines. The sentiments that are at the roots of communism, being of all times, are also of ours. It is true they do not express themselves in each epoch under doctrinal form. But they do not disappear completely just because they are not vigorous enough to give birth to a system which states them methodically. Besides, it is clear that the times when such sentiments are in the best possible condition to manifest themselves are those when, for whatever reasons, they most particularly draw attention to the fate of the suffering classes. And no century has ever been more favorable than ours to the development of communist feelings. Socialism, precisely because it has an altogether different goal, would not know how to satisfy these inclinations. Assuming a socialist state to be realized as completely as possible, there still would be wretched people and inequalities of every kind. The fact that no individual will possess capital will not eliminate inequality of talents, sickness or invalidism. Since in such a view competition is not abolished, but regulated, there will still be services of limited usefulness which, even if regarded and recompensed according to their just social value, will not suffice to give their performer a livelihood. There will always be incapable people who despite themselves will be unable to earn an adequate living, and others who, while earning strict necessities, will not succeed—quite like the workingman today—in having more than a precarious and confined existence, seldom consistent with the effort expended. In short, in Marxist socialism, capital does not disappear; it is merely administered by society and not by individuals. The result is that the method it uses to compensate workers of all kinds no longer depends on individual interests, but only upon general interests. But just because remuneration will be socially just, it does not necessarily follow that it will be sufficient for all. Just as with capitalists, society—if not motivated by other feelings—will have an interest in paying the lowest possible price. There will always be, for ordinary, simple services, within everybody's reach, a widespread demand. Consequently, competition will be so sharp that society will oblige the mass to be satisfied with little. The pressure exerted on the lower stratum would then emanate from the entire community and not from certain powerful individuals, but nevertheless it could still be very strong. Communism clearly protests against such duress and its results. Socialism by no means meets this problem. Should the socialization of economic forces be an accomplished fact tomorrow, communists would be opposed to the excessively great inequalities which would obtain then as now. In a word, there is a place for both communism and socialism precisely because they are not oriented in the same direction.

It happens, however, that communism, instead of remaining what it had been before the advent of socialism—an independent doctrine—was annexed by the latter once socialism was established. In fact, although conceived under entirely different conditions and answering entirely different needs, socialism, just because it was led to take an interest in the working classes, found itself very naturally and particularly susceptible to those feelings of pity and fraternity which were to temper, without contradicting, what still was too harsh in its principle. For reasons that can be seen (but which we will have to examine more carefully later) it was the same spirits who henceforth experienced both the new hopes that gave rise to socialism and the ancient aspirations that created the basis of communism. To give only one reason, how can one feel the need for economic functions to be bound more closely, without at the same time having a general feeling of social solidarity and fraternity? Thus socialism was exposed to communism; it undertook to play a role in it at the same time as it pursued its own program. In this sense it was actually the heir of communism, and, without being derived from it, absorbed it while remaining distinct. Therefore we are inclined to associate the two sets of ideas.

So we see that there are two currents in contemporary socialism which are juxtaposed, which act one on the other but come from very different sources and take courses no less different. One is quite recent; this is the so-called socialist current. The second is the old communist current which joins its waters with the other. The first is dependent on obscure causes which push society to organize its economic forces. The other satisfies needs of charity, fraternity, of humanity. Although they generally flow beside each other, they are still distinct; if the ordinary person confuses them because of their proximity at the source, the sociologist should not expose himself to the same confusion. Besides, we will see that in certain cases they become separate; even in our day it has happened that the communist current again reacquired independence. There was a time in the century when clearly communist systems established themselves alongside of socialist systems.

It is not only from a theoretical point of view that it is important to keep this distinction clearly in mind. If we are not mistaken, the current of pity and sympathy—succeeding the ancient current of communism, which one generally finds again in modern socialism—is only a secondary element. It complements but does not constitute it. As a result, the measures one adopts to stop socialism leave intact the causes which gave birth to it. If the needs socialism expresses are deep-rooted they will not be met by according some satisfaction to these vague feelings of fraternity. But observe what happens in all the countries of Europe. Everywhere one is concerned with what is called the social problem and is impelled to bring to it at least partial solutions. And yet almost all the preparation made for this goal is destined exclusively to ameliorate the lot of the laboring class. That is, to respond only to the generous inclinations underlying communism. We seem to believe it urgent and useful to lighten the burden of the workers, to compensate by liberality and legal favors what is depressed in their situation. We are ready to multiply subsidies, relief, assistance of every sort, to extend as much as possible the circle of public charity, to make laws to protect the welfare of the workers, etc., in order to narrow the distance separating the two classes and decrease the inequality. We do not see —and this happens all the time to socialists—that in proceeding thus, we take the secondary for the essential. It is not by attesting to a generous affection for what still remains of the old communism that we will ever be able to either check or realize socialism. It is not by giving all our attention to a situation found in all centuries that we can bring the slightest alleviation to what dates from only yesterday. Not only do we thus stray from the aim we should keep in sight, but the very aim we propose cannot be reached by the path we are pursuing. For it is in vain that one will create privileges for workers which neutralize in part those enjoyed by employers; in vain will the working day be decreased or even wages legally increased. We will not succeed in pacifying roused appetites, because they will acquire new force in the measure they are appeased. There are no limits possible to their requirements. To undertake to appease them by satisfying them is to hope to fill the vessel of the Danaides. Actually if the social problem were put in these terms, it would be much better to declare it insoluble and strongly oppose it with an absolute bill of exception than to bring it to solutions which are not there. That is why, when we do not distinguish the two streams which give rise to the social theories of our day, we do not understand the more important of the two; why, consequently, we believe we are shaping a social program which in reality does not achieve its ends, and which is even deprived of all efficacy.

Once this distinction is established, people will more easily recognize that the social theories of the eighteenth century have not passed the level of communism. However, communism then acquires a new aspect. Equality is no longer spoken of as a regimen men would do well to impose on their egoism but to which they are not morally bound; it is now considered as being right and necessary. Societies establishing it would not be elevating themselves above nature; they would merely be following the path marked by nature, merely be conforming to the very principle of all justice. By this new note one surmises that the communism of the eighteenth century has been fashioned—at least in part—under new influences and new conditions. It has for its basis a very strong and general collective sentiment, namely, that the social inequalities everywhere visible were not just. Further, as a reaction against what existed, the public conscience went as far as to declare every type of inequality unjust. Granting that in the light of this feeling, some theoreticians examine the most offensive economic relationships, and a whole series of demands—clearly socialist —could not fail to result. There we have indeed a germ of socialism. Only, in the eighteenth century this germ did not receive the development it required. This feeling of protest was not turned against the facts of industrial and commercial life, as they then functioned. It did not attack, for example, the problem of the little dealer or small producer in the face of a large merchant of manufacturer; or the ties of the worker to the employer. It simply blamed wealth in general and expressed itself—at least in the large systems we have spoken of—only in abstract generalities and philosophic dissertations on the social dangers of wealth and its immorality. Its vigor and generality are evidence that it had deep roots in the public conscience and that consequently it attached importance to specific social conditions; nonetheless, as far as regards the economic order, one would say that it remained a stranger to the surrounding life. It has no point of application in contemporary reality, it does not aim at any definite fact, but is taken up only with general and metaphysical notions which are not of any time nor any place. The result is that the thinkers it inspired have generally fallen back on the commonplace topics of traditional communism.

Yet even in this regard some reservations are necessary. There are certain writers of the time for whom this new sentiment of social justice entered more immediately into contact with economic reality and so took a form which is sometimes very close to authentic socialism. This is especially the case with Simon-Nicolas-Henri Linguet. Hardly known today, Linguet was famous during part of the eighteenth century. It was he who took up the defense of Chevalier de la Barre. Adventures of every kind, loud quarrels with economists, encyclopedists, lawyers, and the audacious quality of certain of his ideas attracted attention to him. If we still are not clear about the moral value of his character, there is no doubt that he was an original mind and independent thinker. But in his various works, and more especially in his *Théorie des lois civiles* (1767) and his *Annales politiques, civiles et littéraires du XVIIIᵉ Siècle* (1777-1792) observations are found which even suggest the very language of contemporary socialists.

Linguet, in fact, is not satisfied to discourse on wealth, although on occasion he does not inhibit himself from these fashionable dissertations. He describes at length the contemporary situation of the worker who had only his hands to make a living and (like Karl Marx later) sees in him the heir of the slave of antiquity and of the serf of the Middle Ages. "They moan beneath the disgusting rags which are the uniform of poverty. They never share in the abundance of which their labor is the source. . . . These are the servants who in our midst have truly replaced the serfs." (*Théorie*, II, p. 468.)[9] Even slavery seems a preferable state to him. "It is a question of examining what effective advantage the suppression of slavery procured for him. I say it with as much grief as frankness: all they have gained is to be at every instant tormented by the fear of starvation—a misfortune from which their predecessors in this lowest rank of humanity were at least exempt." (*Ibid.*) In fact, the master was interested in treating his slaves well, because they were his property, and to endanger their health was to risk his fortune. Today, even this bond of solidarity between the employer and those he employs is broken. If they become incapable of rendering the services for which he pays them, he replaces them with others. The liberty the worker has gained is therefore that of dying of hunger. "He is free, you say. Ah! that is his misfortune. He belongs to no one—but no one belongs to him." (*Annales*, XIII, 498.) "So it is a sad irony to say that workers are free and have no master. They do have one—the most terrible, the most imperious of masters. . . . They are not under orders of one man in particular, but under those of all in general." (*Ibid*, XIII, 501.) Economists answered that contracts which fixed wages were agreed upon freely and it was that which made for the superiority of the modern worker. But, replies Linguet, "for it to be so, it would be necessary that the workingman could remain a while without working, in order to make himself needed. But he is compelled to yield because he is obliged to eat, and if it happens that he resists, his ruin—which is inevitable—increases and reinforces his

9 *Théorie des lois civiles*. (1767).

dependence, precisely because the cessation of work has rendered him more needy. If he does not work today at any price, he will in two days be dead of starvation and the curtailment his surplus suffered yesterday is a reason for reducing it tomorrow." (*Annales*, VII, 216.) "For the very insufficiency of wages of the day laborer is one reason to reduce them. The more he is driven by need, the more he sells himself cheaply. The more urgent his necessity, the less profitable is his labor. The temporary despots whom he weepingly implores to accept his services, do not blush to feed him like a fowl, so to speak—in order to be sure that some strength still remains. It is by the degree of his exhaustion that they regulate the compensation they offer him. . . . Such is the state in which nineteen-twentieths of each nation in Europe were languishing since the poisoned gift of liberty." (*Annales*, 1, 98-99.)

This situation is not ancient. On the contrary, it is quite recent and here is how Linguet gives its history. When kings undertook to fight against feudalism, they sought the alliance of the serfs and promised them liberty if they triumphed over their common adversary. What was the result? "They unchained this mass who, knowing the weight of their master's irons and not knowing what those of kings weigh, united joyfully under the latter's banners. This was truly a wooden horse that took revenge on the serf." (*Annales*, I, 94.) For then "society found itself divided into two camps; the rich, owners of money and also commodities, arrogated to themselves the exclusive right to tax the wages of the labor which produced them, and the other, isolated workingmen who—no longer belonging to anyone, no longer having masters nor (as a result) protectors interested in defending them . . . found themselves irretrievably bound to the will of greed itself." (*Ibid.*) This, therefore, is that liberty that caused all the evil, because in liberating the serf, by the same stroke it deprived him of all security. This is why Linguet calls it "one of the most deadly plagues which the refinement of modern times has produced." (*Annales*, I, 101-102.)

Such are the consequences "of the revolution which befell society." (XII, 501.) "Never, in the midst of its apparent prosperity, has Europe been closer to total ruin—all the more terrible as despair will be the cause of it. . . . We have come by a straight road to the point where Italy found itself when the war of slaves inundated it with blood and brought carnage and flames to the gates of the mistress of the world." (*Annales*, I, 345.) Already revolts have broken out in Italy, in Bohemia, in France. Soon perhaps one will see some new Spartacus come to preach a new slave war. Could not one believe he is hearing a socialist of today prophesying social revolution?

Another thinker—though very moderate—Necker, describes the economic situation of his time in colors quite as dark. (See specially *Sur la législation et le commerce des grains*, first part, ch. xxv.)[10] He begins by defining the word "people." "I understand by this word," says he, "that part of the nation born without property, from parents in almost the same condition, and who, having been unable to receive from them any education, are reduced to their native faculties. It is the most numerous and the most wretched class, since its subsistence depends only on its daily labor." The people so defined are condemned to misery because of the "power of the owners to give in exchange for a piece of work desirable to them only the smallest wages possible, that is to say, what represents the strictest necessity. This power in the hands of the owners is based upon their very small number compared with that of men without property, on the severe competition of these last, and principally on the prodigious inequality that exists between men who sell their labor to live daily and those who purchase it in order simply to augment their wealth or wares.[11] One is squeezed by the moment, the other not at all; "one will always make the law, the others will always be forced to accept it." This regime, it is true, is of all time, but two circumstances constantly increase it. "One is that ownership tends to combine rather than divide, . . . small possessions join together

---

[10] *Sur la législation et le commerce des grains.*
[11] The original gives no indication of where the above quotation ends.—A.W.G.

gradually in the hands of the rich, the number of owners diminishes, and they are then able to dictate a more imperious law to the men whose work they buy." "The second circumstance which tends to weaken the resistance of working men struggling for their wages is that as society ages it amasses a great quantity of the wares of industry suited for luxury and comfort, considering that the life of a large number of these articles outlive the span of man, such as jewels, glass, buildings, diamonds, metal ware and many other objects. This accumulation of riches which increases daily creates an insensible and permanent competition with the new labor of workers and renders their claims more powerless." Under these conditions the labor contract "is a bargain of force and compulsion which derives solely from the rule of power and the yoke weakness is obliged to assume." (*De l'importance des opinions religieuses*, p. 239.) And he too compares the lot of workers with that of slaves (p. 496 of the same work).[12]

To these two names it is appropriate to add that of Graslin. In his *Correspondance avec l'Academie économique de Saint-Petersbourg* (Londres, 1779) he enunciated a theory which is none other than that of the "basis of wages." According to Graslin, "in modern society there is a multitude of privileged who take from the sum of labor more than they put into it. These are, first, the owners of land, income, trusts, that is to say, those who put absolutely nothing into the total. Then come those who have a position midway between the privileged and the workers and who receive wages "higher than their due were there equality in sharing work and profits." These are the entrepreneurs of factories, of business, etc.; for their pay is due in part to the accumulated wealth they direct, but which is unconnected with the individual. All these unjustified levys are at the expense of the portion which should revert to the laboring class and which is thus unjustly diminished. Besides, let a discovery come along to reduce still further the quantity of manual labor needed, and the lot of the worker becomes

[12] *De l'importance des opinions religieuses*, edition of 1788.— (M.M.)

still more precarious. "In the present constitution of society," says Graslin, "humanity has more to lose than to gain from inventions that cut down work." (*Corresp.*, 57-58.) Montesquieu had earlier (*Esprit des lois*, XXIII, 15) signalled the social dangers of industrial progress. "These machines, whose object is to cut down skill, are not always useful. If a commodity is of moderate price and equally suits the purchaser and the worker who has made it, machines which simplify the manufacture—that is to say, which reduce the number of workers—would be pernicious."

This is entirely different language than we just lately heard from Morelly, Mably, and Rousseau. This time we are in the presence of, not abstract dissertations on the rich and the poor, but positive grievances which strike at a situation made for the worker by the economic organization of the times. On this point socialists of our day speak no differently. But at first it is only among a few rare writers that the feeling of protest (which we already found at the base of the great communist system) left the sphere of philosophical abstractions to address itself to economic reality. And even in these exceptional cases, if it more closely resembles the state of mind that inspires contemporary socialism, nonetheless it remains midway and has not yet given birth to clearly socialist doctrines. The practical conclusions which the authors we have just spoken of draw from their critiques are rather conservative. Necker, Linguet, insist on the need for maintaining the present social order by all possible means and are satisfied merely to indicate a few measures to render it a little more tolerable. An absolutely equalitarian communism is surely not without temptation, only they well know it is not realizable. But this solution aside, they see no other than the *status quo*, with some modifications of detail. Their socialism is entirely negative. This is interesting to note, for it shows that as early as that time, one of the seeds of socialism was in existence. But it is no less important to notice that it failed to receive full development. We will soon have to ask why.

But this germ of the socialist idea is not the only one

we encountered in the social doctrines of the eighteenth century. There is another, which is found in the same rudimentary state. In order for socialism to be possible, it is necessary that public opinion concedes the state very extensive rights. An established socialist organization might come to have an anarchic rather than an authoritarian character, but, in order to establish it, it may be necessary to transform juridical institutions, to alter certain of the rights individuals then enjoyed. And as these changes can only be the work of the state, it is essential that there be no rights, so to speak, in opposition to its own. On this point all the great thinkers of the eighteenth century—physiocrats excepted—are in agreement. "The sovereign power," says Rousseau, "which has no other aim but the common good, has no limits but those of public utility, broadly conceived." (*Oeuvres,* I, 585.) And in fact, since according to his theory every social order is a construction of the state, it can be modified at will by the state. The contract by which the members of the community bind themselves together can be revised by them at any moment of time and without one's being able to limit the extent of the modifications they make. By resting on this theory of the state Rousseau has sometimes been called a socialist. Montesquieu, moreover, thinks no differently and for him, too, the welfare of the people is the supreme law. (XXVI, 24.) Thus, nothing in the ideas of the time objects to the state's modifying the bases of economic life in order to organize it socially.

However, no one seems to have dreamt that the state could or should use for that end the broad rights allowed it in principle. Without doubt, communists like Morelly, do in a sense have it play an economic role. But at first this role—as they conceive it—is completely negative. They do not demand that the state becoming the center of industrial and commercial life, the mainspring of the entire machine, and regulate its functioning so that it may be the most productive and harmonious possible (which is the characteristic of socialism). Its task, in these systems, would reduce itself to seeing that everybody works and that the products of labor are used in common; to prevent idleness and private ownership from reestablishing itself. Further, it is only in novels whose utopian character is admitted by their authors that its sphere of action is thus enlarged. And whenever it is a question, not of producing a work of speculation and a completely metaphysical fiction, but of proposing reforms applicable to society of the time, the boldest limit themselves to demanding some financial measures or some modifications of the right of inheritance which would stop the inequality of social conditions from becoming still greater. Rousseau had occasion to plan a constitution for Poland, but as far as the economic order is concerned, the design he proposes is very slightly affected by his general theory of the state. The novelties he advises in this area amount to very little. Actually he does not consider his general concepts as being applicable to this category of social functions, and those of his contemporaries who more or less shared his ideas felt the same. There is perhaps one exception to this general remark. There is one economic enterprise which several writers of the eighteenth century wished to have at least more or less closely bound to the state, that is, commerce in grain. According to Necker, if the state itself was not to have charge of it, nevertheless it was to supervise and regulate it. In any event, a positive intervention was considered necessary. Some even demanded that the state take over the direction completely and become a trader. This was the feeling of Galiani (*Dialogues sur le commerce des grains.* Londres, 1770) and of Desaubiers (*Considerations d'économie politique sur le commerce des grains*). Under this plan the state would be charged with an active economic function. This time it is indeed a matter of socialist extension of the state's powers —but this is the only important one proposed. It shows that the conception then held of the state logically led to socialism, but we see that except for this particular point it was prevented from producing the results it implied.

In short, a hope for a more just social order and an idea of the state's rights which, together, are the seeds of socialism, but which were limited at the time to only rudimentary wishes—that is all we find in the eighteenth century. Even under the Revolution one went no further. Baboeuf's doctrine, perhaps the most advanced of the century, did not go beyond simple communism. It differed from the systems of Mably and Morelly only in this particular—that far from considering it utopian, its author tried to realize it—even by force. And since he found collaborators (as this was a real conspiracy), it is an indication that the belief in social justice we spoke of had not only been stirred, but had even begun to apply itself to the concrete facts of economic life, but without resulting in any renovation of the system, or any new orientation in the ideas of the time.

This established, we must take account, that is to say examine: one, where does this double seed come from, how was this new concept of justice and the state constituted? and two, what prevented it from leading to the socialist consequences it implied?

To the first question the answer is simple. In fact it is evident that these ideas are none other than the two fundamental principles on which all the political transformations of 1789 rest. They are the result of the double movement from which the Revolution sprang; the individualist movement and the statist movement. The first resulted in having it admitted as evident that the place of individuals in the body politic should be exclusively determined by their personal value, and consequently of having traditional inequalities rejected as unjust. The second had the result that reforms judged to be necessary were considered realizable, because the state was conceived as the natural instrument of their realization. Besides, these principles are jointly responsible for each other in the sense that the stronger the state is constituted and the higher it is raised above all individuals, of whatever class and origin, the more, therefore, did all individuals appear equal through connection with it. This is where the two tendencies we noted sprang from. They were born for the sake of the political organization and with a view to modifying this organization. They appeared to have so little contact with economic reality because they were formed under altogether different influences. Therefore all the economic reforms they inspired in the eighteenth century present themselves as appendages of political theories. It is political ideas which are the center of gravity of the system.

But the second question remains. How does it happen that once created, these concepts do not apply themselves, through a very natural extension, to economic life? How is it that under their influence the social problem was not posed? Why is it that although the essential elements of socialism were given at the time, it had to wait until the end of the Empire to be established?

One reason given is that one of the ferments of socialist thought was then wanting because the workers' situation had nothing about it which particularly aroused interest. It has been said that the guild-system, by tightening the ties which bound workers to their masters, did not leave them—as completely as today—at the mercy of competition. But, at first, aside from workers' guilds, there were those of manufacturers which were not grouped in the same manner. So it is far from a fact that the corporation had retained in the eighteenth century the beneficial effects it had in the Middle Ages. The line of demarcation between masters and workingmen was sharp. "One has spoken," says M. Levasseur, "of the fraternity reigning in the body of trades. We have already seen by searching in the goldsmith's community what is correct." (*Classes ouvrières jusqu'en 1789*, I, p. 77.) Just as the bourgeois scorned the artisan, the latter scorned the worker who had no apprentice. For a long time the abyss between the two classes was widening. In fact, workers were finding so few protegés through the corporations that more and more they were withdrawing from them to form trade unions which, outside of the corporation, furnished them support against the masters. These associations went back to the seventeenth century. "Police ordinances had been powerless to destroy them. On the contrary, they multiplied and became stronger to the degree that the separation between worker and master broadened." (Levasseur, *Classes ouvrières jusqu'en 1789*, II, p. 218.) Besides, we need only recall how Necker,

Linguet, Graslin, describe the situation of the worker to understand that it was not much better than it is today. Already, in the first part of the century the marquis d'Argenson had used comparable language. "I find myself now in Touraine," he writes in his *Mémoires*, "[and] I see nothing but frightful misery there . . . [the inhabitants] hope only for death and avoid propagating." And elsewhere: "Forty thousand workers in the arms factories of Saint-Etienne-en-Forez have stopped working. They are kept under watch so they will not leave the country. The silk workers in Lyon, similarly, are always kept under surveillance. . . . These things should have an end." "Our principal manufacturers are falling on all sides." (After Lichtenberger, p. 94.) Also riots and strikes were extremely frequent, as early as the seventeenth century, in spite of the resistance and prohibitions of authority. (É. Levasseur, *Classes ouvrières jusqu'en 1789*, II, p. 318.) The best indication of the suffering experienced by the workers, and their state of discontent, is the multitude of orders and precautions taken against them by the authorities. "One question which seems to have been of deep concern to the eighteenth century is that of the discipline of workers. The masters submitted to the law. But beneath the masters there stirred the multitude of wage workers, a restless population that industrial progress made more numerous and which every day became more isolated from the class of employers. This population, enrolled in mysterious trade unions, blacklisting the shops of employers who offended it, at times became formidable to its masters by its passive resistance, or through force of numbers incited defiance of the government. . . . Therefore did the authorities seek every means of binding the worker to his work and to his shop." (Levasseur, *Ibid.*, II, p. 362. Cf. 409.)

These facts are instructive. They demonstrate again how secondary the problem of the worker is in socialism, since as early as then the lot of workers was very much the same as it became later and nonetheless socialism did not exist. Besides, we will see that as early as the beginning of this century the great socialist systems were formed but even under the Revolution we find only their seeds. Now it is impossible that in so brief a span of time the condition of the laboring class had worsened to this point. The conclusion which becomes clear from the above is not purely negative. If one compares two facts with each other: first, that the elements we find in eighteenth century socialism are also those which conditioned the revolutionary events; and second, that socialism [arose from them] on the morrow of the Revolution. If one compares them, I say, one is correct in believing that what was lacking in the eighteenth century to give birth to an authentic socialism was not that the Revolution be once and for all a *fait accompli*, but, in order for these factors to produce their social or socialist consequences they had first to produce their political consequences. In other words, could it not be that the political transformations of the revolutionary epoch brought about the extension to the economic order of the ideas and tendencies of which they themselves were the result? Could it not be that the changes wrought in the organization of society, once realized, demanded others which moreover stemmed in part from the same causes which had engendered them? Could not socialism, from this double point of view, have issued directly from the Revolution? This hypothesis is already in agreement with what we noted and will be confirmed by what follows. This is not to say that socialism is justified by this line of reasoning. But its historic development seems incontestable.

Chapter 4

Sismondi

WE HAVE SEEN that the social doctrines of the eighteenth century had not advanced beyond communism. They displayed all its distinctive signs: conscious and avowed utopianism, a literary and sentimental character, and finally and most important, a fundamental tendency to put everything which concerned economic interests as far as possible outside public life.

It is important to note here that we do not define communism by its equalitarian spirit, as incontestable as that may be. Communism has always required that the fruits of labor be shared equally among all citizens, and it seems difficult—if not impossible—that it could accept any other arrangement. For as soon as we agree that wealth has no *raison d'être* except to the degree that it is indispensable to the maintenance of life and that beyond this limit it becomes morally and socially dangerous, then, since it is equally indispensable to everyone, it should be equally distributed. But equal distribution is only one consequence of the principle that the social role of wealth should be reduced to a minimum and even eliminated if possible. Equal distribution is so secondary and contingent a result that it can very well be reconciled—without any contradiction—with an opposite role for wealth. Indeed, if economic functions are social functions *par excellence,* we may conclude that they should be so organized socially as to become as harmonious and productive as possible. But this will not determine the ways in which this wealth should be distributed.

If, for whatever reason, we believe that the best means of assuring social harmony is to divide the products of labor into equal parts, we may demand equality of sharing just as communists have done, without either affirming the communist theory or contradicting the socialist theory. This, for example, is the thesis maintained by Louis Blanc. Therefore let us not be deceived by appearances—whatever role they may play in present concepts. Let us refrain from defining communism by a superficial characteristic which is neither essential nor unique to it, and let us hold firmly to the distinction we have formulated between the two doctrines. The essential feature of communism is the peripheral position it assigns economic functions in social life; while socialism places them as centrally as possible. The society envisioned by communists is ascetic, while socialist society would be essentially industrial. Those are the two opposing attributes that one should always keep in mind to prevent confusion—all others are secondary and have no substance.

But if communism, so defined, is the social doctrine of the eighteenth century, nevertheless we encountered, as early as that epoch, two important seeds of socialism. They are, first, a sentiment of protest against traditional social inequalities; and second, a conception of the state which allows it the broadest of rights. Applied to the economic order, the first of these factors gave birth to a desire to modify the system and at the same time the second furnished the means and the necessary instrument to achieve these modifications. And yet neither one nor the other accomplished these results. Arising in connection with the political organization, these two ideas were applied to it, they stimulated the transformations which are the work of the Revolution, but they were hardly extended beyond it. How is this? Since these tendencies are precisely those from which revolutionary events derived, we might suppose that before they could cause economic changes they had to transform the political structure. Outright socialist doctrines did not appear as early as the eighteenth century because the Revolution was not yet an accomplished fact. We were about to say that it seems likely that a mature development of society precedes the extension of these two ideas to the economic sphere. Yet, as the present discussion will show, the hypothesis that from the time the Revolution ended, Socialism appeared is confirmed by the facts. It is towards the end of the Empire, but especially at the epoch of the Revolution, that socialism established itself definitely.

Adam Smith's doctrine had just been imported into France by Jean-Baptiste Say, whose *Traité sur d'Économie politique* (which is hardly more than a reproduction of the master's theories) quickly enjoyed great success. Taught by Say, first at the Athenæum, then in an official chair at the Conservatory of Arts and Trades, it rapidly found many followers. But scarcely was it formulated than the opposing socialist doctrine —or what passed for it—asserted itself with no less energy. There is nothing surprising about this simultaneity. In fact we will see that economics and socialism actually derive from one and the same source. They are the products of a similar social condition which they interpret differently. But the identity of the basic social reality is obviously beneath this dual interpretations. These hostile schools have a close kinship. They issued from the same source and so have many more points in common than is ordinarily believed.

Jean-Baptiste Say's book dates from 1803. As early as 1804 Ferrier, in a work entitled *Du Gouvernement considéré dans ses rapports avec le commerce* (which reached its third edition in 1822), attacked the new school and opposed the traditions of Colbert, developed by Necker, to the ideas of Adam Smith. At the same time Ganilh, (*La Théorie de l'Économie politique*), used almost the same language. In 1815 Aûbert de Vitry, in his *Recherches sur les vraies causes de la misère et de la félicité publique,* protested the optimism with which Adam Smith and his disciples regarded an industrialism without regulation or restraint. "It is at least doubtful," says he (p. 30), "in spite of the pretentions of modern economists that our wealth—which according to their maxims should cause the poor to live with the passions of the rich, to augment the external power of nations by the accumulation of internal riches—has done anything but place those who have no gold at the mercy of those who possess it, to break the first by an impotent cupidity, to brutalize them by stupid work, to intoxicate others through the abuse of pleasures, to constantly keep the seeds of disorder alive in the midst of societies by encouraging vile and unbridled passions." But it is mainly de Sismondi's work that gives evidence of the troubled concern of these critics.

Simond de Sismondi had begun as a straightforward disciple of Adam Smith, and in his *Richesse commerciale*, which appeared in 1803, was in harmony with the spirit which had inspired *The Wealth of Nations*. But little by little, as he himself says, "led on by facts, by observations," he had to abandon one after another the principles of the dominant school, and as early as 1819 he published his *Nouveaux Principes d'Économie politique* or *De la Richesse dans ses Rapports avec la Population*, in which an entirely new doctrine was enunciated. We are going to approach this doctrine in terms of his later *Études sur l'Économie politique*, in which the ideas are the same as in the earlier work and the principal chapters of which had been appearing as articles since 1821.

The modern economic system surely presents us with a magnificent spectacle, says de Sismondi. Never has the productive activity of man been carried to such heights. Production "multiplies itself while changing the face of the earth. Stores are filled; in the shops one marvels at the power man has borrowed from wind, water, fire, to accomplish his own ends. . . . Each city, each nation, abounds in riches. Each wishes to send his neighbors those articles which are in excess and new discoveries in science permit their transportation with a speed that astonishes. This is the triumph of the art of acquiring wealth." (Introduction, 9.) But do all these signs of apparent prosperity correspond to real prosperity? The collective comforts of life, the sum total of goods—have they grown in the measure that people have thus heaped up accumulated riches? "More concerned with history than are economists, and in a better position consequently to compare present times with the past, we have examined those who gathered all the fruits of the visible marvels of science; of the flourishing activity which multiplies at once human strength, capital, means of transport, and communication within the whole universe, of this fever which makes us all live so fast, of this rivalry which makes us strain to supplant one another. We searched, and while we found in our century the triumph of things, man seemed to us more badly off than ever." (II, 150.)

Indeed, who are the fortunate in this new regime? Not the workers. In darkest colors de Sismondi describes their situation in the country that can be considered the classic land of industrialism, where one can best observe its effects—that is, in England. (II, 152.) Nor are the heads of enterprises—the masters—the fortunate ones. Necessarily limited in number, this group shrinks every day as a result of the increasing concentration of commerce and industry. Further, the possibility —always approved—of new inventions, or of unforseen rivalries which ruin them, the fear of bankruptcy always on the horizon, especially in industries which develop rapidly—keep these in a state of perpetual anxiety and prevent them from truly enjoying this unstable prosperity. One may reply that it is not the producers but the consumers who profit from this industrial hyperactivity. But for this gain to be real it would have to extend to the large mass of consumers and consequently to the lower classes—since they are the most numerous. But, says de Sismondi, society is so organized that the labor they furnish brings them nothing beyond their subsistence. ((II, 154-155.) Thus they could receive no more than before, while the work exacted from them is much more intense, more unhealthy and more demoralizing. There thus would be an increase in want and misery at the very time a plethora of wealth is produced, at the very time when there ought to be—according to present notions—a widespread abundance.

Such a result seems paradoxical. De Sismondi nevertheless undertakes to demonstrate that it inevitably and necessarily derives from the new conditions of economic organization. His entire demonstration rests on the two following propositions: one, collective well-being implies that production and consumption balance exactly, and two, the new industrial regime prevents this balance from being established in a regular manner.

The first proposition is easy to establish. Imagine an isolated individual who himself produces all that he consumes. Will he produce more than he can consume; will he accumulate wealth? Yes—but in a certain measure only. He will first provide himself with things which are immediately dissipated by being used—such as food; then with those he will enjoy for a long time while using them—like clothing; and finally with those things which, though useful to him from now on through the future, will last longer than he does—such as shelter. Before anything else he will seek to assure himself of the basis of immediate consumption. In addition to this first essential, he will build a reserve if he has the means. To give greater security to his existence, he will not want his daily bread to depend on daily work but will try, for example, to store wheat for an entire year. Likewise, in addition to the clothing he actually wears, he will make more in order to have protection against possible accidents, although he does not expect to use it immediately. But after having in this way provided a supply for use and a fund for reserve, he will stop, even though he could increase his consumable wealth further. He will prefer to rest rather than produce things he cannot use. Society as a whole is precisely like this individual. It has its supply for consumption—everything its members have already acquired for immediate use, and its reserve fund—to provide for possible accidents. But after these two amounts are provided, anything more is useless and ceases to have value. To the degree that accumulated wealth exceeds the needs of consumption, it ceases being wealth. The products of his labor cannot enrich the worker unless he finds a consumer to buy them. It is the purchaser who makes their value; therefore if he is lacking it is nil.

No economist denies this evidence. However, according to Say, Ricardo, and their followers, this necessary balance between consumption and production is self-establishing and inevitably, without anyone's having to concern himself with it, production can not increase without consumption increasing at the same time. Were commodities able to multiply themselves indefinitely, they would always find markets. In fact, they say, imagine that a hundred laborers produced a thousand sacks of wheat, a hundred manufacturers of wool produced a thousand ells of fabric, and to simplify the data of the problem, let us admit they exchange the products of their industry directly among themselves. Then let inventions occur which raise the productive power of both by a tenth. The same men will then exchange eleven hundred ells for eleven hundred sacks and each will thus find himself better clothed and fed. A new improvement will exchange twelve hundred ells for twelve hundred sacks, and so on indefinitely. An increase in commodities will always increase the pleasure of those who produce.

But, replied de Sismondi, this is to attribute to human needs an elasticity they do not possess. In reality the clothier does not have a better appetite because he weaves more fabric, and if a thousand or eleven hundred sacks are enough for his use he will not seek more just because he has something to offer in exchange. The need for clothing is less rigorously fixed. The farmer—in easier circumstances—will order two or three items instead of one. However, even on this score there is a limit that comes from being satisfied, and no one will indefinitely enlarge his reserve of clothing merely because his income increases. What will happen? Instead of demanding more clothes he will wish better ones. He will give up those he is accustomed to and demand finer ones. But then he discourages the present manufacture of common garments and encourages others to replace them and make luxury clothing. Likewise the cloth maker, instead of a larger quantity of wheat—which he would not be able to use—will want a better quality, or else will replace bread with meat. Thus he will not give workers more to do but on the contrary would expect them to be dismissed, to be replaced in part by cattle breeders and the wheat fields by grazing prairies.

Thus it is necessary that all surpluses balance and be exchangeable, and in the same relationship, if they are to raise consumption correspondingly. They no longer serve one another mutually as markets from the moment they are increased beyond a certain point. They tend on the contrary to repel and suppress one another in order to give way to commodities of new and better quality—which they call into being. These latter do not add further to the old but substitute for them. The farmer who produces more than in the past does not utilize, in exchange for this surplus, the excess fabrics which at the same time the manufacturer, by exertion, is able to make. On the contrary, he leaves the latter without work. He will dispose manufacturers, by the very pressure he exerts on them and the prospect of remuneration he offers them, to change their machinery and replace their surplus by products of higher price, and in this way equilibrium will at length re-establish itself. But this transformation is not made *ipso facto*. It constitutes a more or less grave crisis since it implies losses, new expenses, and a whole series of working rearrangements. In fact it supposes that excess commodities have remained unused and lost all value, that the capital engaged in the tools employed to produce them has been destroyed, that workers have remained without employment or had to go into new jobs, that all the losses entailed by the change of work have been undergone by industry, etc. So we are already far from the perfect harmony which would establish itself automatically—according to the English school—between production and consumption.

But this is not all. Balance can re-establish itself in this manner only by the substitution of luxury enterprises for former undertakings. But this substitution is not possible indefinitely, for the need of luxury items is not itself unlimited. The life of luxury is the life of leisure, and the extent of spare time which the average man has at his command is limited. One wears fine clothing when not doing anything; when he works he has no use for them. But the number of men who never do anything is not very large and neither is the time workers devote to rest and entertainment. What is said of clothing can be repeated for all superfluous consumption. Except for the lazy, one cannot spend unlimited hours at the table in good fellowship, or at the theatre listening to good music. So the necessities of life constitute in this way also a limit which cannot be determined precisely but which always is present.

It is therefore not true that production can increase indefinitely while remaining in balance with consumption, for the latter, at a given state of civilization, cannot rise above a certain level. The quantity of objects necessary to life has very narrow limits for certain items and the producer cannot go beyond them with impunity. When that comes he must apply himself to improving quality—but the perfecting of quality itself has limits. The need for superfluities—like the need for necessities—has a limit. Undoubtedly this boundary is not absolute; it can recede with time if the general state of comfort has augmented. The worker then has more leisure time and consequently can better adapt himself to luxury. But it is not overproduction that produces this result, for one does not have greater comfort merely by having more income and one does not have more income just because he has produced more. So at each moment in history there is a point which production cannot pass without disrupting the balance with consumption, and this disruption cannot occur without serious disturbances resulting. For either this useless surplus stays without a buyer—and consequently without value, constituting a kind of *caput mortuum* which will decrease as much as the returns of the producers—or else to sell this excess, the producers will offer it at a low price. But to do so with the least possible loss they will be forced to lower wages, income to the capital employed, rents paid, etc. Imagine general overproduction, and it will be a struggle of all against all, a violent, grievous struggle from which the victors themselves will not really profit. For in order that production may safely free itself from its surplus by letting it go cheap, it must diminish the income of all its associates. But it is by his income that each regulates his expenditures, that is to say, his consumption. If he lowers one, the other diminishes. He is therefore at an impasse. One cannot succeed in artificially elevating the level of consumption in one way except by lowering it in another. Here one loses customers that one gained elsewhere. One flounders endlessly in a situation without solution.

Thus the equilibrium between production and consumption —far from being inevitable—is on the contrary very unstable and easy to disturb. According to de Sismondi, our new conditions of economic life makes this imbalance chronic. Formerly, when the market was very limited, when it did not extend beyond the village, the small market-town, or the immediate neighborhood, each producer could make a careful computation of the needs he had to supply and limit his work accordingly. But today, when the market has become almost limitless, this useful check has disappeared. No longer can one judge precisely the extent of the demand he must supply. The industrialist, the farmer, believe they have infinite markets before them and tend to spread themselves to meet them. These limitless prospects arouse limitless ambitions, and to satisfy the appetites thus stirred each produces as much as he can. Besides, even to be sure of holding onto an acquired position, one is often obliged to try to extend it. For, as one feels himself surrounded by rivals—whom he does not even know—he always fears that a surplus from a more or less distant enterprise will be thrown on the market he now supplies, and he will be dispossessed from it. To prevent an invasion one gets ahead of it by himself invading and one attacks to avoid having to defend himself. He increases his own production in order to prevent overproduction elsewhere from becoming a threat.

In a word, it is because individual interests are discordant and unleashed without restraint today, that the community's interest in a regulated production, in harmony with the needs of consumption, is lost sight of. It is a fight unto death which has imposed itself on those who have engendered this fever, this hyperactivity, which exhausts individuals and society. And this is why the production of wealth, when it has—as today—no regulation, and no planning, causes pain and misery instead of abundance. And de Sismondi concludes in these words: "A thesis results from what we have just explained, and contradicts the accepted doctrines. It is not true that the struggle of individual interests promotes the greatest good of all. Just as prosperity within a family requires its head to adjust expenditures in proportion to income, so, in advancing the public welfare the sovereign authority must supervise and restrain individual interests so as to have them work for the general good. This authority must never lose sight of the acquisition and distribution of income, for it is this revenue which must spread comfort and prosperity to all classes. And particularly it must take under its protection the poor and working class, for it is least in a position to defend itself, and its suffering represents the greatest national calamity." (I, 105.)

The reforms proposed by de Sismondi to remedy these ills do not merit special explanation. Not because he does not consider reorganization of the economic order necessary, but precisely because the needed reorganization seemed so profound that he did not dare formulate a definitive program. Since he believes that such a program exceeds the capacity of an individual mind, he confines himself to describing the discomforts of the present regime, hoping that if they are recognized by all cultivated minds, "the concourse of the wisdom of all will be able to accomplish what a single mind could not." (I, 71.) This analysis is enough to show that this time we are listening to an entirely different language than that of the eighteenth century. If de Sismondi objects to overproduction, it is not because riches themselves seem immoral to him but rather that, if they accumulate without regulation, they cease to be valuable; they are turned against the end which is their *raison d'être,* and engender misery instead of prosperity. Nor does he mean that wealth cannot be expanded greatly in the course of time. The point is, that to develop usefully it must only expand on the demand of consumption. It is necessary that the average income—and consequently the comforts of life—be increased, or else that the population be augmented so that there is reason to raise the level of production. It is demand which should induce offer and which must set the whole machinery going. If, instead of awaiting the impulse which should come from the demand for labor, "one expects to give it by anticipated production, he is doing about the same he would with a watch if, instead of winding the wheel which bears the chain, he violently recoils another. He would break it and stop the entire machinery." (I, 74-75.) The question therefore is not that of communism (that is, to restrain the role of industry), but simply to make industry usefully productive.

However, by reproducing this argument we do not intend to present it as unanswerable and final. First, it can be seen to be essentially logical and dialectical. It expresses how things should logically occur, much more than it establishes the way in which they do actually happen. It consists of saying: this is what ought to happen, and not, this is what is happening. But we cannot settle a question of such complexity with this kind of argument. To solve it, more observation and comparison, and less hypothetical reasoning are needed. (It is true that current criticisms of this argument are of the same nature.) Further, de Sismondi's thesis comes down to emphasizing one of the unfortunate consequences of the present economic regime. But one cannot prevent such results except by reforms which would themselves have inconveniences. How, among these disadvantageous effects, do we decide which is the most significant? According to his temperament, his prejudices, each attaches more importance to one or the other without any objective principle being established. The present situation has all the dangers of absence of control, but all the advantages of liberty. One cannot avoid the first except by in part renouncing the second. Is this good? Is this an evil? We will reply differently to this question—while it is posed in these terms—according to whether we have a greater taste for order, harmony, regularity of functions, or prefer above all else an intense existence and great expenditures of energy.

But even if this and similar theories have limited scientific value, they are important symptoms. They are evidence that as early as this epoch there were aspirations to change the economic order. It matters little from the viewpoint of an exact method how sound the reasons alleged in support of this aspiration may be. The aspiration is certain—and that is the fact which deserves to be retained—for it could not have come into being if suffering had not been actually experienced. The less one views these doctrines as scientific constructions, the more one is obliged to admit they have a basis in reality. One can see even now the nature of the changes demanded. What this doctrine expresses above all is the need for a more controlled and stable industrial life. But where does this need come from? How is it that even then there was enough power in certain people to override, in part, the contrary need? Undoubtedly economic disorder had grown since the eighteenth century, but in so brief a time it could hardly have increased to a degree sufficient to explain this new tenor of social demands. We saw that even before the Revolution this trend was substantial. The point is that in the interval a transformation took place outside the economic order which rendered this imbalance and lack of harmony more intolerable than before. But what was this change? This is what one does not see clearly in these theories. We must presume that their view of the reality from which they derive is a biased one. They focus on one or another of the more or less remote consequences, without returning to the initial situation from which these derived and which, alone, would permit an appreciation of their relative importance.

Chapter 5

The Life and Work of Saint-Simon

BUT ALMOST AT the very moment that Sismondi was elaborating his doctrine, a great system was founded which had a success without equal in the history of the century and which responded to this *desideratum*. It was the system of Saint-Simon. Its author is so misunderstood and, besides, has so original a character that it warrants our pausing. Before studying the doctrine let us look at the man.

Claude Henri de Rouvroy, Count of Saint-Simon, was born on the 17th of October, 1750. He belonged to the family of the author of the *Mémoires*, though of another branch. From infancy he evidenced rare energy and independence of character. At thirteen he refused to take his first communion. For this reason he was imprisoned in Saint-Lazare from which he escaped. Bitten by a mad dog, he himself cauterized the wound with a burning coal. One day when a coachman, in order to pass, was about to interrupt his play, he lay down on the ground in front of the moving carriage. Struck by the extraordinary nature of their child, his parents hurried his education—about which he later complained. "I was weighed down with teachers," said he, "without being left time to reflect on what they were teaching me." However, at an early age he made the acquaintance of d'Alembert who exerted considerable influence—and this undoubtedly is one of the causes which contributed to the development of his scientific mind. This is also, without doubt, the source of his plan—which his school inherited—to rewrite the Encyclopedia of the XVIIIth century in order to harmonize it with the new state of science.

He played successively, in the course of his life, the most diverse roles. To conform to the tradition of his family, he first tried an army career. A captain at the time when war broke out in America, he followed one of his relatives who was in command of the expeditionary force and took part in the war as a staff officer. In the battle of Saintes he was wounded and made prisoner. But on his return to France after peace was concluded, the *ennui* of garrison life became unbearable and he resolved to leave the army.

In the midst of all this the Revolution broke out. He accepted it with enthusiasm but refused to play a role in it, believing that while the battle of parties lasted, former noblemen should keep their distance from public affairs. Still, he was not satisfied to stand by as an inactive witness or passive observer of the events that were unfolding and entered the revolutionary movement through another door. The former soldier made himself a business man and purchaser of national property. In this he was associated with a Prussian, the Count of Redern, who for this purpose placed at his disposal a sum of 500,000 francs. The undertaking which Saint-Simon was to direct alone succeeded beyond all expectations. However, in spite of the proof he thus gave of his confidence in the final triumph of the Revolution, he ended by becoming suspect. Ordered arrested, he was imprisoned at Saint-Pélgie, then at Luxembourg, under the name of Jacques Bonhomme, which he had adopted for his business transactions. The 9th of Thermidor happily came to deliver him.

Then began the third phase in the life of Saint-Simon. The speculator was transformed into a grand lordly friend of luxury and learning. In his magnificent mansion on the Rue de Chabanais he held open house, but it was almost exclusively with artists and especially scholars that he surrounded himself. Monge and Lagrange were his principal companions. At the same time he helped very generously —and even more discreetly—all young men of promise who were referred to him. Poisson and Dupuytren stayed with him a long time. He sought out these contacts in order to educate himself. He even went so far as to become a student again, and set up residence beside the École Polytechnique ere he took courses. Then he moved—again for the same reason—near the École de Médicine. He even assumed the expenses of numerous experiments. I will not discuss his marriage which ended in amicable divorce at the end of a year, as it was an event without significance in his life.

But Saint-Simon's fortune was much too modest for this life of Maecenus to last. We can be sure that in 1797 he only possessed 144,000 livres. He lost his fortune knowingly, and by 1805 nothing was left. Then begins the last period of his life, when he produced all his works. But although productive, life did not cease being hard on this unfortunate thinker who more than once found himself with nothing to eat.

He sought a position, and through the intervention of the Comte de Ségur was named copyist to Mont-de-Pitié, with a stipend of a thousand francs a year. As duties occupied his whole day he was obliged to use his nights to pursue the personal works he has just begun. His health was in a deplorable state (he coughed blood) when chance placed in his path a man (Diard) who had formerly been in his service and who had become wealthy. This good man took him in and Saint-Simon was the guest of his former servant for four years, until 1810. It was at that time that he published his first great work: the *Introduction aux travaux scientifiques du XIXe siècle*. But Diard died, and living again presented difficulties for Saint-Simon. However, in 1814 he seems to have escaped them for a time, although it is not known just how. It is then that he successively had as secretaries Augustin Thierry and Auguste Comte. In 1817 his financial condition even permitted him to give the latter 300 francs a month. Some works he published at this time enjoyed great success and brought him important subscriptions for later works that he had in preparation. Among the subscribers are the names Vital Roux, Perior, de Broglie, La Fayette, La Rochefoucauld, etc. But the daring nature of the author's ideas ended by frightening them. For one thing, Saint-Simon led a very irregular life. He was always extravagant, and poverty began once more. At times during this period, he was tormended by hunger and could not always find—even among those he had previously helped—the assistance he might have expected. Dupuytren, whom he had come across, offered him a hundred sous. Crushed, the philosopher surrendered to despair and on the 9th of March, 1823, shot himself. He lost an eye but his brain remained uninjured, and after 15 days the patient was better. This period of discouragement over, he returned to his work, and this time fortune was good to him. A small group of fervent disciples gathered around and maintained him until death, which occurred on the 19th of May, 1825. He died surrounded by friends, conversing with them about work undertaken in common, and about his next triumph.

It was, as one can see, a singularly unstable life. Nevertheless it was far from lacking in unity. What set its course from the first was the very character of Saint-Simon, which reappears—the same—in all the roles he successively played. What dominated him above all was a horror of everything common and vulgar and a passion for the great and new. From early infancy he had given indications of this. His faith in himself and the grandeur of his destiny were never belied. From the time he was fifteen his valet would awaken him every morning with the words: "Wake up, monsieur le comte, you have great things to do." Later, he related that he had a dream of Charlemagne, from whom his family claimed descent, and the great emperor said to him, "My son, your successes as a philosopher will equal mine as a soldier and statesman." (*Oeuvres*, I, 101.) Dedicating one of his books to a nephew, he wrote him, "My intention in dedicating my work to you is to urge you on to nobleness. It is an obligation for you to do great things." It is this passion that explains the lack of moderation he practiced in life, his wastefulness, and his debauchery, which did him the greatest harm in the eyes of his contemporaries. "I have made every effort," he wrote in another letter, "to excite you, that is to say, to make you mad—for madness, my dear Victor, is nothing but extreme ardor, and enhanced ardor, is indispensable for accomplishing great things. One does not enter the temple of glory except that he has escaped from the Petites-Maison." (*Notice historique*, I, 37.) Hence his prodigality. Money did not matter to him. The feeling he had about himself easily provided him with a domineering and superior air and manner. This very thing caused his break with Augustin Thierry who did not want to submit to all his wishes. But all this rather despotic behavior was tempered by great personal charm, by the respect that his impartiality and the generosity of his feelings inspired. Indeed, he exerted considerable influence on the most distinguished minds of his day: Poisson, Halévy, Olinde Rodrigues, Rouget-de-l'Isle, and finally and above all, Auguste Comte, who owed him much more than he acknowledged.

But his career did not have a merely formal unity, due to the very personal mark his character placed on everything he did. Actually, in everything he undertook he pursued only one and the same end. This dissolute person, who seems to drift according to any circumstance, was a man of a single idea and it was to realize this idea that he passed through all these incarnations. To reorganize European societies by giving them science and industry as bases —that was the objective he never lost sight of. From the time of the American campaign it was on this that he reflected. At that time he was writing his father, "If I were in a calmer situation I would clarify my thoughts. They are still raw, but I have a clear expectation that after they have matured I should find myself in a condition to do a scientific work useful to humanity—which is the principal aim I am setting for my life." It is under the influence of this idea that he devoted himself both to scientific works and large economic enterprises. For his speculations on national possessions were not the only ones. In America he suggested to the viceroy of Mexico a canal between the two oceans. He offered to build a canal from Madrid to the sea for the Spanish Government. Later, he dreamed of a gigantic bank whose revenue would serve to execute useful works for humanity. But in a kind of justification for his existence, he declares that his worldly dissipation and the diversity of his careers were a necessary preparation for the task to which he felt himself called. (*Oeuvres*, I, 81.) In any case, there is no doubt that the last part of his life is the expected, normal, outcome of what had preceded. Despite an apparent desultoriness, it realizes an idea which is that of his life's work.

*   *   *

The external form Saint-Simon gave his work contributed to turning public attention away from it. It is a loose series of papers, innumerable brochures, plans and lists of articles forever outlined but never realized. The author deals simultaneously or successively with the most diversified subjects, passing from astronomy to politics, from chemistry to psychology, repeating himself with a complacency which has no equal except in the abundance of his digressions. So the mind quickly becomes fatigued from pursuing thoughts which occasionally mark time, which spread into endless paraphrases, and at other times, on the contrary, move with dizzy speed across ages and worlds, losing themselves in every kind of turn and detour which conceals their unity. One has difficulty finding his way in the midst of this collection of diverse works despite a bibliography—which is just as confusing. Therefore in order to facilitate knowing the work, one must first attempt to introduce a little order into this mass of seemingly incoherent writings. Actually, its classification is not difficult once one has grasped the principal idea that inspired them. They fall, in fact, into two groups whose close connection we will soon explain. There are those devoted to questions of general science and philosophy, whereas the others are political and social studies—today we would call them sociological.

The first classification consists of:

1. *Lettres d'un habitant de Genève à ses contemporains.* Brochure of 103 pages, written in 1803. Saint-Simon there develops the idea—which is at the basis of his entire system—that it is science which should exercise hegemony over mankind today, at the same time indicating several

ways—in other respects chimerical—to assure this preponderance;

2. *Introduction aux travaux scientifiques due XIXe siècle.* One vol. 178 pages, 1807. Republished in two volumes in 1808;

3. *Lettres au bureau des longitudes,* which appeared in 1808. These are a continuation of *l'Introduction* and have the same ideas developed there. Saint-Simon states the necessity for an encyclopedic philosophy which embraces all the sciences, and sketches his conception of it. At the fifth letter, president Bouvard invites him to discontinue his communications, in a letter which is quite strange in tone and orthography, and which has been preserved. (I, 75.) This outline of the new encyclopedia was taken up again in several books, very brief, some of which we have had access to:

4. *Mémoire sur la science de l'Homme et Travail sur la gravitation universelle.* 1813. Copies of this work, on which we will spend some time, were sent to several persons, accompanied by a letter asking help. "For fifteen years," Saint-Simon wrote, "I have been eating bread and water; I work without a fire and have sold everything but my clothes, to cover the expenses of copying the work. It is the love of knowledge and the public good, the desire to find a means of terminating, in a moderate way, the frightful crisis in which all European society finds itself, that has caused me to fall into this state of distress. It is without shame therefore that I can confess my misery and ask the help necessary to place me in a position to continue my work."

Following are the principal works which are of special interest to the sociologist:

1. *Réorganisation de la société européene,* 1814, by M. le comte de Saint-Simon and Augustin Thierry, his pupil.

2. *L'Industrie.* The first part, entitled *La Politique,* was signed by Augustin Thierry, adopted son of Saint-Simon;

the second and ninth volumes only are Saint-Simon's alone (1816-1817), except for the first three books of the latter which are Auguste Comte's. But they appeared under the name of Saint-Simon;

3. *L'Organisateur* (1819);

4. *Du Système industriel* (1821-1822);

5. *Catéchisme des industriels* (1822-1824);

6. *Nouveau Christianisme* (1824).

The six works contain the social system of Saint-Simon. Some other works must be added, which were not published until after his death and whose dates we do not know:

De l'Organisation sociale (fragment of an unpublished work.)

De la Physiologie appliquée aux améliorations sociales (which he calls, in the course of the book, *de la Physiologie sociale*.)

For a long time these works remained dispersed and as they had originally appeared. In 1832, Olinde Rodrigues combined the most important into one volume. In 1859-1861, another edition, more complete, of *Oeuvres choisies*, was published by Lemonnier in three volumes. Finally, in 1865-1878, the members of a council founded by Enfantin to execute his last wishes published *Les Oeuvres de Saint-Simon et d'Enfantin* in 47 volumes. The volumes devoted to Saint-Simon are numbered separately and it is according to this special numbering that citations will be made.

Chapter 6

The Doctrine of Saint-Simon: The Foundation of Positivism

FROM THE ENUMERATION (of the works of Saint-Simon) which we have just touched on, it appears, at first, that Saint-Simon's thinking pursued successively a two-pronged goal. In fact we have just seen that he concerned himself first with matters more particularly philosophical, and only later with social problems. But is there really a duality in his thought? Had he not come to sociology, to scientific politics, only through inability to satisfy his early aspirations for a total science? Was not his interest in social matters—as has been maintained (Michel, *Idée de l'État,* 173.)—merely the result of his renunciation of loftier speculations, and the sociologist in him merely a philosopher frustrated and discouraged by failure? To fail to appreciate at this point the unity of his system, is to disregard what is its fundamental principle. Quite the contrary, his sociology and philosophy are so intimately joined that far from their being extrinsic to each other it is actually difficult—almost impossible—to separate them or explain one independently of the other.

In point of fact the idea from which he takes his departure and which dominates his entire doctrine, is that a social system is only the application of a system of ideas. "Systems of religion, of general politics, morality, of public instruction," says he, "are nothing else than applications of a system of ideas, or if one prefers, it is the system of thought considered under different aspects." (*Mémoire sur la science de l'homme,* XI, 18.)[1]

---

[1] Peoples do and must organize themselves differently according to the manner in which they view the universe and themselves, according to whether they see reality as, for example, the creation of a free will or as the product of a necessary law, or whether they accept one or several gods. The form of each society therefore depends on the state of its knowledge. (Added by Durkheim)

Elsewhere he says (*Ibid.*, p. 191) that undoubtedly scientific revolutions have alternated with political revolutions, that they have been successively the cause and effect of each other, and he cites examples of this alternation. For example, according to him it is the establishment of positive science in the sixteenth century that determines the organization of Protestantism and, consequently, the political transformations in northern and even the whole of Europe. For the political bond, which until then united the different European peoples, from then on became weak. But these changes in the political organization in their turn gave rise to knowledge—for example Galileo's completion of the Copernican system and the appearance of the Baconian method. Nonetheless, and although these two factors mutually engendered each other, he is far from putting them on the same plane. It is the idea, that is, knowledge, which according to him is the moving power of progress. Although at each phase in history it receives the reaction of movements it previously induced, nevertheless, it is the motive cause *par excellence*. For it is the positive source of all social life. A society is above all a community of ideas. "The similarity of positive moral ideas," he says in a letter to Chateaubriand, "is the single bond which can unite men into society." (II, 218.) Institutions are only ideas in action. (*Industrie*, III, 39.) It is religion which, up to now, has been the soul of societies but "all religions were based on the scientific system" of their time (*Science de l'homme*, XI, 30.) They are the knowledge of peoples without science or the things that science is made of.

This granted, one can easily perceive the bond that unites the philosophy and sociology of Saint-Simon; both have a social and practical goal. For this reason, and not to satisfy a purely speculative curiosity, Saint-Simon addresses these lofty problems. This is how he was led there. At the time he believed that "the single object a thinker can propose to himself," is to examine the moral system, the religious, the political—in a word, to determine "what is the system of ideas—however one views them"—that the state of European societies at the beginning of the nineteenth century demands. But this system of ideas is only the result of the system of science. It is its abridged and condensed expression, provided one gives the word "science" its broad meaning, that is to say, provided one understands it to be the whole ensemble of knowledge acquired in the corresponding epoch. What unites men into society is a common way of thinking, that is, of picturing things to themselves. But at each moment in history the manner of representing the world varies with the state reached by scientific knowledge —or what is considered such—in other words, with what passes for positive fact. It is therefore by systematizing the latter that one can define what, at a given epoch, should be the consciousness of a certain people. But on the other hand this systematization is the very object of philosophy. For the philosopher, as Saint-Simon conceives him, has as his aim some reality or other which escapes other branches of human knowledge, since these latter by definition embrace everything that can be attained by thought. Only, each of them studies one and only one part of the world, one aspect of things and only one. There is, then, room for a special system which ties all these fragmentary and special learnings to each other and gives them unity. This is philosophy. This supreme effort of reflection has as its goal, not to reach beyond reality because of the unknown means and methods of the so-called sciences, but simply to organize the useful conclusions they lead to, and to restore them to unity. It is their synthesis, and as the synthesis is of the same nature as the elements of the philosophy, it is itself a science. "The particular sciences are the elements of the general science, to which one gives the name philosophy; thus philosophy necessarily had and always will have the same character as the particular sciences." (*Mémoire introductif*, I. 128.) "It is," he says elsewhere, "the compendium of acquired learning," the great book of knowledge. (*Correspondance avec Redern*, I, 109.) It is, therefore, an encyclopedia. Saint-Simon thus takes up again the idea of the philosophers of the eighteenth century. Only, between this encyclopedia that he exhorts with vows and that of the pre-revolutionary epoch, there is all the distance that separates these two moments of history. The latter, as every work of the eighteenth century, was above all critical. It demonstrated that the old system of ideas was no longer in harmony with the new discoveries of science, but it did not say what ought to be. It was a weapon of war, made to destroy, not to reconstruct. But today reconstruction is needed. "The authors of the French Encyclopedia demonstrated that the generally accepted patterns of thought could not serve the progress of science . . . but they never indicated the ideas needed to replace those they discredited." "The philosophy of the 18th century was critical and revolutionary, while that of the nineteenth will be inventive and organizational." (*Ibid.*, I, 92.) This is how he conceives it. "A good encyclopedia would be a complete collection of human knowledge classified in such a way that the reader could proceed by equally spaced gradations from the most general scientific concept to the most particularized ideas." (I, 148.) Thus it would be the perfect science. But it is impossible to realize its perfection. For that, it would be necessary that all the particular sciences had been developed fully, whereas it is in their nature to develop endlessly. "The tendency of the human spirit will therefore be always to compose an encyclopedia, while its perspective is to work indefinitely toward the accumulation of materials which the construction of the scientific edifice demands, and towards the improvement of this design—without ever completing the supply of these materials." (*Mémoire sur l'Encyclopedie*, I, 148.) It is a work that is always necessary, but which it is not less necessary to revise periodically since the particular sciences it systematizes are perpetually in process of evolution.

So conceived, philosophy has an eminently social function. In periods of calm and maturity, when society is in perfect balance, it is, the guardian of social conscience because it is its culminating part and like the key to a vault. In times of trouble and crisis, when a new system of common beliefs is straining to be worked out, it is philosophy that must direct this elaboration. Thus there is no separation between the two kinds of study that Saint-Simon successively devoted himself to, for both have the same goal, since his philosophic works have a social end as do his sociological works. In this way philosophy appears as a branch of sociology. "Every social regime is an application of a philosophic system and consequently it is impossible to institute a new regime without having previously established the new philosophic system to which it must correspond." (*Industrie*, III, 23.) He has the same end in view always. But there is more, and the unity of his thinking is even deeper. "The philosopher places himself at the apex of thought; from there he envisages what the world was and what it ought to be. He is not merely a spectator. He is an actor of the first rank in the moral world, for it is his opinions on what the world should be that rule human society." (*Science de l'homme*, XI, 254.) From the above one can easily see that it is under the influence of the same practical preoccupations that he successively worked at both philosophy and sociology; but it is still not apparent why he went from one to the other. Why was not philosophy sufficient for the social task he contemplated? How is it he was unable to immediately deduce from it the practical conclusions he was moving toward and which he believed necessary to elaborate in the different writings which filled the second part of his career, and to lay the foundations of a special science of society? In other words, if the unity of the goal he pursued springs from what we just said, it is not the same with the unity of means he used. He seems to have successively employed two kinds, without one's immediately seeing why. Although the paths he followed converge at the same point, he seems to have followed two different ones and to have tried one only after having abandoned the other. But we will see that this duality is only apparent. It is philosophy itself which led him to sociology as its natural complement. The path we see him take in the second case is merely the result and extension of the first.

In fact, for this systematization which constitutes philosophy to be logically possible, it is necessary that it comprise only elements of the same nature. One cannot integrate in a coherent manner theological concepts, devoid of any positive basis, having no authority but that of a claimed revelation, and scientific knowledge, established by observation and in the light of free examination. One could not form a unity, single and organic, of ideas as heterogeneous and from sources as disparate as the conjectures of priests, on the one hand, and propositions demonstrated by scholars, on the other. But all the subordinate sciences which deal with inorganic bodies—astronomy, physics, chemistry—have definitely taken on a positive character. There is nothing further to alter. Consequently, the philosophic encyclopedia is possible without discrepancy only if other knowledge— and especially the science of man—assume this same character, and only if they themselves become as positive. But they have not yet reached this stage,[2] at least it is only partially or fragmentarily that certain scholars have treated them according to the same principles and procedures as other sciences. As a result, if philosophy includes only present acquired results it can be only an ambiguous system, without unity. Undoubtedly since the Renaissance one is content with this equivocation, one lives in this antinomy. But as we see it, it is precisely this contradiction that causes the critical situation of modern societies, which, by preventing them from being in harmony with themselves, from being freed of the contradictions which beset them, places an obstacle before all harmonious organization. It is essential to get out of this impasse. There is no choice except between the two following courses. Either be resigned to a philosophy which embraces only the sciences of inorganic bodies, or else, if one wishes to enlarge the basis of comparisons and generalizations, it is necessary to first establish the science that is missing. Either remove its part of the void, or else supply it. No other expedient is possible. But the first of the solutions is not a solution. For so curtailed an encyclopedia would not play the social role which is its only *raison d'être*. It would be of no use. In fact, it is not by gathering the knowledge that we have about things that we can ever succeed in discovering the means of keeping men united in societies. It is not by systematizing the most general conclusions of physics, chemistry,

[2] "Physiology does not yet warrant being classed among the positive sciences." (*Science de l'homme*, XI, 27.)

or astronomy that one can establish for a people a system of ideas which may serve as a foundation for its moral, religious, and political beliefs. It is not that these sciences are not elements of this system; but by themselves they are insufficient to build it. In fact, they have long occupied a leading position and exercise a kind of preponderance, precisely because they are the most advanced. But their moral impotence becomes only too manifest by the state of crisis that European societies are going through. Chemists, astronomers, physicists, exclaims Saint-Simon, "what right have you to occupy at this moment the place of *avant-garde*? Humankind finds itself engaged in one of the greatest crises experienced since the beginning of its existence, but what effort are you making to end this crisis? . . . All Europe is slaying itself (1813) and what are you doing to stop this butchery? Nothing, say I! It is you who are perfecting the means of destruction; it is you who are directing their use. In all armies, one sees you at the head of the artillery; it is you who are conducting the execution of the attack! What are you doing, I say again, to re-establish peace? Nothing. What can you do? Nothing. Knowledge of man is the single thing that can lead to the discovery of the means of reconciling peoples' interests, and you study this science not at all. . . . Stop directing the scientific laboratory. Allow us to rekindle the heart of him who was immobilized under your supervision and to recall his whole attention to deeds which can bring back general peace by reorganizing society." (*Science de l'homme*, XI, 40.) So one must go forward and apply himself to the task, if one wishes to render humanity the service it so badly needs. What has not been done must be done. It is necessary to extend the positive spirit, which inspires astronomy and the physico-chemical sciences, to man and societies, to establish anew and on new foundations the system of human learning relating to this double objective; to place them in harmony with what we previously knew concerning inorganic things, and to make possible the unification of the world. This is why, in order to attain the goal philosophy pursues, it is not enough to build the system from such sciences as exist. You must begin to complete it by founding a new science—the science of man and societies. Saint-Simon does not use the word sociology—which Comte will coin later; he uses "social physiology," which is its equivalent.

We can now account for the unity of the doctrine. We now perceive the different parts it consists of and what binds one to the other. In order to liberate the body of ideas on which the social structure should rest, it is essential to systematize the sciences—in other words, make a philosophic encyclopedia of them. But this encyclopedia can fulfill the social role that has fallen to it only if a new science is added to the series of established sciences. This is social physiology. And that is how, in order to approach the single and unique aim he had in mind, Saint-Simon was led to depart from purely philosophic considerations and address peculiarly sociological matters. It is because the study of the second is indispensable to the advancement of the first. It is the necessary condition of its ability to produce results. However, he did not pass from one to the other without the notion of returning. Quite the contrary— once the science of societies will have been created, he will have to resume the encyclopedic task, suspended only for the moment. For then it can synthesize all human knowledge and embrace the whole universe, while remaining homogeneous. In fact, no longer consisting of any but positive sciences, it will itself be positive, in its ensemble as in its parts. "It can be seen," says Saint-Simon, "that the particular sciences are elements of general science; that the general science, that is to say, philosophy, had to be conjectural as long as the individual sciences were . . . and that it will be completely positive when all the particular sciences are. This will occur when physiology and psychology (which comprise social physiology) are based on observed and examined facts, for no phenomenon exists which is not astronomical, chemical, physiological or psychological." (*Science de l'homme,* XI, 18-19.) And with this positive philosophy one will finally be able to establish the system of ideas which Saint-Simon aspires to above all else, which he never loses sight of—without the system whose highest form is religion. So these turns and detours are merely apparent; they never separate him from his original goal. On the contrary, in the end they lead him back to his point of departure. This explains how Saint-Simon, after beginning with philosophic writings, went on to political studies, and finally crowned his intellectual career with his book *Nouveau Christianisme*.

*   *   *

Having indicated the place of social studies in the work of Saint-Simon, let us look more closely at how he conceived of them.

What preceded has already permitted us to determine one of their essential characteristics. In fact it follows from what we just said that these studies will have to be made in the same spirit and according to the same principles that served to make the sciences of inorganic bodies. Human sciences have to be constructed in imitation of the other natural sciences, for man is only one part of nature. There are not two worlds in the world, one which depends on scientific observation, and the other which escapes it. The universe is one, and the same method must serve to explore it in all of its parts. Man and the universe, says Saint-Simon, are like a mechanism on two scales—the first is a reduction of the second but does not differ from it in nature. Man is related to the universe like "a watch enclosed within a great clock from which it receives movement." (*Introduction aux travaux scientifiques due XIXe siècle. Oeuvres choisies, I, III.*) Since it is demonstrated that the positive method alone allows us to know the inorganic world, it follows that it alone is suited to the human world, also. The tendency of the human spirit since the fifteenth century "is to base all its reasoning on observed and examined facts. Already it has reorganized astronomy, physics and chemistry on this positive basis. . . . One concludes necessarily that physiology, of which the science of man is part, will be treated by the method adopted for the other physical sciences." (*Science de l'homme*, XI, 17.) And since it is the necessary condition, if thought is to have practical results, there is nothing more urgent than to give this science that same character. "At the present time, the best use we can make of the power of our intelligence is to impress a positive character on the science of man." (*Science de l'homme*, XI, 187.) It is to be so completely integrated in the cycle of natural sciences that Saint-Simon considers it only as a branch of physiology. "The domain of physiology viewed as a whole is generally composed of all facts relating to organic beings." (*Physiologie sociale*, X, 178.) It is true that conceived in this way it appears to have no other object than the individual. But this is not so. Physiology consists of two parts: one which deals with individual organs, the other with social organs. "Physiology is not only the science which, addressing itself to our organs one by one, experiments on each of them . . . to better determine the spheres of activity. . . . It does not consist only in this comparative knowledge which draws from the study of plants and animals valuable ideas on the functions of the parts we possess in common with these different classes of organic beings." In addition to this special physiology there is another, a general physiology which, "rich in all the facts discovered through valuable pieces of work undertaken in these different directions, addresses itself to considerations of a higher order. It towers above individuals, looking upon them merely as organs of the social body, whose organic functions it must examine, just as specialized physiology studies those of individuals." (*Physiologie sociale*, X, 176, 177.) This general physiology has a special object, as distinct from the physiology of human individuals as is the latter from the physiology of animals and plants. The social being is not a simple aggregate of individuals, a simple sum, but a reality *sui generis* which has a distinct existence and a nature which is peculiar to it. "Society is not at all a simple conglomeration of living beings whose actions have no other cause but the arbitrariness of individual wills, nor other result than ephemeral or unimportant accidents. On the contrary, society is above all a veritable organized machine, all of whose parts contribute in a different way to the movement of the whole. The gathering of men constitutes a veritable being whose existence is more or less certain or precarious according to whether its organs acquit themselves more or less regularly of the functions entrusted to them." (*Physiologie sociale*, X, 177.) This is the social organism. This general and social physiology naturally embraces morality and politics which consequently must themselves become positive sciences. Once physiology is advanced, says Saint-Simon, "politics will become a science of observation, and political questions handled by those who would have studied the positive science of man by the same method and in the same way that today one treats those relating to other phenomena." (*Science de l'homme*, XI, 187. Cf. *Oeuvres*, III, 189-190. *Science de l'homme*, 17-19, and 29 and fol.) And it is only when politics are dealt with in this manner, and when, as a result, it can be taught in schools like other sciences, that the European crisis can be resolved.

But this *sui generis* thing—the object of this new science —what is the proper perspective for it to be viewed in order to study it? Today it is generally acknowledged that to have as complete as possible knowledge of it, it must be considered successively from two different aspects. One can consider human societies at a determinate and fixed moment in their evolution and then examine how, in this phase, their different parts act and react on each other— in a word, how they contribute to the collective life. Or else, instead of fixing and immobilizing them artificially in one moment of time, one can follow them through the successive stages they have travelled in the course of history, and then propose to find how each stage has contributed to determine the one that followed. In the first case one attempts to determine the law of social organization at such and such a phase of historic development, while in the other, one inquires about the law according to which these different phases have succeeded each other, what is the order of succession and what accounts for this order—in other words, what is the law of progress. In the eyes of Saint-Simon the second point of view is the more important. Therefore it is the only one at which he places himself. Indeed, if at each moment of its existence the social organization gives an account of things then observed, it still does not explain itself. To understand it, one must go back further; one must connect it with previous conditions of civilization which have given rise to it and which alone can account for it. Then, in order to explain these, one must go back still further. Consequently the real explanation consists in relating to each other—by always moving further into the past—the succeeding forms of civilization and in showing how they were brought about. The dominating fact in social physiology is the fact of progress. In this Saint-Simon ties himself to Condorcet, whom he addresses as his master and precursor, although he might have had a very different conception of human progress.

In fact, according to him, the law of progress dominates us with an absolute necessity. We submit to it—we do not make it. We are its instruments—not its authors. "The supreme law of progress of the human spirit carries along and dominates everything; men are but its instruments. Although this force derives from us, it is no more in our power to withhold ourselves from its influence, or master its action, than to change at will the primary impulse which makes our planet revolve around the sun. All we can do is to obey this law by accounting for the course it directs, instead of being blindly pushed by it; and, incidentally, it is precisely in this that the great philosophic development reserved for the present era will consist." (*Organisat.*, IV, 119.) From a superficial and yet very general view of historic matters, it appears that there are great men who have been the authors and guides of progress, that they have directed it according to a preconceived plan toward the goal they assigned to it. But in reality they are themselves the products of this movement; they merely summarize everything the spontaneous advance of the human spirit had prepared before them and without them. The business of progress is essentially impersonal and anonymous, because it is necessary. (IV, 178.) But precisely because at each epoch of humanity progress was unable to be anything but what it was, it is always—at least on the whole—all that it should or can be. "Nature has suggested to men, in each period, the most suitable form of government. . . . The natural course of things has created the institutions necessary for each age of the body social." (*Physiologie sociale*, X, 190.) Its determinism thus induces an optimism which, in addition, is the very base of the historic method. For the historian is obliged to postulate that human institutions have been—at least in general—in harmony with the state of the peoples who have established them. It is this principle that Saint-Simon especially reproaches Condorcet for not having understood. Without considering the extreme variety of religious systems, Condorcet had presented religion as an obstacle to the happiness of mankind—"an essentially false idea," says Saint-Simon. Religion had its role—and an essential one—in the development of the human spirit. (*Corresp. avec Redern.* I, 115.)[3] Similarly, Condorcet, and with him a multitude of historians, had seen in the Middle Ages only a period of chaos and confusion, a regrettable consequence of a kind of aberration of the human mind. For the same reason Saint-Simon objects to such a conception. It is the Middle Ages out of which modern times sprang; they were thus a necessary antecedent and consequently constitute an essential stage, indispensable to our social evolution.

So we see both how the problem of social physiology is posed and by what method it must be resolved. Since the progress of human societies is subjected to a necessary law, the primary aim of science is to find this law. And once discovered, it will itself indicate the direction progress must follow. To discover the order in which humanity developed in the past, in order to determine what this development should become—that is the urgent question, *par excellence*, which imposes itself on a thinker. In this way politics can be treated scientifically. "The future consists of the last items of a series of which the first composed the past. When one has properly examined the first terms of a series, it is easy to postulate those following. Thus, from the past, deeply observed, one can with ease deduce the future." (*Mémoire*

[3] Durkheim adds in the margin, "Reread the entire discussion of Condorcet."—(M.M.)

introductif, I, 122, and *Mém. sur la science de l'h.*, XI, 288.) The fault of statesmen, usually, is to have their eyes fixed on the present. And thus they expose themselves to inevitable errors. For how, if one limits oneself to the consideration of so brief a period, distinguish "the remains of a past which was disappearing and the seeds of a future which is arising?" (*Syst industr.*, V, 69.) It is only by observing series of broadly extended facts, as a result of searching deeply into the past, that one can disentangle among the various elements of the present those large with future from those which are no more than monuments of a past that has outlived itself. Since it will be easy to establish that the former belong to an ascending series and the latter to a regressive one, it will be relatively simple to make a selection and to orient progress.

The nature of the problem determines the method. To find the law of progress it will be necessary to organize factual series as broad as possible. (*Science de l'h.*, XI, 22.) That, says Saint-Simon, is the only solid part of our knowledge, and to establish these series we must address ourselves to history. The method of social physiology will therefore be historic. But for history to serve this purpose, it is essential that it be entirely transformed. Up until now it has merely been a branch of literature. For too long it has been seen as "just a biography of power in which nations figure only as instruments and victims." And although "enlightened men today feel that history does not consist of a stupid tableau of dramatic elements of guile and force, there are few of them—even few historians—who have understood the actual object of great historic works." The proof is that "the ancient division by dynasties and reigns has been maintained as if it were always merely a question of the biography of sovereign families." (*Organisat.*, IV, 71-72.) So conceived, history is nothing but a succession of narrations and anecdotes, without practical applications. "History, it is said, is the breviary of kings; but from the way kings govern, one can well see that their prayer books have no value; in fact, history, from a scientific aspect, has not yet abandoned the language of infancy. This important branch of our learning still has no other existence than as a collection of more or less well established facts. These facts are not united by any theory; they are not all linked in the order of consequences. So history is still an inadequate guide for kings as well as their subjects and furnishes neither one or the other a means of judging what will happen, from what has happened." (*Science de l'h.*, XI. 246.) To become the instrument *par excellence* of social physiology, it must make itself scientific. And to do this it must raise itself above the national viewpoint—which can be nothing but descriptive—and no longer consider this or that people, but all humankind, in its progress. From then on the framework of history necessarily transforms itself. It can no longer be a question of using only kings and vanished dynasties to mark out this history. The division of epochs is made according to the differences which the movement of humanity presents across the centuries, and corresponds to the great phases of human development. Then, the knowledge of peoples can truly serve to enlighten the future, whereas today we wander at random, not even knowing what is before us and what behind. "Proceeding almost with eyes shut along a path we do not recognize, we sometimes believe ourselves close to what is far away and . . . a great distance from what is close by." (*Organisat.*, IV, 74.) So imbued was he with the conviction that if one wishes to understand the present, one cannot plunge too deeply into the past, Saint-Simon goes as far as to extend these series of facts which serve as a basis of his inferences, beyond human history. In his comparisons he introduces animal history, which he links to the latter without a break in continuity. By starting with animals he attempts to find the law which dominates mental evolution and the advance of civilization. So for him social physiology—like psychology—is only one branch of physiology, strictly speaking. (See *Science de l'h.*, XI, 188.)

At this point, and although we still have not fully expounded the doctrine of Saint-Simon, we cannot fail to be aware of the importance and grandeur of the fundamental conception on which it rests. The most impressive event in

the philosophic history of the nineteenth century was the
founding of positive philosophy. In the presence of the increasing specialization of sciences and their increasingly positive nature, one might wonder whether humanity's early
aspiration for unity of knowledge could henceforth be considered an illusion, a deceiving perspective, which it was
necessary to renounce. One might fear consequently that
the sciences, and thus their unity, were more and more
fragmented. Positive philosophy was a reaction against this
tendency, a protest against this renunciation. It asserts that
the eternal ambition of the human mind has not lost all
legitimacy, that the advance of the special sciences is not
its negation, but that a new means must be employed to
satisfy it. Philosophy, instead of seeking to go beyond the
sciences, must assume the task of organizing them, and
must organize them in accordance with their own method
—by making itself positive. An entirely new vista was thus
opened up for thought. This is why it can be said that,
aside from Cartesianism, there is nothing more important
in the entire history of French philosophy. And at more
than one point these two philosophies can legitimately be
reconciled with each other, for they were both inspired by
the same rationalist faith. But we have just seen that the
idea, the word, and even the outline of positivist philosophy
are all found in Saint-Simon. He was the first to conceive
that between the formal generalities of metaphysical philosophy and the narrow specialization of the particular sciences, there was a place for a new enterprise, whose pattern
he supplied and himself attempted. Therefore, it is to him
that one must, in full justice, award the honor currently
given Comte.

But this is not all. One of the great innovations positive
philosophy brought along with it is positive sociology. As
has been said, it is the integration of social science into
the circle of the natural sciences. In this regard, one might
say of positivism that it has enriched human intelligence,
that it has created new horizons. To add a science to the
list of sciences is always a very laborious operation, but
more productive than the annexation of a new continent to

old continents. And it is at once much more fruitful when the science has man for its object. It almost had to do violence to the human spirit and to triumph over the keenest resistance to make it understood that in order to act upon things it was first necessary to put them on trial. The resistance has been particularly stubborn when the material to be examined was ourselves, due to our tendency to place ourselves outside of things, to demand a place apart in the universe.

Saint-Simon was the first who resolutely freed himself from these prejudices. Although he may have had precursors, never had it been so clearly asserted that man and society could not be directed in their conduct unless one began by making them objects of science and further that this science could not rest on any other principles than do the sciences of nature. And this new science—he not only laid out its design but attempted to realize it in part. We can see here all that Auguste Comte, and consequently all that the thinkers of the nineteenth century, owe him. In him we encounter the seeds already developed of all the ideas which have fed the thinking of our time. We have just found in it positivist philosophy, positivist sociology. We will see that we will also find socialism in it.

* * *

In explaining the fundamental concepts of Saint-Simon we were able to see what Comte owed him, and we will have occasion to discover this same influence in the details of the theories. However—with the exception of Littré—the Comtists have denied this affiliation. They have even gone so far as saying it was to Comte that Saint-Simon owed everything that was accurate and original in his doctrine. But the facts refute such an interpretation. It was only about 1817 that regular relations were established between the two philosophers and there is no doubt that the essential lines of Saint-Simonianism had been drawn well before that date. The *Mémoire sur la Science de l'homme* and the work on *Gravitation universelle* dated from 1813, and all the principles of the system are expressly formulated there.

Actually we primarily used the first of these books to explain the way Saint-Simon conceived of philosophy and the science of societies. There one finds the entire program of positive philosophy and positive sociology, and the same ideas had already been more than sketched out in his earlier writings. So one can but regret that, not only Comte's school, but Comte himself had so completely failed to recognize his most immediate and important predecessor. In fact, not only is Saint-Simon not even mentioned in the chapter of the *Cours de philosophie positive* in which Comte poses and examines the tentative facts before him in order to lay the foundations of social physics, but further, in the *Système de politique positive* (II, preface, p. xv and xvi.) he shows no hesitation in speaking with anger of the "morbid liaison of his early youth with a depraved juggler."

He confesses to having been captivated at the very first by Saint-Simon, but adds, "Later, I recognized that such a liaison had allowed no other result than to shackle my spontaneous reflections, previously guided by Condorcet." This was to forget that Saint-Simon himself was attached to Condorcet, had studied and meditated about him and that, as a result—on this point their research being oriented in the same direction—could not conflict. Besides, it is only too easy to oppose Comte to himself. At the very time he was expressing himself with such severity about his old friend and referring to the same book where the phrase we just cited is found, Comte, in letters to his friend Valat, acknowledged all the benefits he reaped from his dealings with Saint-Simon. Positive politics, he says there, is purely the influence of Saint-Simon, and "this influence strongly served my philosophic education." And he adds, "I certainly owe a great deal intellectually to Saint-Simon, that is to say, he contributed powerfully to launching me in the philosophic direction that I clearly created for myself today and which I will follow without hesitation all my life." (Cited according to Weil, *Hist. du mouy, sac.*, p. 206-207.)

In 1818 he was writing to this same correspondent, "I have learned through this relationship of work and friendship with one of the men who sees furthest in philosophical politics. I have learned a mass of things I vainly would have sought in books, and my mind has made more headway these six months of our liaison than it would in three years, had I been alone." And he paints an enthusiastic portrait of Saint-Simon, his genius and character. Finally, even *Politique positive,* which is Comte's first great sociological work and which was later presented by him as an original work, unconnected with any Saint-Simonian influence, was to appear originally under the name of its author, in the *Catéchisme industriel.* In view of this special edition, Comte had prepared an advertisement, which has been preserved, in which he declared himself the grateful pupil of Saint-Simon. "Having reflected for a long time," he says, "on the main idea of Saint-Simon, I applied myself exclusively to develop and perfect that portion of the views of this philosopher which relates to scientific direction. . . . I believed I had to make public the preceding statement so that, if my works appear to deserve some approval, it may go to the founder of the philosophic school of which I am honored to be a part." (*Oeuvres,* IX, 9.) Comte later explained this statement as "a single act of kindness" designed to mollify any bad feeling Saint-Simon might have had about him. But such a consideration does not easily explain away so formal an acknowledgment. In any case, it cannot excuse him.

It is indisputable that between these two men there were essential differences, of which Comte was very soon aware. In strange unsigned letters which he sent Saint-Simon towards the end of 1818, at the time of the publication of *l'Industrie,* and which have been published by the *Revue Occidentale* (VIII, 344) he indicates very plainly where the real line of demarcation between his master and himself was located. Comte recognized that the fundamental idea of *l'Industrie,* that is to say positivism, is "the real and only means of raising the social organization, without disruption, into the realm of daylight." But before anything else he had to apply himself to deducing all the scientific consequences of this idea. "It was necessary to discuss its influence on the theory of social science," to erect political economy on a positive basis, and morality on an economic basis. Instead of following this path, Saint-Simon was wrong to pass suddenly to questions of application. Even before his idea had undergone all the scientific elaboration it required, he wanted to draw practical conclusions from it, an entire plan of social reorganization. Thus he placed the cart before the horse. He hurried too much; he wanted, for utilitarian ends, to prematurely use a hastily constructed science. And in fact what differentiates Comte and Saint-Simon is that the former separated science from practice more clearly, but without disinteresting himself in the latter —at least during the better part of his career. Once given this idea of a positive science of societies, he undertook to realize it, not from the aspect of this or that immediate end, but in an abstract and disinterested manner. Although he was always convinced that his theoretical works could and would finally have an effect on the course of events, he understood that before all else he had to produce a scholarly work, to pose the problems of science in all its generality. And although he expects, at the end of his studies, to find solutions applicable to the difficulties of the present time, he believes they must result from an established science, although not contesting these so-called ends as essential. Saint-Simon did not possess the same degree of scientific patience. A definite social crisis had stirred his thought, and it was entirely to solve it that all his efforts were bent. His entire system, consequently, has a practical—not a remote—objective which he hastens to attain, and he has science do nothing but approach this goal. Therefore, although he was the first to have a really clear conception of what sociology had to be and its necessity, strictly speaking, he did not create a sociology. He didn't use the method, whose principles he had so firmly stated, to discover the laws of evolution—social and general—but in order to answer a very special question—of entirely immediate interest —which can be formulated as follows: what is the social system required by the condition of European societies on the morrow of the Revolution?

Chapter 7

Historic Origins of the Industrial System and the Doctrine of Saint-Simon

THE ANSWER TO the question raised by the title of this chapter constitutes the positive content of the Saint-Simonian system, and we are now going to take it up.

We find the new science limited to a single and unique problem, whose interest is more practical than speculative. But at least Saint-Simon undertakes to treat it according to the scientific and positive method whose fundamental rules we saw him formulate earlier. It is not a question of inventing a new system, created out of many pieces—as do utopians of the eighteenth century and other periods—but merely of discovering by observation what is in process of being worked out. "One does not create a system of social organization. One perceives the new chain of ideas and interests which has been formed, and points it out—that is all." (*Organisateur,* IV, 178-180.) Saint-Simon often returns to a notion of spontaneous social organization, especially in relation to the role of banks. (*Catéchisme industriel,* passim; *Système industriel,* V, 46-47.) All one can do is to be aware of the direction the development is taking; next, to distinguish, among the elements of which the present is made up, those which are developing more and more— and developing more completely—and those which more and more are ceasing to be; finally, to recognize the future behind the survivals of the past which conceal it. To do these things, it is necessary to study the growth of our societies since they were definitively established. According to our author, it is in the Middle Ages—the eleventh and twelfth centuries— that they were formed with all their essential characteristics. That epoch is consequently "the most suitable point of departure" for "that philosophic observation of the past" which alone can enlighten the future.

Let us see what societies were like at that time and how they evolved since.

What gave them an organized character when, toward the tenth century, they began to free themselves from the chaos produced by barbarian invasions, was that the social system revolved completely around two centers of gravity, distinct but closely associated. On the one hand, there were the chiefs of the army, who constituted what is since called feudalism, and to whom all of secular society was closely subjected. All property, real and personal, was in their hands, and workers—individually and collectively—were dependent upon them. On the other hand, there were the clergy, who controlled the spiritual direction of society, generally and specifically. Their doctrines and decisions served as guides to opinion; but what overwhelmingly established their authority was their absolute mastery over general and particular education. In other words, the entire economic life of society depended on the lords, and all intellectual life on the priests. The first ruled supremely over productive operations, the second over consciences. Thus all collective functions were strictly subjected either to military power or religious authority, and this double subjugation constituted the social organization. That is why Saint-Simon calls the system military and theological; occasionally he also uses the expressions feudal and papal. But although he dwells on the confining submission implied in this organization, he does not suggest it was imposed or maintained by violence and repression alone. He keeps repeating, on the contrary, that this arrangement of European societies establishes itself spontaneously, because it alone corresponded to the state of civilization. War was then chronic. It was the one field open to the activity of peoples, the only way for them to enrich themselves; consequently it was natural that only those capable of directing it were invested with the highest degree of authority and respect. Likewise, as the clergy was the only group which then possessed learning, it was out of real necessity that it exercised an absolute power over minds. Thus this two-pronged supremacy was based on the nature of things. It corresponded to a social superiority of these two classes which was real and which it merely expressed.

This is the origin. Let us now see what this organization became in the course of history.

It is a general rule that the apogee of a social system coincides with the beginning of its decadence. In the eleventh century, spiritual and temporal powers were definitively established; never was the authority of clergy and lords more undisputed. But coming into existence at that very moment were two new social forces. Being opposed to the preceding ones, they entered into struggle with them, gradually destroyed them, and thus disintegrated the system whose parts had been bound together only because they were all subjected to the all-powerful action of the double authority. These two forces were the free commune and exact science.

What had accounted for the strength of feudal organization was the subjugation of the industrial class by what then took its place, the military class. The former had no influence of its own, but received all its direction from the latter. Thus everything tended toward the same end. All economic life was subordinated to the interests of war and warriors. But with the twelfth century began the great movement of the emancipation of the commune. Villages, by payment of silver, were freeing themselves from seigneurial tutelage. And they were totally composed of artisans and merchants. A whole segment of the economic structure thus found itself detached from the others who until then were forcing their control on it. Transformed into a special, relatively independent, organ, henceforth the villagers were going to live their own lives, to pursue their particular interests—outside of any military influence. As a result, the whole collective life no longer revolved exclusively around the two centers we just named.

Liberated industry was going to be able freely to realize its own nature, to propose for itself purely industrial ends, which not only differed from but contradicted those the system had forced upon it.

A new force, *sui generis*, had entered the heart of the social body, and as by nature and origin it was foreign to

the old organization—and could only disturb it—it was inevitable that its very presence would disconcert the latter's
functioning and would develop only by destroying it. At the
same time the exact sciences were imported into Europe by
the Arabs. The schools they founded in their conquered
parts of Europe were quickly imitated elsewhere. Similar
establishments arose in all occidental Europe, "observatories,
dissection rooms, study rooms for natural history were set
up in Italy, France, England, Germany. As early as the
thirteenth century, Bacon was brilliantly cultivating the physical sciences." (*Organisat.*, IV, 84.) Gradually, in opposition
to the clergy, a new body was forming, which like the preceding one aimed at directing the intellectual life of society.
These were the scholars who, in their relation to the clerical
class were in exactly the same situation as were the enfran-
chised communes—that is, the corporation of artisans and
merchants—*vis-à-vis* feudalism. Thus two seeds of destruction were introduced into the theological-feudal system, and
in fact from that moment the two forces which were the
source of its strength began to grow weaker.

But although the conflict never ceased, it was some time
before it produced visible results. The old system was too
solidly entrenched, and too resistant, for obscure causes to
immediately manifest their action through exterior and apparent effects; actually it never enjoyed greater splendor.
But in reality, "all this brilliance rested on hollow ground."
(*Organisat.*, IV, 89.) It is through failing to recognize the
importance of this subterranean process that one so often
sees the Middle Ages as a dark era in which a veritable
intellectual night reigned, and that consequently nothing
about it was related to the period of light which followed.
In reality, it was the Middle Ages which paved the way
for modern times. It contained them in embryo. "If historians had analyzed and examined the Middle Ages more
deeply they would not have spoken to us only of the visible
part of that period. They would have recorded the gradual
preparation of all the great events which developed later
and would not have presented the explosions of the sixteenth
and following centuries as sudden and unforseen." (*Ibid.*)

There are two facts which more than all others contributed to predetermine what was to follow; first, the invention of printing, which put an enormously powerful instrument of action at the disposal of science, and second—and above all—Copernicus' discovery, later taken up and verified by Galileo, whose influence on the system of theology has been as considerable as it has been little acknowledged. "In fact," says Saint-Simon, "the whole theological system is founded on the supposition that the earth is made for man and the entire universe for the earth. Remove this supposition and all religious doctrines crumble. But Galileo demonstrated that our planet is one of the smallest, that it differs in no way from the others, that it revolves in a mass around the sun. The hypothesis that all nature is made for man now so plainly shocks good sense, is so in contradiction with the facts, that it cannot avoid seeming absurd and soon being overthrown—dragging with it all the beliefs of which it was the basis." (*Organ.*, IV, 100.) In fact, even if it were not proven that religion was irretrievably irreconcilable with the new concepts, they were indeed sure to overturn the system of accepted ideas, to cast out humanity from the central position it believed it occupied in the universe to some point or other at the periphery. There is no doubt that the abandonment of the anthropocentric point of view—first in the natural sciences, and then with Auguste Comte in the sciences of man—has been one of the most important conquests of science and one which had the greatest effect in orienting the mind in a new direction. To think scientifically —is it not to think objectively, that is, to divest our notions of what is exclusively human in them in order to make them a reflection—as accurate as possible—of things as they are? Is it not, in a word, to make the human intelligence bow before facts? One cannot exaggerate the significance of a discovery which logically obliged reason to assume toward the world the attitude demanded by science.

Nevertheless, however important this preliminary evolution might have been, it is only in the sixteenth century that the forces antagonistic to the old system found themselves strong enough to come into the open, in such a way that the results could be perceived by anyone. At first these forces were directed against theological rule; Luther and his co-reformers upset pontifical authority as a power in Europe. At the same time in a general way they undermined theological authority "by destroying the principle of blind faith, by replacing it with the right of examination which—restrained at first within quite narrow limits—was to inevitably increase . . . and finally to embrace an indefinite area." (*Organist*. IV, 89.) This two-fold change operated not only among the peoples converted to Protestantism, but even among those who remained Catholic. For once the principle was established, it extended well beyond the countries where it had first been proclaimed. As a result, the bond which tied individual consciences to ecclesiastical power—although not shattered—was loosened, and the moral unity of the social system definitely unsettled.

The entire sixteenth century was seized by this great intellectual revolution. But it was at its close that the struggle—begun against spiritual power—proceeded against temporal power. It took place at almost the same time in France and in England. In both countries it was led by the common people, with one of the two branches of temporal power as leader. With the English, feudalism placed itself at their head to combat royal authority; in France royalty made itself their ally against feudal strength. Actually the coalition —in both peoples—had begun as early as the enfranchisement of the lower class, but it is only in the seventeenth century that the domestic rearrangements on both sides of the channel came into the open and battle was joined in broad daylight. Here Richelieu, then Louis XIV shattered seigneurial power; there, the Revolution of 1688 broke out, limiting royal authority as much as was possible without overturning the old organization. The final result of these events was a weakening of the military system in its entirety. It was weakened, first because it lost unity due to a schism between the two elements of which it was formed—and a system cannot be disunited without being enfeebled—and then because one of these elements departed from battle crushed. Therefore, although at this time feudalism—at least in France—seemed to burn with strong flame, in reality these magnificent external appearances concealed a state of internal deterioration which events of the following century soon made clear.

In fact, until then feudalism had been the object only of partial assaults, directed against this or that part—first against the spiritual power then against the temporal. There had been a series of blows, more and more violent but always limited. But in the eighteenth century the shock had gone so deep, the feudal order's resistance became so weak, that the attack on it became generalized, and directed against the whole of its organization. One then sees the principle of the right of examination in religious matters extended to its extreme limits. Theological beliefs were entirely upset "with too much imprudence, precipitation and caprice; without doubt, with a too absolute forgetfulness of the past and with too confused and uncertain views on the future. But finally this is what they were and they were unable to change themselves." (*Organisat.*, IV, 102.) Moreover the discoveries then being made in all sciences contributed more to this result than all the writings of Voltaire and his colleagues, whatever their importance. (*Ibid.*, 105.) At the same time, criticism spread from spiritual to temporal power all the more as there was a close bond between royalty and clergy; the reform of both was based on the same doctrines. So we see the Regency to Louis XV, Louis XV, to Louis XVI, going from failure to failure, and approaching ruination.

Thus the history of the old system from the time when, towards the tenth century, it reaches maturity, up to the eve of the Revolution, shows us a spectacle of an uninterrupted decadence. But at the same time that this regressive process was developing, another was occuring in reverse direction with no less significance. Industrial and scientific forces, once formed, did not manifest themselves exclusively by destructive effects, that is, by overthrowing the old social order. They gave rise to another. They did not limit themselves to detaching consciences and individual wills from the centers which until then, by providing a similar direction, had made a single body of them. But to the degree they acquired more energy, they themselves became foci of common action and centers of organization. Around them gradually formed the social elements which the old forces —more and more powerless to keep them subordinate— were allowing to escape. Under these new influences, a new social system was slowly arising in the bosom of the old, which was disintegrating.

As long as arts and crafts had been narrowly subordinated to theological and military authority, having to serve as instruments for ends which were not their own, they had been impeded in their progress. But as soon as they began to be free—thanks to the liberation of the common people—they took flight and developed so quickly that they soon became a social force to be reckoned with. Little by little all society fell into dependence upon them, because nothing was any longer possible without them. Military force itself was subjected to them, once war became a complex and costly thing, once it demanded not merely native courage and a certain disposition of character, but money, machines, arms. More and more, improvements in industry, the inventions of science, and finally wealth, were proving more vital to success in arms than innate bravery. But when a class acquires greater importance and respect, when the functions it fulfills become more essential, it is inevitable for it to wield greater influence on the direction of society and increased political authority. This in fact is what occurred. Little by little one sees representatives of industry admitted to governmental councils, playing a greater and greater part, and as a result having a larger share in determining the general course of society. It is especially in England that this phenomenon manifests itself. Gradually the common people—in other words, the classes which fulfill only economic functions—obtain first a consultative voice in the tax vote, then a deliberative voice, then the exclusive right to vote on budget. They substitute themselves for the old temporal power in one of its most important functions, and are able henceforth to act in conformity with their own interest in the direction of society; they modify its orientation, since they have altogether different ends than the military classes. In other words, the social system begins to revolve about a new center. (*Organisat.*)

This is not all. One of the essential prerogatives of feudal power consisted in administering justice. Seigneurial justice was one of the essential characteristics of feudal organization. But once the villages were freed, one of the rights considered most important to achieve was the administration of justice. "From then on municipalities were formed and entrusted with this care. Its members were designated by the citizens and for a limited term." It is true that the importance of these municipal tribunals dwindled under the influence of various circumstances. But commercial and industrial matters remained assigned to them. "Such was the origin and nature of the commercial tribunal which at first were nothing more than municipalities." (*Industrie*, III, 135 and fol.) But the appearance of these tribunals is an important event in the process of organization we are tracing. From this moment, in fact, the industrial class had a judiciary organ which was its own, in harmony with its special nature, and which contributed to complete the system which was in process of formation.

But this spontaneous organization was not reduced to the creation of a few outstanding organs like those mentioned. It extended to every detail of collective life, to the whole mass of the population which it affected in an entirely new way. Before the liberation of the communes, the people— in secular matters— had as their only continuing leaders the chiefs of the army. But with enfranchisement, they gradually became detached, and organized under the leaders of the arts and crafts. They bargained with the others over practices of order and subordination, which—without being rigid—served to assure stability in the transacting of business, and harmony in society. It is especially due to the institution of permanent armies that this new grouping of social forces could separate itself completely from the old and become independent. In fact, from this moment on, the task of soldiering was a special function, separated from the remainder of the population. As a result, "the mass of people no longer had any connection with the military heads. It was organized only industrially. He who took up soldiering no longer considered himself—and was no longer looked upon—as belonging to the people. He passed from the ranks of the new system into those of the old, from the communal he became feudal—that is all. It was he who dehumanized himself—not the system of which he formerly was a part. . . . Let one consider the state of people today and he will see that they are no longer in direct and continuing connection with temporal matters except through their industrial chiefs. Imagine any workman in his daily relations—whether in agriculture, in manufacturing, in commerce—and you will find he is habitually in contact with and in lower rank only to the leaders in agriculture, manufacturing or commerce." (*Organisateur*, IV, 149.)

Just as with industry, science, as it grew, developed an organization appropriate to its own character, and very different, consequently, from that permitted by theological authority. Scholars became esteemed personages whom royalty more and more made a habit of consulting. It is as a result of these repeated consultations that great scientific bodies were gradually established at the pinnacle of the system. These are the academies. Thereafter there arose all kinds "of special schools for science where the influence of theology and metaphysics were, so to speak, nil." "A larger and larger mass of scientific ideas entered ordinary education at the same time that religious doctrines gradually lost influence." (*Organisateur*, IV, 137.) Finally, just as with industry, this early organization did not remain confined to the higher levels of society, but extended to the mass of people. With respect to the body of scholars, they were in a state of subordination analogous to their former position vis-à-vis the body ecclesiastic. "The people, organized industrially, soon perceived that their usual works of art and craft were not at all in rapport with their theological ideas . . . and wherever they could be in contact with savants they lost the habit of consulting priests, and acquired the custom of placing themselves in touch with those who possessed positive knowledge." (*Organisateur*, IV, 153.) And since they found themselves benefitted by the counsel given them, they ended by according "the unanimous opinion of the scholars the same degree of confidence that in the Middle Ages they accorded the decisions of spiritual power. It is by a kind of faith of a new type that they successively accepted the movement of the earth, modern astronomical theory, the circulation of the blood, the identity of lightning and of electricity, etc., etc." "So it is proven," concludes Saint-Simon "that people have become spontaneously confident in and subordinate to their leaders in the fields of science, just as they are temporally with regard to their industrial leaders. I have, consequently, the right to conclude that confidence as well as social rankings are developed within the new system." (*Organisateur*, IV, 155.)

The results of this double evolution can be summarized as follows: In the measure that the ancient social system gave way, another was formed in the very bosom of the first. The old society contained within itself a new society, in process of formation and every day acquiring more strength and consistency. But these two organizations are necessarily antagonistic to each other. They result from opposing forces and aim at contradictory ends. One is essentially aggressive, war-like, the other essentially pacifist. The one sees in other peoples enemies to destroy; the other tends to view them as collaborators in a common undertaking. One has conquest for its aim, the other, production. Similarly, in spiritual affairs the first calls on faith and imposes beliefs which it puts beyond discussion. The second calls on reason and even trust—it requires a type of intellectual subordination which is essential to rationality, a commitment to further exploration and testing. Thus these two societies could not coexist without contradicting each other. In spite of this antagonism, we saw that industrial society had succeeded in spontaneously providing itself a certain organization but one which could hardly be regarded as adequate.

Shaken as it was, the past was still alive everywhere and opposed definitive establishment of the present. Feudal and religious power had been obliged to yield some place to savants and producers in the political system of society.

But it was for the old regime and not for the new that this system had been made. Industry had utilized it as much as possible, but had not replaced it with one truly created in its own image and adjusted to its needs. The modifications it introduced are important to note as they show how much a rearrangement of landed property was needed— but they cannot be regarded as transformations. A social constitution made for war and destruction cannot easily adapt itself to essentially peaceful and productive activity. Therefore satisfying these new needs required the creation of an adequate political order. Similarly, the old morality and law were discredited in the new world which was arising; but a new juridical and moral order, without which the new system could not be considered organized, did not come into being automatically. Thus, scientific industrial society reached out for an appropriate social organization which was not yet in existence. To succeed, it had both to overcome the inertia of the old and to shape the new. As long as this two-fold result was not achieved, it was inevitable that disorganization and conflict would be severe and would affect the whole of society.

Such was the situation on the eve of the Revolution, and out of it the Revolution was born. "This tremendous crisis did not at all have its origin in this or that isolated fact. . . . It operated as an overturning of the political system for the single reason that the state of society to which the ancient order corresponded had totally changed in nature. A civil and moral revolution which had gradually developed for more than six centuries engendered and necessitated a political revolution. . . . If one insists on attributing the French Revolution to one source, it must be dated from the day the liberation of the communes and the cultivation of exact sciences in western Europe began." (*Syst. Ind.*, V. 77.) A two-fold need gave rise to it: the need of being extricated from the past and the need to organize the present; the Revolution met only the first of these needs. It succeeded in striking the final blows at the old system. It abolished all that remained of feudalism—even royal authority —and all that survived from the old temporal power. It gave to freedom of conscience the juridical consequences it implied, whereas before it had only the weight of moral sanction. This was solemnly inscribed in the foundation of our law.

But on the land thus cleared, the Revolution built nothing new. It asserted that one was no longer obliged to accept the old beliefs but did not attempt to elaborate a new body of rational beliefs that all minds could accept. It destroyed the foundations on which political authority rested but failed to establish others of any stability. It proclaimed that political power was not to belong to those who had monopolized it until then, but did not assign it to any definite organ. In other words, it neglected to state what it was for—which was to make of it a *res nullius*, an instrument suited to all possible ends, but not a definite factor with a defined objective. An action so exclusively destructive, far from attenuating the crisis which had given rise to it, could only make the evil more acute and intolerable. For the absence of organization from which industrial society suffered became far more perceptible once all that remained of the old had disappeared. The weak cohesion of this dawning society became a much graver social peril once the old social bonds were completely destroyed. The social body, uprooting these ties, even the most . . . in order to attain its end, did it [so well] (?) that it no longer had any at all.[1] It is certainly from this that there stemmed a kind of uncertainty, an exasperated anguish, which is characteristic of the revolutionary epoch. "For long," says Saint-Simon, "the impotency of the old, general ideas was felt; for long their domination had become inconvenient. One did not forgive oneself for failing to throw off this moral despotism, already labelled prejudice, but to which one still submitted for lack of anything better." "Philosophers more fearless than wise, struck at antiquated views with premature blows —blows however weak and superficial—which made the system of general ideas crumble and society fall apart. No longer having anything left that was agreed upon, people separated and became enemies. It was a struggle of all

[1] The original manuscript is incomplete here.—(M.M.)

whims, a battle of all imaginations." (*Industrie,* II, 206.)
This was one indication of the partial miscarriage of the
Revolution. As a society so disoriented cannot live, one soon
sees reborn from their ashes certain of the destroyed institutions. Royal authority was re-established. But these revivals
of the past did not constitute a solution. So the problem is
posed on the morrow of the Revolution, at the start of the
nineteenth century, in the same terms as on the eve of 1789,
only it has become more pressing. The denoument is more
urgent if one does not wish to see each crisis produce another, exasperation the chronic state of society, and finally,
disintegration more or less the result. One must take a
stand. Either completely restore the old system or organize
the new. It is precisely this that is the social question.

As we view it, it cannot be posed with greater profundity.
The originality of this historic analysis is that Saint-Simon
very correctly felt that the changes spontaneously produced
in European societies since the Middle Ages had not simply
acted upon this or that particular characteristic, or on such
and such a detail of the governmental mechanism, but that
the social organism had been affected to its very foundations. He understood that the liberal movement—of which
the Revolution was only the culmination, but which had been
incubating for centuries before it—had not merely the effect
of unchaining citizens from burdensome shackles as an end
in itself. He saw the dissolution of the old order of things
that had resulted, that this dissolution had not solved the
central problem but was making such a solution more immediately necessary. He understood that to reorganize society it was not enough to destroy the old system of forces
which unified it, and that once this destruction is accomplished social equilibrium itself—as essential as it might
otherwise be—in its turn becomes precarious, is maintained
only by a miracle, and can fall with the slightest wind. Consequently, it is necessary to rebuild on new foundations and
according to a plan which is not simply a reproduction of
the old. Thus the great contemporary questions are found to
be related to the whole course of our historic development.

*   *   *

As we observed, Saint-Simon judges the work of the Revolution with independence—sometimes even with severity. If he considers for example, that in certain aspects it was imprudent and precipitous and in any case does not constitute a solution of the crisis, it would be a mistake to see a condemnation in his criticisms. First, he postulates the principle that it was necessary and inevitable; our history —the whole of it, since its beginnings— is but its long preparation. Further, he reproaches the men of the Revolution for having overthrown the ancient institutions without determining what to put in their place. He considers this destruction as indispensable to the building of a new regime, and the night of August 4th was one of the great dates of history for him. The French nation, says he, "proclaimed its maturity the night of August 4th by abolishing all institutions derived from the state of slavery." (*Catéch.*, X, 12.) Besides, it is to the beneficent influence of the Revolution that he attributes the relatively favorable situation in which we find ourselves with regard to social questions. "The Revolution" he says, "Whose great moral effects are beginning to develop, has made the French people enter into lively contact with politics; one should not be surprised that today they are showing themselves superior in organic concepts to the English." (*Organisation sociale*, X, 148.) In short, he objects not to its having been, but to its not having been all that it might, and especially all that it had to be.

But why had it stopped midway? What prevented it from ending in positive results? The explanation Saint-Simon gives deserves consideration.

It is in the nature of man, he says, to be unable to pass without intermediary from one doctrine to another, from one social system to a differing system. That is why the authority of science and industry would never have been able to replace that of clergy and feudalism unless—when the first began to arise and the second weaken—there had not constituted itself between the two "a temporal and spiritual power of an intermediary kind, illegitimate, transitory, whose unique role was to direct the transition from one social system to another." (*Syst. Ind.*, V, 80.) Thus between the feudal body and the industrial body appeared the class of lawyers. Lawyers, just as workers, had been at first merely agents of the lords. But gradually they formed a distinct class, whose autonomy kept growing, whose action, consequently, opposed feudal action and modified it "by the establishment of jurisprudence, which had merely been an organized system of barriers opposed to the exercise of force." (*Ibid.*, 81.) An equity was then established which was not purely feudal, and military power found itself subject to limitations and rules drawn in the interest of commercial men—for these latter necessarily profited from any restriction brought against the antagonistic power they fought. In the spiritual realm similarly, metaphysicians—rising from the very heart of theology—wedged themselves between positive science and clergy, inspired at once with the spirit of both. And without ceasing to base their reasoning on religious foundations, they nevertheless modified theological influence by establishing the right of examination in matters of law and morality.

These are the two intermediate and fused forces which occupied the political stage almost exclusively until the Revolution, because by their composite and ambiguous nature they corresponded better than all others to the equally ambiguous state of civilization. Without doubt they thus rendered the greatest services and contributed in large measure to the final liberation of science and industry. Thanks to one, the working world escaped feudal tribunals. Thanks to the other, the idea took hold more and more that society could maintain itself without individual consciences being subordinated to theological doctrines. Their authority was so great when the Revolution broke out that quite naturally people took direction from them. Manufacturers and scholars believed they could do no better than blindly entrust their cause to them. Thus the men of law and the metaphysically-trained almost exclusively composed the revolutionary assemblies and inspired their actions. But in this novel situation they could exercise no action other than conforming to their nature and their past. Since they had had no other function until then except to limit governmental powers, they continued unremittingly to apply new limitations, until, by being restrained, these social forces found themselves reduced to naught. But if these lawyers and metaphysicians were admirably prepared and organized to lead this revolutionary work to its final goal, they possessed nothing of what was required to erect a new system. For, although they did not understand this, it was from the past, from the old order of things, that they inherited the whole groundwork of their doctrines. How could jurists bring themselves to a conception of a social order different from the one they had just destroyed, since "their political opinions are inevitably deduced, for the most part, from Roman law, from the ordinances of our kings, from feudal customs—in a word, from all the legislation which preceded the Revolution," (*Sur la querelle des Abeilles et des Frelons,* III, 219.) How could metaphysicians—the entire philosophic school of the eighteenth century —establish a system of ideas and beliefs in harmony with a particular social condition when, under the influence of the theologic spirit which continued to animate them, they were aspiring in all practical questions to absolute solutions, independent of any consideration of time and place, any historic condition? The effective role of both was therefore reduced to merely destroying. "When they wished to go further, they were thrust into the absolute question of the best government imaginable, and—always controlled by the same habits— treated it as a question of jurisprudence and metaphysics. For the theory of the rights of man—which has always been the foundation of their work in general politics—is nothing other than an application of high metaphysics to high jurisprudence." (*Syst. Ind.,* V, 83.)

We can see that this fashion of conceiving and evaluating the historic role of lawyers should not be attributed simply to the personal prejudices of Saint-Simon—to the antipathy, for example, of an intuitive and creative genius for the somewhat dry dialectic of jurists. Law is the form social relations have taken through the effect of custom and tradition and becomes fixed habit. It is the past, therefore, that it expresses. By the very way it is formed, it corresponds much more to the state of things that has disappeared than that which is striving to establish itself. For this very reason it embarrasses—usefully in many cases—projects of social reform, and in consequence those who have had custody of the law appear to the innovators as enemies rather than collaborators.

But in addition to this very general reason, there is a particular one which specially animated Saint-Simon's feelings. Industrial society, as he conceives it, demands, because of its extreme complexity, an organization which is equally complex. As it must be able to adjust with facility to circumstances of time and place, and though it rests everywhere on the same very general foundations, it cannot be identical everywhere, today and tomorrow. It cannot be fixed within rigid and defined formulae; it cannot subject itself to an absolutely uniform and fixed rule once and for all. Only its principles can be defined with exactness. Consequently, the juridical form required by this society cannot be completely detached from the social matter to which it is applied, so as to be considered distinct, in the abstract, and to become the object of special study and elaboration. Separated from the concrete social, particular, variable facts in which it exists, it can consist only of blind formulae, foreign to the reality they ignore. But this abstraction is implied in the point of view of jurists. They have no *raison d'être* except in the measure that law can be isolated from the social functions it regulates. For only under this condition can there be a question of establishing a body of special functionaries—namely jurists—charged with understanding and interpreting it. Therefore, since such dissociation is impossible in an industrial society, the so-called jurists could have no place in it. In such a system, it would be to men of commerce—and to them alone—that would belong the application of general principles of law to the diversity of individual cases. For they alone are close enough to the details of social life to be able to take into account all possible combinations of circumstances and not clumsily impose uniform precepts on differing situations. One can thus better understand the great importance Saint-Simon attributes to the accession of commercial tribunals. He sees in them the model of a new judicial organization in which men of industry have as their judges only peers and colleagues, while the role of legal specialists is reduced to a minimum. For this basic reason, the legal specialists could not effectively fulfill the office of directors of social evolution since they lacked what was necessary to lead it to its natural end—namely, close contact with collective reality. The reason Saint-Simon holds lawyers in suspicion is that, according to him, an incompatibility exists between the rigidity of juridical discipline and the infinite flexibility of industrial organization. Law must become built into society through industry in order to be able to express all shades and variations, and must cease being the material of a special function.

It seems clear that the highly developed economic life of modern societies cannot be organized except with the aid of a system of law far more supple and malleable than that of the codes, and is consequently inseparable from the social relations to which it is applied. On the other hand, it appears necessary in the practical management of our societies that men of law do not play a preponderant part, a preponderance which, as Saint-Simon sees it, traces its origin to the earliest struggles against feudalism.[2]

Even as they stand, Saint-Simon's observations are noteworthy. But they represent still another significant point in the history of ideas. If, in fact, one relates them to what was previously said, one arrives at the conclusion that according to Saint-Simon, European societies have passed successively through three social systems; the theological or feudal, the metaphysical or juridical, and the positive. We recognize in this formula the famous law of three stages which Comte was to make the foundation of his doctrine. However, it is of Saint-Simonian origin.

It is a very profound observation to have noted in this political revolution not only a fortunate abatement of feudal despotism but the coming of a new form of collective life— the first attempts at a social organization resting on an economic base. His views on the establishment of standing armies and their consequence are no less noteworthy.

It would take too long to point out all the fertile ideas contained in this broad tableau of our historic development. It is Saint-Simon who was the first, before Guizot, to understand

[2] And which has no reason for being once the latter has disappeared.

the full social significance of the communal movement and the ties which bound it to the Revolution and to current problems. He was also the first to judge the work of the Revolution with the impartiality of history, without condemning it in general—as did the defenders of the old regime—and without systematically extolling it—as did the liberals of his time—and on this point again Comte was his heir. On the whole, one must admire his complete absence of all prejudice, and the feeling for historic continuity he discovered in the role of every period—even the most discredited, like the Middle Ages—in the uninterrupted course of transformations which bind the society of the tenth century to contemporary times.

Chapter 8

The Organization of the Industrial System

LET US NOW return to the practical question noted in this historical analysis. Granted that our present societies contain in them two different, and even contradictory, social systems—one which is becoming weaker and weaker, the other emerging more and more—how can the crisis resulting from their antagonism be solved?

Will one try to compromise the contradictions and give each side a share of this system? But a nation does not constitute a true political association unless it has a common goal for activity. It cannot—without being divided against itself—pursue two contradictory ends. This is the case with England, whose constitution rests at once on industrial and military principles. The result is that each institution has, so to say, its opposing contra-institution. Thus, impressment of sailors coexists there along with the liberal law of *habeus corpus;* the industrial city of Manchester has no representative in Parliament, while tiny villages do; the English government attempts to subject all nations to its maritime hegemony and yet asserts the equality of all peoples by demanding suppression of the slave trade, etc., etc. An organization so chaotic destroys itself; and the people it embraces cannot advance in one direction or another since they cannot take a step in one without then taking another in the opposite direction. Such a condition is a state of crisis and disorder which cannot endure. (*Catéch.*, X, 82.) It is necessary to choose resolutely between the two ends that can be proposed for social activity. But could not one preserve the military system by introducing improvements which would place it in harmony with the new exigencies of industrial life? This, replies Saint-Simon, is to attribute to social institutions a plasticity they do not possess. "Institutions, like the men who create them, are modifiable—but they cannot be denatured. Their primary character cannot be entirely effaced." (*Catéch.*, VIII, 34.) They can therefore "be improved only up to a certain point, beyond which the principles which served as their foundation can no longer bend sufficiently to admit the modifications one would want them to undergo." (X, 162.) Consequently, it is not by retouching details that one can eliminate from modern societies the contradictions which plague them. Such measures are merely provisional and temporary solutions, useful in their hour—and Saint-Simon even believes this hour has passed—but which in any event could not be definitive. They could not stop the crisis since they permit its causes to survive. In order to radically end it, one cannot hesitate between the two following courses; either wholly restore the ancient system or else produce another which integrates—as did the preceding one when it was intact—the whole of social life.

At the time, the first course was recommended by representatives of the reactionary school—by Maistre, Bonald, Lamennais. Saint-Simon does not lack respect for their doctrine, which at least seemed to be logical and consistent. But, he says, societies do not flower twice in the course of history. "A system which the centuries have built and destroyed cannot be re-established. The destruction of old doctrines is complete, radical and irrevocable. They will always be remembered with gratitude and veneration by all true thinkers and all people of probity, for the innumerable and eminent services they rendered civilization during the long era of their maturity. But henceforth their place is only in the memory of true friends of humanity and they can make no claim to vigor." (*Syst. Ind.*, VI, 50 and 51.)

Even if the movement which leads humanity in its present direction only had its birth in Christian societies, and while a duration of several centuries may make it impossible to view it as a simple accident, still one could justifiably believe that some day it will come to an end—just as there was a day when it began. But in reality its origins are much more remote. It was only to avoid needlessly extending the field of historic research that Saint-Simon took this date as a point of departure for his observations. If you go back still further—if you start, for example, with the societies which preceded the Middle Ages—you will see that even then social evolution was taking the same direction.

In the Greco-Latin world the industrial class was merged with the class of slaves. It was the slaves who were the producers, and the slave was the direct property of the master—he was his thing. The substitution of serfdom for slavery—such as occurred in Christian societies—was a first liberation for industry. For the serf depended on military power in only an intermediate and indirect way, through the mediation of land to which he was attached. He was bound to the earth, not to the lord, and the latter could not do with him as he wished. The liberty of his movements therefore became greater. (*Industrie*, III, 142.)

On the other hand, in Rome and Greece spiritual and military powers were fused. It was the same class that held both. This diffuse state resulted in a strict subordination of intellectual life to military power, which ceased the day that the two domains were definitely separated by Christianity. This separation has been a primary liberation for the human mind—a profound view which can today be treated as an acquisition of history. The great service Christianity performed for thought was to make it a social force, distinct from governmental powers and equal—even superior in certain respects—to them. Henceforth, the mind has a field which belonged to it in its own right and where it could develop its nature.[1] Thus the growth of the communes and the importation of positive sciences into Europe are not the first beginnings; since the existence of humanity it has moved toward the same goal. It is its nature to go in this direction and to seek to drive it back is vain.

[1] "This division, which did not exist among the Romans, is probably the outstanding improvement in social organization made by moderns. It is the one that earliest created the possibility of making a science out of politics, by permitting it to distinguish theory from practice." (*Organis.*, IV, 85.)

Since this progressive disappearance of the old system "is a necessary result of the course pursued by civilization" (*Organis.*, IV, 63), one has only to inquire if it is useful. And since it is necessary, whatever one may think of it, one can only concur. But actually it is easy to see that this development conforms to the true interests of humanity. From military—which it was formerly—the human spirit became pacific. Industry was offering nations a means—as fruitful as war—of becoming rich and powerful. As a result, military strength lost its old significance. Besides, the conjectural propositions priests were teaching became useless, since science showed the superiority of demonstrated propositions. The representatives of the old order of things no longer render effective service, and maintain themselves only through force of habit. This is what Saint-Simon tried to make clear in a famous pamphlet. "Imagine," he wrote, "that the nation loses Monsieur, princes, cardinals, bishops, judges, and in addition, ten thousand of the richest property owners among those who live off their incomes without producing. What would the result be? This accident would certainly afflict all the French because they are good . . . but no political harm to the state would result. There are a great number of Frenchmen who are able to exercise the functions of the king's brother as well as does Monsieur. . . . The anterooms of the chateaux are full of courtiers ready to occupy the places of the great officers of the crown. . . . How many assistants are our ministers of state worth? . . . As for the ten thousand owners—their heirs will require no apprenticeship to do the honors of their salons as well." (*Organisateur*, IV, 22-23.) But the same ready substitution could not be made if France were to lose, not thirty thousand personages of this kind, but only three thousand producers—whether of the intellectual or the economic order. Then, it "would become a body without a soul" and would need "at least an entire generation to repair the damage." (*Ibid.*, 20.)

So it is neither possible nor useful to restore the old system in its entirety. But on the other hand we know that every eclectic combination is contradictory and incoherent, that a social organization cannot be regarded as stable except as it is entirely homogeneous. In other words, society must be based on only one of the two conflicting principles, and the other be excluded. It follows that modern societies will be definitely in equilibrium only when organized on a purely industrial basis. Let us pause for a moment at this conclusion and the argument it is deduced from, for in it we find one of the important characteristics of socialism—I mean its radical and revolutionary spirit. I am not implying that socialism is constrained to employ violence to attain its goal. In any event such a proposition could not be applied to Saint-Simon since to him violence never accomplishes anything and is only a weapon of destruction. (*Catéch.*, VIII, 9.) I refer only to the very general tendency of socialist doctrines to make a *tabula rasa* of the past in order to construct the future. Whether, in order to proceed to the work of overthrowing, they merely recommend recourse to legal measures or condone insurrection, whether they believe it necessary to control changes or not, does not matter. Almost all say there is complete incompatibility between what ought to be and what is, and that the existing order must disappear to give place to a new. In this sense they are revolutionary—whatever precautions they may take to mitigate the effects of this revolution. We have just seen—through the example of Saint-Simon—where this subversive spirit comes from. It is due to the integral character their demands assume. Feeling very keenly the new needs which trouble society, they no longer share the sentiments of others. Fascinated by the goal they pursue, they believe they must realize it in all its purity, without any alloy to corrupt it. Therefore it is necessary that societies be organized completely—from top to bottom—so as to assure this integral realization. But now today's societies are constituted to realize quite other ends. Consequently their present organization, being an obstacle to what must be established—must disappear. Social elements must be freed so that they may be organized according to a new design. The social body must die in order to be reborn. Saint-Simon does not see this argument as a contradiction of his premises. If—as he keeps repeating—each period of history originates in the one preceding, the old is found again in the new, and so persists throughout changing forms. What will be comes from what has been; what was could not cease to be, for the cause survives in its effect, the principle in its consequences. Nothing is destroyed. Since the future has issued from the past, it cannot free itself from it. One must take a choice. Either future institutions are merely old institutions transformed—and in this case the latter are found within the former—or else the first are not born from the second. But then, from where do they come? Historic continuity is broken and one wonders how such a hiatus can exist without the course of social life itself being suspended at the same time.

At any rate, on this point—granted that the new system must differ completely from the old—how can one proceed to sketch its design? Obviously, to the degree that it does not exist, it must be invented. "It is clear that the industrial regime, unable to be introduced either by chance or routine, had to be conceived *a priori.*" (*Catéch.*, VIII, 61.) On the other hand, it is neither necessary nor even possible to invent it out of whole cloth, for we know that it already exists in part. Under feudalism an industrial organization existed which has gone on developing since the Middle Ages. But what is to be established cannot be anything other than what preceded, strengthened and enlarged. As it stands it is inadequate, but only because it does not as yet embrace the whole of social life, confined as it has been until now by vestiges of the old regime. It remains only to acquire awareness of the features it presents, and to see what they should become. If this system —instead of being subordinated to another—remains itself and is extended to all collective functions without exception; if the principle on which it rests becomes the very basis of social organization in its totality—then, in short, everything is reduced to observing the essential properties of the industrial order as it was spontaneously established, and to generalizing them.

The most vital trait of this spontaneous organization is that its goal, and its exclusive goal, is to increase the control of man over things. "To concern itself only in acting on nature, in order to modify it as advantageously as possible for humankind," has been the unique task of the communes since their enfranchisement—that is, of the new society in process of formation. Instead of seeking to extend the national domain, instead of diverting the attention of men from worldly wealth, it addressed itself, on the contrary, to peacefully increasing their well-being through the development of arts, science and industry. It has had as its unique function the production of useful things for our worldly existence. Consequently, since all reform consists of extending to all of society what until now has been so only for a portion of it, the crisis will only be resolved when all social life converges toward this same goal, to the exclusion of every other. The only normal form that collective activity can take henceforth, is the industrial form. Society will be fully in harmony with itself only when it is totally industrialized. "The production of useful things is the only reasonable and positive end that political societies can set themselves." (*Industrie*, II, 186.) Military virtues, like the asceticism religion preaches, henceforth have no reason for existing. Things of war—like those of theology —no longer interest any but a small minority and, no longer serving as an objective for the ordinary concerns of men, cannot supply the material of social life. The only interests now capable of playing this role are economic interests. "It is a class of interests felt by all men and which belong to the maintenance of life and well-being. This group of interests is the only one in which all men understand each other and have to agree on, the only one on which they have to deliberate, to act in common—the only one, therefore, around which politics can be exercised and which should be accepted as the single criterion of all institutions and social matters." (*Industrie*, II, 188.) Society must become a vast production company. "All society rests on industry. Industry is the only guaranty of its existence . . . The most favorable state of affairs for industry is, for this reason, the most favorable to society." (II, 13.)

From this principle flows a significant conclusion. It is that "the producers of useful things—being the only useful people in society—are the only ones who should cooperate to regulate its course." (*Industrie,* II, 186.) It is therefore to them and them alone that law-making belongs. It is in their hands that all political power should be deposited. Since, hypothetically, the whole fabric of social life would be made up of industrial relationships, is it not obvious that only men of industry are in a position to direct it? The vital rationale consists of two stages: 1. Since in this system there is nothing more socially central than economic activity, the regulating organ of social functions should preside over the economic activity of society. There is no longer place for a central organ with a differing objective since there is no longer other material in the common life; 2. This organ must necessarily be of the same nature as those which it is charged with regulating—that is to say, it must be composed exclusively of representatives of industrial life.

But what is understood by "industrial life?" According to a concept found at the basis of a great number of political constitutions, the most qualified representatives of economic interests would be the property owners. For Saint-Simon, on the contrary, the owner who is merely an owner, and who does not himself exploit his capital, is hardly qualified to fill such an office. He is not even a part of industrial society, for it embraces only producers—and he does not produce. He is a drone, whereas it numbers only bees. He is therefore as completely a stranger to it as are the nobles and functionaries of the old system. There are, says Saint-Simon, two major groups: one consists of the immense majority of the nation—that is to say, all workers—and which Saint-Simon calls national and industrial; and the other, which he labels anti-national, because it is like a parasitic body whose presence only interrupts the play of social functions. In the latter are included noblemen . . . and "owners living like nobles, that is to say, doing nothing." (*Parti national*, III, 204.) This opposition between owner and industrial appears constantly in his writings and under all forms. In one of his last works (*Catéch. Industriel*) the owner is even designated by the most modern word, "bourgeois." "It is not the industrials who caused the revolution, it is the bourgeois." But it is important to note that it is not all capitalists who are placed beyond the pale of regular society, but only those who live on unearned income. As for those who themselves make their wealth productive, who enrich it with their toil—they are industrials. Consequently, industrial society comprises all those who actively participate in the economic life, whether they are owners or not. The fact of possessing does not provide access to it but does not preclude them from it.

But how are idlers to be eliminated? The logical result of what preceded would be denial of possession without working, and consequently the prohibition of accumulating wealth to a degree which would permit idleness. Saint-Simon does not go as far as this. He is satisfied to place the useless in a state of legal tutelage. They will not participate in political power. They will be tolerated in society but will have the status of aliens. For, lacking representation in the councils which direct collective activity, they will not affect its course. To arrive at this result without delay—since under the Restoration one was a voter only on condition of paying a certain amount of direct taxes—it would suffice to legislate that only the industrials would be allowed to pay this tax. In this way, industry would quickly and easily be mistress of the chambers. This is the import of a measure Saint-Simon recommends, and which at first seems quite strange. He demands that henceforth the land tax directly affect, not the owner of land, but the farmer, the tenant. This is not in order to burden these producers—on the contrary we will see that he is concerned with bettering their situation—but so that they alone may have the right of electing representatives. It is a way of eliminating the idle owner from political life. If Saint-Simon does not demand the same reform for owners of personal capital, it is because they were not covered by a direct tax high enough to provide electoral qualification. (*Industrie*, II, 84-96).

But if owners are not to be considered producers, it is not the same with scholars, who are the indispensable auxiliaries of industry. "The social body," says Saint-Simon, "consists of two great families: that of intellectuals, or industrials of theory, and that of immediate producers, or scholars of application." (*Industrie*, III, 60.) Consequently they too have the right to be represented in the managing organs of society, and this representation is actually indispensable since industry cannot do without the knowledge of science. It is necessary therefore that the supreme council of industry be assisted by a supreme council of the learned. However, the two organs—though united—must be distinct, for the two functions—theory on one side and practice on the other—are too different to be fused. "The division of society and all that concerns it—temporally and spiritually—must obtain in the new system as in the old." (*Organisateur*, IV, 85, n.l.) This is a victory of Christianity which it is important not to lose. Thinkers must be able to speculate with complete independence and without servilely capitulating to the needs of practice; but it is essential that the practical men decide finally on all that concerns execution. Moreover the two organs should not be placed on the same footing; there must exist between them a certain hierarchy. It is to the industrials that the principal role should belong, for it is on them that the existence of the thinkers depends. "Scholars render very important services to the industrial class, but receive services from it that are much more important. They receive existence. . . . The industrial class is the fundamental class, the providing class of society." (*Catéchisme*, X, 25.) The learned form but "a secondary class." (*Ibid.*) Between the two, finally, are the artists, whose position in the system is less clearly fixed. Occasionally Saint-Simon seems to treat them as a class apart, represented by a special organ in the managing centers of society; at other times they disappear into the industrial class.

In summary, granted that social functions can be only secular or spiritual—that is, turned towards thought or towards action—that in the present state of civilization the only rational form of the temporal is industry and of the spiritual, science, Saint-Simon concludes: 1. That normal society should consist only of producers and scholars; 2. That as a consequence it should be subordinated to directing organs composed of similar elements, with a certain preeminence of the first over the second. This is the fundamental principle of the new system. But before going into the details of the means of application, we should understand their significance.

Occasionally their significance has been misunderstood. In making himself the "apostle of industrialism" it is said that Saint-Simon has only "completed Adam Smith and Jean-Baptiste Say" (Weil, 168) and it is only in the light of the details, not in the fundamental principle of the system, that an early form of socialism is found. But in reality socialism is already quite complete in the doctrine we just presented. What in fact was its final goal, if not to bind economic life to a central organ that regulates it—which is the very definition of socialism? The nature of this organ matters little, and likewise its relationship with the governmental organ—which we will take up later. From all that preceded, it would seem that the central organ has nothing—and could have nothing—more important as its function, since henceforth economic life constitutes the whole of social life. It is, from this time on, centralized. If this consequence of the principle was not perceived, it is because reform was thought of—incorrectly—as limited to the manner in which this council or sovereign assembly would be composed. From this point of view, Saint-Simon seems satisfied to call for sounder recruitment of political assemblies, and to limit himself to demanding that a greater representation be given to industry. But it is not noticed that another change was to occur at the same time. Not only is political power no longer in the same hands, but it affects an altogether different class of interests than before—namely, that of economic life. The latter becomes not only an object, but the only object, of collective action. Industry is now to be regarded as a social function, or rather as *the* social function *par excellence;* in replacing military functions, it took on all their social characteristics. Although in Saint-Simon's thinking economic life should continue to be conducted by individuals, and although he does not conceive of it except as an ensemble of individual undertakings—that is to say, in the form it now presents— still he regards this aggregate as a system which has unity, all of whose parts should function harmoniously and consequently must be subordinated to a directing social agency.

There are many passages in which this attitude is expressed. In some very remarkable sentences in the *Système Industriel* he shows that as a result of the division of social labor, individuals would today be more jointly responsible and more dependent on the mass. "In the measure that civilization makes progress, the division of labor—considered from the spiritual as from the secular side, grows in the same proportion. Thus men depend less on others as individuals, but more on the mass—and precisely in the same relationship." (V, 16.) And this action of the mass is natural and useful, because "the organization of a well-ordered system requires that the parts be strongly tied to the whole and subordinated." (*Ibid.*) It is in order to assure this dependence, this superiority of the whole over the parts, that a directing agency is necessary. Its role is to combine efforts with a view to a common goal. "Until now, men have exerted energies upon nature which were purely individual and isolated. . . . With this in mind, one can imagine what point humanity could reach if men . . . organized themselves to apply combined efforts to nature, and if nations, among themselves, followed this same practice." (*Organis.*, IV, 194.) It is precisely to assure this combination that the entire system should strive. This is possible only when through the effects of the division of labor, unity of the industrial body already exists in fact. It is necessary, beforehand, "that in the large majority of the nation, individuals be joined in industrial associations, more or less numerous and connected . . . to permit their formation into a generalized system by being directed toward a great common industrial goal." (*Syst., Ind.,* VI, 185.) This is where Saint-Simon distinguishes himself from the system of the classic economists. For them economic life is completely outside politics; it refers wholly to the individual. For Saint-Simon it is the whole substance of politics; not only is there a politics of economic interests, but there is no other. "Politics is the science of production." (*Industrie,* II, 188.)

*   *   *

The entire doctrine of Saint-Simon hinges upon the following problem: "What is the social system required by the present situation of the European peoples?" To answer this question, Saint-Simon examines history. It reveals that modern societies carry within themselves two social systems—not only different but contradictory—which have been developing in opposite directions since the early Middle Ages. One has as its key military force and the unreasoned prestige of faith; the other, industrial capacity and the freely accepted authority of the learned. Temporally, one is completely organized for war, for depravation—the other for peaceful production. Spiritually, the former systematically turns men's minds away from all that is earthly, whereas the latter centers them on things of this world. Such an antagonism precludes mixed and eclectic solutions. At least, these cannot be useful except temporarily and only to the extent they lead to a radical and definitive solution. Such makeshifts cannot avoid the final solution, except for what can be indefinitely put off. A society cannot be consistent and stable as long as it rests concurrently on two principles so manifestly contradictory. It cannot be in equilibrium unless it is organized completely in a homogenous fashion—that is unless all collective forces move in the same direction and around a single and identical center of gravity. It is therefore necessary to choose firmly between the two systems. Either wholly restore one, or else extend the other to the entirety of social life. But the first is impossible; for even though it might be useful, in no event could one revise the course of history. So we are left with the second. The only way to solve the crisis is to eliminate from society all that remains from the past, all survivals—now without reason—of the feudal and theological regime, and to no longer tolerate as regular members any but producers of useful things—the industrials, as Saint-Simon again says. Society must rid itself of parasitic agencies—which persist from habit and which absorb part of the collective vitality—in order to become a system of economic functions, a vast association of production, and which, as a result, is organized.

Formulated in this way, Saint-Simon's thesis could be accepted by even the most classic economists. In fact they too maintain that present societies should be essentially industrial, that economic relationships are the substance, *par excellence*, of collective existence. But here is where the divergence between them and Saint-Simon reveals itself. In the eyes of the economists, economic actions—though most vital in contemporaneous societies, though keeping the others in dependence—are nonetheless exclusively private matters. For Saint-Simon, however, the industry of a nation is a system which has unity, and by virtue of this must be subject to a directing influence, to an action exercised by the whole over the parts. And since from his point of view the industrial system is at one with the entire social system, it is from society that this influence must emanate; it is the collectivity which should control this activity. In other words, for both, social life should be at one with industrial life. But by seeing the latter as only combinations of individual interests, the disciples of Smith and of Say at one stroke rob it of all social character, and arrive at the strange conclusion that there is nothing in society clearly social. For they have withdrawn from it all the old content—namely, the passion of national glory, the respect for common beliefs, etc.—and have put in its place only things and feelings of a private order. More in keeping with his principle, Saint-Simon, having established that henceforth the only normal manifestation of social activity is economic activity, concludes that the latter is a social thing, or rather that it is *the social thing*—since nothing else is possible—and that it must be regarded as such. It must indeed have a collective character unless there is something else that has—in other words, unless there is something more common among men. Society cannot become industrial unless industry is socialized. This is how industrialism logically ends in socialism.

However, this socialization of economic forces is not conceived by Saint-Simon under a rigorously unitary form. He does not even have the notion that commerce and industry can be conducted through any other means than that of individual enterprise. He only asks that the system formed by means of private exploitation be subject to the control of regulating agencies, of controlling councils which maintain unity by assuring harmony. We can now examine the way these councils are to be composed and their mode of functioning.

First, as concerns their recruitment and organization, there are in Saint-Simon's works several plans which do not entirely agree among themselves. The most complete is that of the *Organisateur;* in it are three Chambers. The first, or chamber of invention, will consist of three hundred members chosen from among engineers and artists. It will draw up projects "of public works to be undertaken to increase France's wealth and to improve the condition of its inhabitants." (IV, 51.) It will also have charge of formulating plans for public celebrations. The second, or chamber of study, will consist of an equal number of members, but is composed entirely of scholars—a hundred mathematicians, a hundred physicists and one hundred physiologists. It will study the projects of the first chamber, and in addition, direct public education. This will be its principal function. Finally, a third, the chamber of execution, will be the Old Chamber of Communes or Deputies. It will be recruited only from among the heads of all branches of commercial farming and manufacturing industries. Only through it—and it alone—can projects conceived by the first chamber and examined by the second be achieved.

This is why the instrument of collective action, namely, the budget, depends on it and it alone. These three chambers will form the Parliament.

In the *Système Industriel* we find another less utopian program. Saint-Simon is content to ask that the establishment of the budget and the use of funds be assigned to the representatives of industry, and that the Institute be utilized in such a way as to substitute for the clergy in the exercise of spiritual power. To attain the first objective, it will suffice to reorganize three ministries: finance, interior, and marine. The Minister of Finance could only be an industrialist who had practised his profession for ten consecutive years; further, he would be assisted by a council of twenty-six members—likewise chosen from industry—called the chamber of industry, which would determine the budget. The Minister of the Interior would have to have spent at least six consecutive years in industry. Attached to him and charged with determining the use of the funds granted the Minister by the chamber of industry, would be a council composed of scholars and engineers. Finally the Minister of Marine affairs must have been a captain for ten years, and the council associated with him would consist of thirteen members named by the captains of our great ports. (V, 106 *et seq.*)

As for spiritual authority, it will be even easier to organize. Granted that "the strongest bond uniting members of society consists of a similarity of principles and knowledge, and that this similitude can only result from the uniformity of instruction given to all citizens" (VI, 238), it will suffice to call upon the Institute to formulate "a national catechism which will include the elementary teaching of principles which serve as the basis of social organization, as well as summary instruction in the principal laws governing the material world." (VI, 237.) In addition that same body will supervise public instruction so "nothing can be taught in the schools contrary to the national catechism." (VI, 239.) One can see that as he advances, Saint-Simon sought to reduce and simplify the reforms he demands in order to show that they are easily and immediately applicable. However, in the *Catéchisme Industriel*, going back to the question of the reorganization of spiritual power, he proposes a modification in the constitution of the Institute to enable it to best fulfill its new functions. There would be two Academies in it: one, corresponding to the Academy of Sciences, and composed of "scholars in political economy," which would have as its function setting up the code of interests, in other words, formulating the rules to which industry should conform in order to be as productive as possible. The other Academy, which was found in principle in the group of moral and political sciences instituted by the Revolution—but was later abolished—would be charged with establishing the code of feelings—in other words, a system of moral rules in harmony with the conditions of existence of an industrial society. It would consist not only of moralists, but of lawyers, theologians, poets, painters, sculptors, musicians. Finally above these two Academies, a supreme scientific College named by them would coordinate their work, set up in a body of doctrines the principles and regulations established by them, and serve as intermediary between them and the council entrusted with the exercise of temporal authority. (X, 25 *et seq.*)

It is unnecessary to expound in detail these schemes of reform which are patently not relevant to the system. Whenever a reformer is not content to postulate general principles, but undertakes to show in a detailed plan how practical they are, it is difficult for him to avoid falling into a utopia—sometimes even into childishness—or difficult at the least to avoid giving the impression of it. In this respect there are merely differences of degree in the programs of Thomas More and Campanella and Saint-Simon, and this common appearance has certainly contributed to the historic error which makes of socialism a simple derivative, a new variation, of ancient communism. What gives all these doctrines this same look, when they attack problems of application, is the separation which exists—and is felt to exist—between the obviously abstract and vague character of social forms which are completely imagined, and the eminently concrete nature of those before our eyes. Whatever may be the ingenuity of their inventors, the reality they construct through the sole effort of thought is indeed poor and pale beside that of actual experience and present contact. Their contours, in spite of everything, are very uncertain, the lines irresolute. We are aware that social life is too rich, too complex, to be neatly arranged in advance. All these schemes appear artificial and unreal—a feeling which stems from the very efforts made to prevent it —by wanting to foresee all, in other words, by multiplying the details of the execution. A program of reform cannot but be schematic, and the less it wants to be, the more it arouses our suspicion. It is appropriate therefore not to linger over the details of the measures proposed by Saint-Simon—especially since the system is not to be judged by them. Let us see them only as an illustration of principles, which alone warrant being retained and which, themselves, have not changed. They are found again, completely the same, at the base of the different plans we just explained, and can be summarized as follows: 1. Granted that social life should be completely industrial, the regulating agency of social life should be so constituted as to be able to direct it competently—that is to say, it should be composed of industrials; 2. Granted that industry can do nothing without science, it is necessary for the supreme council of industry to be assisted by a council of scholars; 3. Granted that science and art, theory and practice, the spiritual and the temporal, constitute two functions—at once distinct and jointly responsible—it is necessary to give each a distinct organization, while establishing a system of constant communication between them.

Two important propositions thus were established. The first is that collective affairs require special abilities—just as do private matters. As a result the system formed by the group of industrial professions cannot be advantageously administered except with the aid of professional representation. At a stroke the revolutionary principle which attributed uniform competence to everyone in social matters was rejected. There is nothing Saint-Simon fought with greater vigor. The second is that practice presupposes science but is not to be confused with it. Human conduct is intelligent and enlightened only to the degree it is directed by theory—though theory cannot be productive except on condition of its not being limited to pursuit of practical ends. In this light, science ceased to be a simple private occupation, a simple matter of individual curiosity. It became a social function *sui generis,* since one could expect from it common principles according to which both interests and feelings were to be regulated. It was therefore called upon to play in society—with respect to industry—the role which intelligence, and especially reflective intelligence, plays in an individual with regard to activity. By assigning it this task, Saint-Simon did not assign it a new mission, but only made it conscious of the functions it actually fulfilled. What is it, in fact? Is it anything but the pre-eminent form of collective intelligence?

Now that we know how these councils were to be composed, let us examine the way they are to function.

The first problem is that of knowing what relations they will maintain with what one commonly calls the State or the government—in other words, with the constituted bodies which control the material force of society—army, police, etc. Since, until the present and among all known peoples, government has exercised preeminence over all social functions, one might suppose that the industrial organization will equally be subordinated to it in the future, that industry will submit to its action and be only what it permits it to be. In fact is it not through government that all corporations within society have their existence, and is it not a rule that they are subjected to its control? But such a hypothesis is excluded by the principle which requires special ability of all who participate in the administration of industrial life. Precisely because the functions government fulfills are not of an economic order, it is not to intervene in the play of economic functions. "Government always injures industry when it mixes in its affairs. It harms it even in instances where it makes an effort to encourage it." (*Industrie,* II, 186.) Moreover, history shows that the industrial world established itself spontaneously outside of all governmental action. It was born under the influence of internal causes, progressed silently, without—for a long time—the State's being conscious of the great transformations in process. Even industry developed only because certain parts of the social body, subjected until then to governmental authority—that is, to feudal power—gradually freed themselves from it, and thanks to this liberation were able to give themselves a special organization. What then, in the new society, is the task of government? Since it cannot and should not influence the actual foundation of communal life, it can fulfill only a subordinate and negative role. It will defend producers against the idle who wish to consume without producing. It would be completely useless if there were only workers in society. "But circulating in its midst is a mass of parasitic men who produce nothing but want to consume —just as if they were producing. Through their power these people live on the toil of others—whether one gives it to them or whether they take it. In a word, they are idlers, that is to say, thieves. Workers therefore run the risk of seeing themselves deprived of the pleasure which is the goal of their work." As a result, there is a place for a special undertaking which seeks "to prevent the violence with which idleness menaces industry." (*Industrie*, II, 129-210.) It follows that it has merely secondary functions since it does not contribute directly and in a positive way to the *raison d'être* of society, namely, the production of useful things. It is dependent upon the industrials, who remunerate it for the very special service it renders them. "As long as governments protect the learned, in theory and practice, one remains in the old regime. But from the moment the learned protect governments one really begins the new regime." (*Industrie*, III, 29.) Thus it is the supreme councils, composed as we have stated, which alone have the capacity to authoritatively determine the progress of society.

Out of this proposition grows another, of no less significance. Since government is foreign to industrial organization, the latter is indifferent to all possible forms of government. It lends itself as well to one as to another. In fact Saint-Simon shows through examples that peoples, although subject to a similar governmental regime, present the most striking contrast in their economic situation. He states further that it is not without reason that industrials are disinterested in these questions since "they are without the vote or a political party of their own." (*Catéch.*, VIII, 11.) They have a deep conviction that all these controversies do not concern them, that economic life is independent of all constitutional particularities. But if this is so, in an entirely and exclusively industrial society—such as Saint-Simon announced—it is clear that all these questions can be of only secondary interest, since the orientation of society does not depend on them. It is therefore necessary not to invest them with an importance they do not have; one would neglect the real difficulties of the present time. This is the error that the revolutionary assemblies and all that followed them committed. It was thought the most urgent thing was to apply one's self to the study of the best possible government, without seeing that all these combinations of political metaphysics were not getting to the bottom of things. While a wealth of ingenuity was being expended on these superficial arrangements, industrial society remained in the state of disorganization or imperfect organization, from which the crisis resulted, and which made it continue. This method must be rejected and all these problems of pure politics put in their true place which is a secondary one. There is even no occasion to deal with them *ex professo* and in general, and the best thing is to resolve them according to circumstances—in other words, to conserve the form of government which exists, whatever it may be, aristocratic, monarchic, republic, etc.—provided that it presents no obstacle to the definitive establishment of the new regime.

Let us stop for a moment at this concept, which accounts for an important fact. A very particular characteristic of the social theories of the nineteenth century—which is not found at all in those of the eighteenth—is that now two types of questions are distinguished and separately treated even though they are considered connected. On the one hand are the "political" and on the other, "social" problems. Further, it is clear that the more one advances in time, the more public attention turns from the former and looks to the latter. What went before permits us to understand how this distinction occurred, what it signifies and from whence comes this progressive effacement of political questions. It is because these last directly or indirectly refer to the form of government. Social questions, on the contrary, are those to which the economic state of modern societies give rise; what accounts for them is that industrial functions have assumed an importance and development which do not permit their being left in their unorganized state. And these questions are called social precisely because, as Saint-Simon demonstrated, economic relations have become either the unique, or in any case, the principal substance of social life.

Thus there are two very different orders of problems: the one deals at length with the highest spheres of society, which are—or rather which have been until the present— the most conspicuous; the other is concerned with organization of the lower portions. It is evident that it is not by resolving the first that one can ever find the solution of the second, that it is not by combining in this or that fashion the various elements of government, that one can give the industrial world the organization it demands. Under these circumstances, one immediately sees that political questions have lost their interest, since they concern merely a small portion of society, since they relate only to a special function, whereas with the others, it is the whole positive content of collective life which is involved. That is what accounts for the opinion—rather general today—that events occurring in the upper regions where governmental acts are elaborated, do not cause very profound repercussions. It is because we are aware that it is not there that the vital mainspring of society is located, that it is beneath this superficial surface that great social interests live and move. If, formerly, political questions had an altogether different significance, it is because the role of government was then altogether different. As long as the foundation of social life was made up of common beliefs and traditions, it was the government which, by embodying these traditions, unified societies. Through it these latter acquired awareness of themselves, so that all manifestations of collective activity were jointly responsible for the form of government. Suppress the Roman patriciate and there is no longer the city of antiquity. Without feudal loyalism, without monarchial loyalism, the societies of the Middle Ages, and later those from the six-teenth to the eighteenth century, could not maintain them-selves.

But where economic relations form the basis of communal life, social unity is above all the result of a solidarity of interests; it is therefore due to internal causes, to the bonds of interdependence which unite the various parts of society, and not to this or that characteristic of the governmental agency. Each people today forms a homogeneous whole, not because it acquired the habit of identifying itself with such and such a function or class, but because it is a system of functions, inseparable from one another and mu-tually complementing each other. Government is only one of these functions, it no longer has the grand role which it formerly fulfilled. Therefore one can believe that what best characterizes our present democracies, what makes them su-perior to other kinds of government, is precisely that gov-ernmental forms are reduced to a minimum. As a result, they in no way disturb the underlying organization which is striving to emerge. Perhaps also it is there that one should seek the difference which separates them from primitive de-mocracies, with which they have so often and so carelessly been confused.

But let us resume the course of our exposition. We have just seen that the directing councils of industrial life are independent of the governmental agency and are even su-perior to it. But if they are destined to be placed above government, would it not be on the condition of their be-coming the government? If they make it step down from the preeminent position it had occupied until now, would it not be quite simply because they themselves have the councils and powers? But is it necessary to represent them as administering the industrial life of society according to processes which governments have always employed in the direction of communal affairs? Would they not be merely a state of a new type, faithful to all the traditions of the state and functioning in the same way? "This," says Saint-Simon, "would be to completely misunderstand the nature of the regime which alone can suit industrial societies."

These latter do not merely require that the councils which direct them be organized differently from the old governmental councils. It is necessary in addition that the directing activity they exercise make itself in an entirely new way, according to an altogether different method, so that it may be in harmony with the special conditions in which these societies are found. They must have a specific mode of functioning, which it is important to determine.

What characterizes governmental activity among all known peoples is that it is exercised by men on men. Governments have always been made up of individuals who dictated to other individuals; wills were subjected to other wills. And it could not be otherwise since force was the only principle of the social organization of military societies. By definition, military society implies that certain people hold power and that others are excluded from it; the first are the masters of the second, but the latter obviously do not accept their state of submission since it is imposed on them. The whole order rests on a dictatorial foundation. While it is imperative, and because it is imperative, governmental action is necessarily arbitrary, for the men who command govern as they desire. The sovereign will, to which the others are subjected, twists and turns in any direction it pleases; the very essence of despotism is will. One often complains of the arbitrariness, of which history furnishes so many examples, and reproaches the governments themselves. This is wrong, for it is not simply an accidental result of individual faults, but inevitably a consequence of the old social order. And it cannot fail to be such as long as society is coherent only because some wills are subjected to other wills. One must particularly guard against believing that such a state of affairs is due to this or that form of government, that for example—according to a common opinion so often repeated—it has as its unique cause monarchical despotism. (*Org.*, IV, 191 in note.) It is not less so under parliamentarianism. The arbitrariness of majorities is no better than that of monarchies. In one case as in the other, it is men who give orders to men and who make them obey. It matters little that the master will is that of an individual, of a caste, or of a group designated by choice.

The behavior of the regulating agencies of industrial societies must be altogether different. In fact here it is not the strongest who control but those most capable in science or industry. They are not summoned to office because they have the power to exercise their will but because they know more than others, and consequently their functions do not consist in saying what they want, but what they know. They do not dictate orders, they only declare what conforms to the nature of things. The scholars show what the laws of social hygiene are; then, from among the measures they propose as a result of these laws, the industrials choose those which experience has proved most practicable. The first will say what is healthful and what is not, what is normal and abnormal; the second will execute. The one will teach what is true; the others will draw from these teachings the practical consequences they imply. Things will occur as they are now occurring in industry, where, for example, chemists can tell us of the laws of combination of bodies, physicists of their resistance, and engineers deduce their applications, without any place provided in all this for the play of capricious and impersonal [sic][2] wishes. It is no longer men controlling men. It is truth alone which speaks; it is impersonal, and nothing is less capricious. In short it is things themselves—through the mediation of those who understand them—that indicate the manner in which they should be handled. "In the old system," says Saint-Simon, "society is governed essentially by men; in the new it is governed only by principles." (*Org.*, IV, 197.) But principles, to be obeyed, have no need to speak with the tone of command. Nor do they need to force their wishes. One submits to them voluntarily because they are what they are, because they are the truth. One cannot want to act otherwise than in conformity with the nature of things. So, with caprice, governmental repression disappears.

[2] Considering the next two sentences, it would seem that Durkheim meant to say "personal" wishes here, rather than "impersonal."—A.W.G.)

One can say that in such a society there are no longer inequalities, for there no longer are privileges. Those who direct are not above those who are directed; they are not their superiors. They fulfill a different function—that is all. They say what is and what is not, what is good and what bad; the others act, and that is all. And as each has the role which fits his capacity, all are equally treated. "True equality," says Saint-Simon, "consists in each drawing benefits from society in exact proportion to his social outlay, that is to his real capacity, to the beneficent use he makes of his abilities. And this equality is the natural foundation of industrial society." (*Syst. Indus.*, VI, 17.) "The industrial system," he says elsewhere, "is founded on the principle of perfect equality. It is opposed to the establishment of all rights of birth and even all types of privilege." (*Catéch.*, VIII, 61.) Under these circumstances the social order does not need to be imposed. It is naturally and voluntarily desired by all since each finds in it the necessary arena for the free development of his nature, and bows only to the necessary principles derived from the nature of things. It is under these conditions, and only these, that society can truly exercise sovereignty—"sovereignty which does not at all consist of arbitrary opinion built into law by the mass, but of principle derived from the very nature of things, whose justice men only need to recognize and proclaim the necessity for." (*Organ.*, IV, 198.)

To distinguish this way of conducting social affairs from what until then had been employed by governments, Saint-Simon proposes to call it by a special name—he calls it "administrative," in contrast to the other, which he terms "governmental." "Humankind," says he, "has been destined by nature to live in society. It was summoned, first, to live under governmental rule. It is destined to pass from governmental or military rule to administrative or industrial rule." And he uses this expression because this is the rule now utilized in the management of large industrial companies. They are administered and not governed. The adminstrative bodies which direct them do not impose arbitrary wishes upon them. They speak only in accordance with what the scholars teach them, according to what statisticians inform them as to what is proper to do or not do. They are not invested with a quasi-religious authority which makes one obey them. They are simply better informed than those who execute what they have decided. Their whole function consists in setting up the best possible budget in the common interest. It is this type of conduct that must be introduced into the governing of social interests. "The establishment of the Bank, insurance companies, savings banks, companies for the construction of canals and the formation of a multitude of other associations which have for their object the administration of very important matters—all these have accustomed the French to the administrative mode of conducting great affairs. And as a result this method can be applied to the management of general interests without innovation in the top direction of public affairs causing either surprise or shock." (*Org. soc.*, X, 148.) In a word, industrial society should be conducted industrially.

Let us correctly understand Saint-Simon's thinking. We have just seen, in succession, first that government, strictly speaking, was to be reduced to the subordinate role of police, then, that the regulating agencies of the new society had to perform their activities in an altogether different manner than governments had previously employed. The result is that in industrial society governmental activity, if it is not completely nil, is reduced to a minimum. But Saint-Simon foresees a time when it will become almost needless.

When organization is finally established, the number of idle, of parasites—and consequently thieves—will be reduced to naught; for being unable to maintain themselves, and being sure of finding in the social organism a place suited to their abilities, those who resort to violence in order to subsist will be rare indeed. Thus government will be more or less completely without reason for existence. Whatever it may be in the future, imperious authority should now no longer have a place in the conduct of common affairs. In industrial society, there will not be government in the sense we use the word. For to say "govern" is to say "power to compel," and here, everything is voluntary. The society of Saint-Simon is not an army which has no unity except through submission to its leaders and which docilely performs according to their orders. To be precise, it has no leaders. Each has the position which is natural for him to occupy, and executes no measures except those ordered by the nature of things. Everything is done of itself. If therefore, following usage, every social theory in which governmental form is more or less completely suppressed is called "anarchistic," one must also give this name to the doctrine of Saint-Simon.[3]

Here we see confirmed a proposition we enunciated in our first lesson. It is that socialism, far from being authoritarian —as is so often said—far from demanding a stronger organization of governmental powers, was, on the contrary, in one sense, essentially anarchistic. We find the same attitude, even more pronounced, in Fourier as in Saint-Simon, in Proudhon as in Fourier, in Marx as in Proudhon. But what is no less important to note is that on this point again the two opposite doctrines, socialism and communism, present the most striking similarity. It is also known that at every period orthodox economists have maintained that the social order was voluntary and that, as a result, governmental action was normally unnecessary. They too want to reduce government to the role of police, hoping that the role itself will become more and more unnecessary. And this coincidence between the two systems is not the result of a fortuitous accident; it comes from the fact that both rest on the same principle, namely, industrialism. If the substance of social life is made up exclusively of economic interests, then there is no need for compulsion to urge people and communities to pursue their interests and government authority has no reason for existing. There is nothing to do but allow men to act according to the nature of things and of their needs. It is not necessary to force people to run after their happiness—it is only a matter of telling them where it is. In both systems people have no other aim but their temporal well-being. Society has no other goal than itself and it would seem clear it has no need to be

[3] He who seeks his well-being in a doctrine which he knows to be harmful to society is always punished by the inevitable effect of the laws of organization. (XI, 165.)

led or dragged toward it by a coercive power. So the more
we go on, the more we see communism paralleling socialism,
and if we stress this relationship, it is because it will help us
understand better the meaning of these doctrines, and the way
"social" questions are posed in our time.

*   *   *

After having pointed out that industrialism was the foundation of the new society whose coming Saint-Simon forecast—
or rather, discovered—we began an exposition of the consequences implied in this principle. The three following propositions have been successively established: 1. Since industry is
destined to become the unique substance of social life, the
councils charged with managing society should be so composed as to be able to administer national industry competently—in other words, it should comprise only producers; 2.
Government, in the ordinary sense of the word, i.e., executive
power, should be reduced to a subordinate police role, from
which it follows that industrial organization is indifferent to
all forms of government. It is to the supreme council of industry that the conduct of society belongs and it can equally
acquit itself of this office under all constitutions; 3. In exercising its functions it will proceed according to an entirely
different method than that which governments of all times
have employed. As its authority stems not from the fact that
it is strongest but because it knows what others are ignorant
of, its actions will have nothing arbitrary or coercive about it.
It will not do merely what it wishes, but what fits the nature
of things, and as no one wishes to act other than in conformity with the nature of things, one will do as it says without its
having to compel it. One will voluntarily follow its directions,
just as the sick man follows his physician's, the engineer that
of the chemist and mathematician, the worker that of the
engineer. Thus there will be no need to arm it with the imperative authority which until now has been characteristic of
governments. It will not be above those it directs, but will
simply have another role. In other words, it will not be a
government, but the administrative council of the great industrial company formed by the whole of society. It follows

then that with all strictly governmental activity being abolished in industrial society, the latter is anarchistic. Order will be maintained by the simple working of individual volition, without requiring coercive discipline.

At first such a conclusion may be surprising, for it seems to contradict the authoritarian character which the Saint-Simonian system presents in certain passages. For have we not seen Saint-Simon demand that a national catechism be established and that all contrary instruction be prohibited? But what makes this contradiction disappear—at least what lessens it—is that, if Saint-Simon does recognize an authority, it is exclusively that of science, and this authority, having no need of force to be accepted, impresses him as differing radically from what until now has been the attribute of governments. And if he does assign science such efficacy, it is because—seeing in society only a system of economic interests —it appears to him that from the moment one knows where his interest lies one cannot fail to proceed to it voluntarily. Force is unnecessary where attraction suffices, and consequently the role of the managers of society is needed only to apprise men where their advantage lies, that is to say, what modes of conduct are implied in the nature of things. The only important difference between this anarchistic concept and the economist's is that for the latter society is already capable of voluntary harmony without the need to base it on new foundations, whereas for Saint-Simon it is only in a reformed and reorganized society that this automatic accord of all social functions is possible. For the one, this suppression of all enforced activity is now realizable and desirable; for our philosopher it must necessarily result from the complete transformation of the social order which it requires—but it cannot come until then. But—and this is the essential point—both agree that governmental force or, more generally, social force, is destined to disappear.

Now that we know what the regulating organ of industrial society consists of and the nature of its activity, let us see in what direction this action should be exerted—in other words, what goals it should propose for itself.

Then, as today, according to the school that for this very reason has assumed the name "liberal," the only goal the directors of society—whatever their name—can set for themselves is the maintenance of freedom. "But," answers Saint-Simon, "what do we understand by that word? Does one refer to political liberty, that is to the right accorded every citizen —whoever he may be—to interest himself in public affairs without any proof of ability?" But far from being able to serve as an objective for public activity, such a right is, in itself, monstrous. It would never even have been imagined but for the looseness and uncertainty in which ideas referring to social matters are still draped. In fact, no one dreams of proclaiming that "Frenchmen who pay a thousand francs of direct tax (referring to the electoral qualification) are likely to make discoveries in chemistry." How then can one lay down "an absolutely like principle for politics, which is still much more difficult and important than chemistry?" It is because "chemistry is today a positive science, whereas politics is still only a conjectural doctrine which does not deserve the name of science. It is in the nature of metaphysics—precisely because it teaches nothing of reality—to assume that it is appropriate to everything without having to study anything in a specialized way. . . . But when politics ascends to the rank of the exact sciences . . . stipulations of ability will become clear and fixed and the cultivation of politics will be entrusted exclusively to a special class of scholars who will impose silence on prattle." (*Syst. Ind.*, V. 16-17, note.) This meaning discarded, does one understand liberty to mean the right of individuals to move with independence in the midst of society? Liberty, so conceived, is assuredly an object of primary concern, but it could not be the aim of human association, for the latter is only possible through a mutual interdependence, which lessens this very liberty. "By no means does one associate in order to be free. Savages combine to hunt, to wage war, but surely not to gain liberty; for in this respect they would do better to remain isolated." So, in general, liberty could not constitute a goal of action, for it implies it. It is but a means, a means which is legitimate only when employed with a view to a legitimate end. "Real liberty does not consist of standing with arms crossed if one wishes, in an association—such an inclination should be severely suppressed everywhere it exists. It consists, on the contrary, in developing, without hindrance and with every possible extension, a temporal or spiritual capacity advantageous to society." (*Ibid.*, 15.)

But then, what is the task of what we just now called the administrative council of industrial society? On what will it exercise its activity? It should set itself a double objective, the one more especially economic, the other moral.

Since a nation is—or ought to be—only a vast society of production, its first objective should be to organize production in such a way as to be as fruitful as possible. But to do so, it is essential that the instruments which serve to produce be in hands most capable of making the best use of them. But it is not always the most capable who are the owners. The law of property, therefore, will have to be reformed. "Property will have to be reconstituted and founded on bases which can render it most favorable to production." (*Org.*, IV, 59.) This is the first and most fundamental rule of industrial politics; this is the first thing the new Parliament must do. Saint-Simon returns at every instance to the primary importance of this reform. As early as 1814 he was writing: "There is no change whatsoever in the social order without a change in property." (I, 242.) Thus he views the law defining property rights as the cardinal law of every state. "The law which establishes the powers and the form of government is not as important and does not have as much influence on the welfare of nations as that which establishes ownership and regulates its exercise." (*Industrie*, III, 82.)

This unfortunately is what the Revolution did not understand. It believed it could solve the crisis by constitutional contrivances, which prevented it "from discussing in a general way the law of property, and searching for a means by which property could be established for the greatest advantage of the nation." (*Indust.*, II, 82, note.) And yet, even the ideal of individual liberty, which some wanted to make the only aim of the social contract, could not be achieved except by means of a more rational reconstitution of the system of ownership.

And it is because the peoples of Europe did not take, to arrive at this goal, the only path which could lead them there, that in the end they miscarried. "The English people for more than a hundred and fifty years have been striving to achieve liberty and establish it firmly. The remainder of the nations of old Europeans . . . are concerned for the past thirty years with this same problem, and the natural means—that of re-constituting ownership—has not occurred to any of them." (*Ind.*, III, 126.) In fact, if the system of ownership does not allow the most capable to take advantage of their capacity, if they are not able to freely command the things which are necessary in order to act, in order to fulfill their social role, their liberty is reduced to nothing.

But such propositions clash with the theory which makes the right of property something untouchable. Saint-Simon recognizes that the existence of property rights, defined and sanctioned by law, is the indispensable condition of every social organization—whatever it may be. "The establishment of the right of ownership and arrangements to make it re-spected is indisputably the only possible basis of political society." (*Industrie*, III, 89.) But if this institution is necessary, it is not necessary that it have this or that form. "From the fact that this law is fundamental, it does not follow that it cannot be modified. What is needed is a law which establishes the right of property, and not a law which establishes it in this or that manner." (*Ibid.*) In fact it is—like all human works—subject to the historical future. "This law," says Saint-Simon, "itself depends on a law superior to and more general than it, on the law of nature, by virtue of which the human mind makes continual progress, a law by which all political societies have the right to modify and perfect their institu-tions, a supreme law which forbids binding the generations to come by any disposition whatsoever." (*Ibid.*) And Saint-Simon concludes in these significant words. "Therefore, these questions: What are the things capable of becoming property? By what means can individuals acquire these properties? In what way do they have the right to use them when acquired? These are the questions legislators of all lands and all times have the obligation to deal with every time they consider it appropriate, for the individual right of ownership can be founded only on the common and general need . . . a need which can vary according to the times." (*Ibid.*, 90.) But to return to our point of departure—what the general need requires is that property should by no means be separated from capacity. "It is true that it is property which makes for the stability of government, but it is only when property is not detached from intelligence that governments can rest on it. It is therefore fitting . . . that talent and possession should not be separated." (*Réorganisation de la Société européenne*, I, 200.)

Here is enunciated in the most categorical manner the principle we will find later on under different forms, in all socialist theories. But after postulating it, Saint-Simon applied it formally in only one case, namely, to landed property, and applied it only very moderately. The reform he proposes has for its point of departure this observation: that the farmer finds himself face to face with the landed property owner in a far more subordinate position than that of the merchant or manufacturer dealing with money lenders. In commercial or manufacturing industry, the producer (the dealer or manufacturer) has the right to use, in the manner he judges to be best for the good of his undertaking, the capital he is charged with turning to account. He invests it as he sees fit, lends it if he wishes, or else makes use of the real estate or machines in which he has invested to guarantee new loans that he contracts. In agricultural industry, on the contrary, the industrial, that is to say, the farmer who does not own the funds he uses, is only a tenant who in no way can dispose of the capital confided to his care. He can do nothing without the consent and agreement of the owner. If he needs money, he cannot make use of the land to obtain a loan. He cannot transform it as he wants, and in any event, if he increases its value, does not benefit from this added worth. The result is that in no way are the rights of property and industrial capacity more completely separated, since the former belong completely to him who does not cultivate. Nowhere does the producer have the instruments of production less freely at his command. Such a system is therefore eminently unfavorable to the progress of agricultural industry and consequently—in view of the principle enunciated earlier—it is important to put an end to it.

To achieve this result, Saint-Simon proposes the three following measures: 1. Land will be appraised when the cultivator takes possession of it, and then at the time the lease comes to its end; the farmer will share benefits with the owner if an increment in the capital is found—just as he will bear half the losses if there has been a deterioration. This clause will be obligatory. The parties will not be free to insert it or not in their lease; the latter will have no legal weight and will not be obligatory upon the contractors except when containing it. 2. The farmer will be able to require the owner to lend amounts needed to make those improvements the property is capable of by mortgaging it, and to the former will belong the administration of the funds resulting from these loans. In case the owner refuses, arbitrators would be charged with ruling on the difference, and if they justify the farmer, the loan will be contracted officially. 3. To facilitate these loans, real property would be converted into personal—in other words, it would be represented by titles, analogous to the actions and obligations of industrial companies and endowed with the same mobility. In this way one would be free of all the formalities that stand in the way of transactions in which landed property is the object, and land banks—whose usefulness is generally accepted in Europe—would become a simple and infallibly successful institution. (*Industrie*, III, 102-114.)

The reform is modest in appearance. In reality, however, as M. Janet says (*Saint-Simon*, p. 39) it touches "the foundations of our social organization." For it has the effect of withdrawing certain rights from the land owner in order to transfer them to the producer. The latter would become, in effect, by the mere fact of his work, co-owner of the land he cultivates, since he would share the increased values it might offer—whatever their origin—and since in addition, even without the consent of the owner, he could employ the real estate capital entrusted to him to secure a loan. Such a right, in effect, permits the farmer the right of definitively compromising the property which serves as security, since the loan—if it happens that it cannot be repaid—leads to expropriation. But the reformist boldness of Saint-Simon goes no further. He does not go so far as to claim—as will his disciples—that there is no legitimate property except what is entirely due to the labor and the ability of the one who possesses it. He admits that it might have another origin—for example, inheritance—but it is enough for him, at least for the time being, that the incapable and idle cannot have, over the things they possess, excessive rights which hinder production. He does not suggest organizing property according to the principles of a perfectly equitable distributive justice, but simply in a way most profitable for economic activity. He does not demand modification of the system of personal wealth, because by its nature personal property is much more dependent on the person utilizing it industrially than on its owner. The former can make of it what he wishes, while the latter cannot extract profit from it without the first. Under these circumstances, rights of ownership are not a noticeable inconvenience for the industrial and this reform was perhaps only a first beginning and an opening move.

We must not forget that in industrial society the right of owners who are only owners is singularly threatened, since their interests would not be represented at all in a parliament that would include only producers. That perhaps is what explains a passage of *l'Organisateur*, where after having said that the most urgent task was to re-establish the system of property on new foundations, Saint-Simon adds that a loan of two billion would be necessary "to indemnify persons for the harm caused financial interests by the establishment of the new political system." (IV, 60.)[4] We do not see how this new regulation of the farm contract—whose principles we ex-

[4] In the *Système Industriel*, equally, he seems to allude to a much greater modification of the right of property. "The ancient civil code," he says, "aims to fix poperty as far as possible in the hands of families who possessed it, and the new one ought to propose an absolutely opposite end; that of facilitating for all whose labors are useful to society, the means of becoming owners." (V, 178.) Is it not inheritance he envisaged in so expressing himself? One can only offer hypotheses on this point.

plained—could give rise to such an expense. For nowhere is it a question, in Saint-Simon's works, of any reform but the preceding. Perhaps this silence is explained by the fact that Saint-Simon proposes above all to pose principles, to indicate how the councils charged with applying them should be composed, but does not himself seek to deduce the whole succession of possible applications. He endeavors above all to indicate the goal to be attained but as for the means, in large measure, he places the burden of finding them on the competent bodies he calls for. Besides, by nature he was unfitted for this latter task. An intuitive and generalizing genius, he foresees—often with a rare clairvoyance—what orientation, in a general fashion, society tends to follow, but he has too little taste for precision to anticipate the progress in its detail. It is only rarely that he sketches plans of reform as complete as those we spoke of above. This must be kept in mind if we want to understand him properly. And this is why his works contain so many seeds which are not developed, so many principles whose consequences remain implicit and have been deduced only by his successors.

For a long period Saint-Simon appears to have assigned no goal to practical activity other than increasing production. In *l'Industrie*, in *l'Organisateur* it is the entire thing. This is how at the end of this last work he defines the aim of social organization as he conceives it: "Thus we believe it possible to grant in principle that in the new political order social organization should have as its only objective to apply as far as possible, and to the satisfaction of man's needs, the knowledge acquired in sciences, in fine arts, and in professions and crafts." (*Org.*, IV, 193.) But gradually he approached the idea of a more clearly moral end which he superimposes on the preceding one.

It is not that moral preoccupations had been absent from his early writings. He understood clearly that the social organization could not be changed without a moral transformation. In the first volume of *l'Industrie*, he points to the absence of a system of morality adequate to the new situation, as one of the causes of the crises which French society suffers. "The French," he says, "have abandoned their ancient system of morality because they have found it was not sufficiently sound. And instead of zealously working to re-place it with a better one, for over twenty-five years they have permitted their entire attention to be absorbed by discussions of petty politics." (*Industrie*, II, 221.) He could no less disinterest himself from moral questions, since for him morality is not at all distinct from politics. "Politics is a consequence of morality. The latter consists of the knowl-edge of rules which should preside over the relationships between the individual and society so that both may be as happy as possible. But politics is nothing but the science of these relations and the rules which are important enough to organize them. . . . Thus politics derives from morality, and the institutions of a people are only the results of its ideas." (*Oeuvres*, III, 30.) At the same time he sketches with deci-sive strokes the plan of this reorganization. What character-izes industrial societies is that, freed of every theological idea, they rest on purely secular foundations. A morality, which alone can suit these types of societies, should have the same character. It too ought to be exclusively temporal, both in the principles it rests on and in the ends it assigns human conduct. It should assume authority for one reason; it should interest man only in things of this world. "In a word, it is necessary to pass from celestial morality to ter-restrial morality. Without discussing here the objections to be found in basing morality on theology, it is enough to observe that in fact supernatural ideas are almost everywhere destroyed; they will continue daily to lose control and the hope of paradise and the fear of hell can no longer serve as a basis for the behavior of men. . . . The era of positive ideas is beginning; no longer can one assign to morality motives other than palpable interests, certain and present. . . . This is the great step civilization is about to take; it will consist of the establishment of an earthly and practical morality." (*Industries*, III, 38.)

But for some time he was satisfied to pose the problem without seeking to resolve it. This is because at the time moral ends—as he conceived them—were not very clearly distinguished from purely economic ends. It seemed to him that in a well organized society, individual interest had to voluntarily agree with the general interests; consequently egoism had to serve the moral, along with the economic order. All that was necessary was for each to acquit himself actively of his office, that is, work, and morality appears to him to exist entirely in the maxim which commands work. This is the idea which is developed in *l'Introduction aux travaux scientifiques*. In these circumstances, what was most pressing, was not to combat or constrain egoism, but to find the social organization which permits it to be utilized. "Opinion," he says in the *Lettres d'un habitant de Genève*, "is still divided on the question of selfishness. . . . The solution of the problem consists in opening a path common to individual and general interest." (I, 44, note.) To find this path is his aim, and from this point of view it was natural that he should feel less need to subordinate economic precepts to clearly moral precepts. But in the *Système Industriel* (1821) a completely new note is sounded. A change took place in Saint-Simon's thinking. He understands that even in a perfectly organized society selfishness is not satisfactory. The spectacle of events unrolling before his eyes seemed to make him understand that, however prescient the social mechanism may be, individual interests divide men more than they unite them. "Society," he exclaims, "is today in extreme moral disorder, egoism is making frightening progress, all is tending to isolation. If these disruptions of social relations are not greater nor more numerous, it is due wholly to the highly developed state of civilization and knowledge which produces in most individuals profound habits of sociability and the sentiment of a certain community of the most common interests. But if the cause of the evil were prolonged further, these customs and this feeling would be insufficient to serve as a brake on general and individual immorality." (*Syst. Indus.*, VI, 51-52.) And he attributes the cause of the evil to the fact that ancient religious beliefs, which restrained egoism, gave way without anything's replacing them. The habits they created continue for some time, but as they weaken, the future becomes threatening. It is important therefore to "fight egoism," for this passion "would of necessity finally result in the dissolution of society." (*Syst. Ind.*, VI, 104.) This is the first time he uses such language.

But what can be opposed to this egoism and dissolution? It could not be a matter of neutralizing them by subjecting them to supernatural ends. Saint-Simon remains faithful to the principle he had acclaimed earlier; the morality of an industrial society can have only earthly ends. Therefore it is among the things of this world that one must seek a goal capable of moderating and constraining egotistical motives. To repeat the expression used by Saint-Simon, the morality of a society organized wholly by the producer can have no other motives than "palpable interests, certain and present." But outside an individual's interest there exist only those of other men which could be taken as the goal of activity. Thus, the only possible checks on personal feelings in a rational and humane morality are sentiments which have other people as their objective. What must be opposed to egoism in order to limit it is philanthropy, and the fundamental rule of morality is the Christian aphorism, "Love one another," which Saint-Simon inscribes as a motto on the first page of his *Système Industriel*. "The fundamental principle established by the divine author of Christianity commands all men to regard themselves as brothers and to co-operate as completely as possible for their well-being. This principle is the most general of all social principles." (*Syst. Ind.*, VI, 229.) Still, it is not enough to repeat it purely and simply as the early Christians formulated it—it must be given an extension which until now it has not received and which it was formerly unable to.

The founders of Christianity undoubtedly made it the basis of an entire doctrine, but this doctrine was only a moral principle for them—it did not become one of the controlling principles of society. It did not give rise to practical institutions which would have made it a reality. It remained an exhortation addressed to the great of the earth. It could, indeed, to the degree it was followed, partially temper the rigors of the social organization but was by no means its soul. "It was (moreover)," says Saint-Simon, "all that was possible at the time, and this triumph—although incomplete—has been an immense boon to the human species." (*Syst. Indust.*, VI, 230.) But the time has come when this maxim must cease being purely platonic. The great moral reform needed today consists precisely "in organizing temporal power in conformity with this divine axiom," so that it is no longer—as it has been until now—a simple recommendation, abandoned to private interpretation, but the very pole towards which political evolution should orient itself. As befits a morality essentially earthly, it must be given all the earthly consequences it implies. So conceived, it is capable of assuming another form which is not merely a translation and application of the preceding one but which is more definite. Philanthropy must naturally affect those men who have the greatest need of it, that is, the most unfortunate, those who live only by their hands, the property-less workers, the proletarians (this expression is used by Saint-Simon himself). And from this flows the rule: "to improve as much as possible the fate of the class which has no other means of existence but the labor of its hands." (VI, 81.) And it has a right to it, not only because it suffers the most, but also because it is the most numerous. "This class forms the majority in a more or less high proportion of all nations on earth. Therefore it is the one which governments should principally concern themselves with while actually it is the one whose interests they look after the least." (*Syst. Ind.*, VI, 81.) And the same idea recurs constantly in the *Système Industriel* and in the *Cathéchisme Industriel* in almost identical terms.

Moreover, in making charity an obligatory rule, Saint-Simon does not believe he contradicts the principle—enumerated earlier by him—that individual and general interests are naturally harmonious in industrial societies. (Cf. *Syst. Indus.*, V, 177.) In fact he considers it in the interest of the rich to concern themselves with the poor, for everyone would profit from a broadly practiced charity. "By improving the fate of the mass," says he, "one assures the well-being of men of all classes." In fact, there are but two ways of keeping the mass of individuals, who are not owners, bound to society: Either keep them in a state of subjection which (materially) prevents them from rebelling, or else arrange it so they do not have the desire. Either impose the social order on them through restraint, or else make them love it. For long the first means alone has been possible, although it has been used with increasing moderation. In fact, the individuals who made up the majority were in a state of ignorance and improvidence which did not permit them to imagine they could derive the benefit they were actually securing from the social order. They were not even capable of freely managing their own affairs. It was therefore necessary for them to be held in tutelage, and social forces were employed mainly to restrain and guard them. But today their situation is no longer the same. Since the Revolution, this most numerous class has demonstrated that it has become mature. From its ranks have come those in agricultural industry who have succeeded the dispossessed nobles, and those who in manufacturing have replaced thousands of enterprises ruined by revolutionary events, by the "law of the maximum" and the wars of the Empire. Due to them, the most essential social functions were not suspended by these crises. Thus the social role they played is the first of the advances made by their knowledge. Therefore there is no longer any reason to treat them as domestic enemies. They can be directly interested in public tranquility by being called upon to participate further in the services of the association. One can admit them into the rank of partners, properly so-called, that is, make of them adherents of society, not because they cannot do otherwise but because they are voluntarily attached to it. And if it can be done, it should be, for it is in the common interest to renounce a system of repression which is so costly and unproductive—costly because it exacts a large removal of funds, unproductive because it does not produce by itself and in addition does not permit deriving from the social energies it suppresses all they can yield. The energies saved by abandoning these ancient practices could be employed more usefully, and the work of individuals is more fruitful when voluntary. It is precisely towards this transformation that the moral rule, just posed, tends. It is essential to improve the fortune of the laboring classes so that by profiting from the social organization they respect it without its having to be imposed on them. "The minority, no longer requiring forceful means of keeping the proletarian class in subordination, should commit itself to those arrangements to which proletarians will be most strongly attached by their interest in the public peace." (X, 127.) And so each has an interest in not confining himself to pure selfishness. This is the price of a truly fruitful social peace.

Here then is a new form assigned to collective activity. The action of the directing councils of society will be obliged not only to aim at regulating property so that industry can be as productive as possible. It would be necessary further to use the products so obtained to improve the situation of the workers. But here, as in preceding cases, although Saint-Simon strongly poses the principle of the reform he demands, he does not draw the practical conclusions which must realize it, except in a hesitating and vague manner. If he indicates the goal with insistence, he is much more sober and less specific as to the means. "The most direct means," he says, "to accomplish the moral and physical amelioration of the majority of the population consists in considering, as primary expenses of the state, those required to procure work for all able-bodied men in order to assure their physical existence; and those which seek to spread acquired knowledge as fast as possible to the proletarian class; and, finally, those which can guarantee individuals composing this class pleasures and gratifications appropriate to the development of their spirit." (X, 128.) Thus large public works, free and advanced education, intellectual recreation placed at the disposal of the workers, are the three means recommended by Saint-Simon. But as to what these great undertakings will be, if they are to be private or consist of a kind of national workshop, whether a minimum wage is to be fixed to assure the physical existence of the employed, etc. —nowhere does Saint-Simon express himself explicitly.

Whatever may be the details of the measures which will permit the realization of this principle, its meaning is not doubtful. He gives an important place in his system to the question of the rich and poor. The feeling which inspires this entire portion of the doctrine is compassion for the unfortunate, along with a fear of their dangers to the social order. It is a deep sympathy for those who suffer most from social inequalities, along with a dread of the hatreds and danger that can rise in their hearts and make them enemies of society. Thus we are finding here sentiments which are the basis of communism. As we previously said, socialism—while distinguished from ancient communism—inherits the motives which gave rise to it. It absorbs it—without being at one with it. In fact it is clear that this latter concern is indeed far from being the only one to shape Saint-Simon's thinking, since for a long time it had been completely absent. Undoubtedly it is completely at home here. From the moment one postulates society has only economic interests, then the single means of binding the mass of workers to social life is to have them share, to the greatest degree possible, in the products of this economic activity and to seek to better their lot. But this is only part of the system and besides was superimposed later on. Everything we said about industrialism, of the social organization destined to grant industry superiority, was raised at the start of this order of considerations. And in Saint-Simon's thinking it is particularly because of maximum production that it is important to practise the Christian maxim. This maxim, modernized, has in view a completely economic and temporal benefit.

The best proof, moreover, that communism is not the same as socialism, is that, if it is found there, it is under entirely new forms. According to communism, the only way to prevent social evil was to make those in all situations poor. To prevent hostility between rich and poor it was necessary to suppress the rich; it was essential to teach men to scorn material well-being, to be content with strict necessities. But it is in an altogether different direction that Saint-Simon, and later socialism, seeks to construct a new society. It is by doing away with the poor that he intends to reconcile the two classes. Far from seeing something desirable in temporal well-being, he makes it the only desirable goal. Consequently, the only way to establish social harmony is to produce the greatest riches possible, in order to satisfy the greatest possible needs as completely as possible.

We have finished explaining the organization of industrial society. In resumé, it is composed uniquely of workers; it would have at its head a council formed solely of the elite of producers. This body would have dependent on it what today constitutes the government, but would take its place without making use of its ancient dogmas, its traditional methods. It would not have to impose the ideas or even the mere whims of a dominant party, but merely declare what is in the nature of things—and it would be voluntarily obeyed. Its role would not be to discipline subjects, but to enlighten minds. As for the direction in which it should exercise this action, it is imposed by the double (?) end just explained.

Chapter 9

Internationalism and Religion

WE UNDERSTAND WHAT an industrially organized society would be, the elements it should be composed of, what would direct it, their mode of functioning, and the directions their action would take. But it is in the very nature of this organization to be unable to confine itself within the limits of a given society. A narrow particularism is incompatible with its constitutive characteristics and, of itself, it tends to take international form.

At first it is practically impossible for this great work of reorganization to take place in any one of the European peoples without simultaneously being produced in others. "The great moral movement which should make society pass from the modified despotic regime to one most advantageous to the majority of society, cannot be effected except by being common to the most enlightened peoples." (*Syst. Ind.*, VI, 80.) "The French nation cannot be treated and cured in isolation; the remedies which can cure it must be applied to all Europe." (*Ibid.*, 100, cf. *Ibid.*, 23, in note.) In fact, a people cannot in the first place adopt an organization so essentially pacific unless others are ready to follow its example. It can disarm only if its neighbors, likewise, renounce militarism. But there is a deeper reason for the need of internationalism. It is that, as of now, there is such solidarity among the various European nations that they cannot proceed except at the same pace along the path of civilization. They do not in effect constitute heterogeneous personalities, foreign to each other and each living a distinct life. Invisible bonds exist among them which render their destinies mutually interdependent. "France does not by any means have a moral life all its own. It is merely one member of European society and a forced community exists between its political principles and those of its neighbors." (VI, 112-

113.) "It finds itself," he says elsewhere, "in a position which makes it, up to a certain point, dependent on its neighbors, and establishes a kind of political solidarity between it and other peoples of the continent." (p. 100.)

The reason for this solidarity is that European societies, since the time they were established, belong to a similar social type. They all began by being subjected to the feudal regime, at the same time that they were practising a similar religion and obeying a similar clergy, which itself was subordinated to a single head independent of all individual governments. But when neighboring societies are similar to this degree, all important changes produced in one have repercussions among the others. When fundamental social innovations appear in one of these peoples, this kind of common atmosphere—in the midst of which they all were immersed and lived until then—for that very reason finds itself modified. It is therefore impossible for them to permit one of their group to become reorganized after its own fashion, as if this reorganization concerned it alone and was not to have an impact beyond its own frontiers. They mutually check each other and consequently cannot be transformed except by a movement of the entire group. In fact, all great changes that have taken place in Europe since the Middle Ages have been common to all European societies. And just as their organization was the same at the beginning, disorganization proceeded among all *pari passu*. Almost at the same moment the feudal regime began to be destroyed everywhere and the Christian religion lost its early unity. The formation of the Holy Alliance is the most recent manifestation of this inevitable solidarity. (VI, 99 and 100.) It is likely that this last fact particularly struck Saint-Simon. Never, in fact, had the impossibility of various countries of Europe isolating themselves from one another, nor the need for them to coordinate their efforts if they wished to join together, been asserted with greater force.

But then, it seems we may be enclosed in a vicious circle. On the one hand, the Saint-Simonian ideal cannot be realized —and consequently the military rule cannot disappear— except by virtue of a kind of international accord; and on the other, military rule, as long as it exists, through the rivalries and hatreds it induces, is an obstacle to such an accord. The situation in fact would be without solution if under the feudal system there did not gradually develop the industrial spirit, which acts in an opposing way; it binds peoples instead of dividing them, and in itself develops the very organization it requires. In effect, "industry is one" and everywhere has the same interests. All those who share in it—whatever society they may belong to—"are united by the general interests of production, by the need they all have for security in work and liberty in exchange. The producers of all lands are therefore essentially friends. Nothing stands in the way of their uniting, and the coalition of their efforts is the indispensible condition if industry is to attain the ascendancy it can and should enjoy." (*Ind.*, III, 47.) In fact, international coalitions among workers of the same kind came into being spontaneously. "At the same time that scientific activity was established and extended further and further into each European nation, the organization of scientific forces in the different countries was also increasingly effected. Nationalistic sentiments have (in this regard) thinned out, and scholars in all parts of Europe formed an indissoluble bond; they have always tended to regard as 'European' the scientific progress made at any particular point. This blessed alliance, against which the old system has no means of resistance, is better equipped to direct the organization of the new system than is the coalition of all European bayonets to stop or merely impede it." (*Org.*, IV, 141.) It is true that such integration of the industrial capacities of the various European nations took place to only a lesser degree. This is because "the feeling of national rivalry, the passions of ferocious and absurd patriotism, created and carefully preserved by the old system, have still conserved a very considerable influence over temporal affairs." (*Ibid.*) But this is but a survival of the old regime which cannot be long in disappearing. Little by little the cosmopolitanism of the learned will carry along that of the industrials. (IV, 142.) Then we will see a vast party established which will include all workers of European society and "from the organization of European industrials into a political party the establishment of the industrial system in Europe will result." (*Catéch.*, VIII, 52.)

The point which Saint-Simon emphasized deserves to be appreciated, for it is highly characteristic of our time. Undoubtedly, in some shape or form internationalism is observed at all moments in history, for there has never been a people who lived in a state of hermetic isolation. Every society has always had something in common with the neighboring societies it most resembled. It thus was led to form associations with them that were more or less stable, more or less definite, more or less broad, but which—whatever their nature—opposed a counter-weight to strictly national egoism. Thus in Greece, above the city was Pan-Hellenic society; similiarly, above the Kabyle[1] tribes was a confederation of related tribes, etc. But until our day, international bonds so formed had this particularity—they bound all the members of each society to all the members of others—indiscriminately. They were not a result of the fact that certain parts of different social groups were more especially attracted to each other; the affinities that produced them were general. The Hellenic confederation, for example, was formed not because the patricians of various cities—feeling themselves particularly close to one another—specially joined together, or that plebians, on their side, followed the same example, but because a general movement led the totality of each city toward the whole of the others. The fusion did not occur exclusively or deliberately at certain limited points; it took place equally over the entire breadth of the social masses. Therefore, in general, what gave rise to all these international combinations is that—in spite of the distinguishing differences which continued in each nationality—nonetheless there was a sufficient number of sentiments, interests, recollections, equally common to all classes and all professions of these societies which united them, so they could support each other. But in our day an internationalism of an entirely new type has appeared—professional internationalism. The rapprochement did not operate exclusively from people to people, but from professional group to pro-

[1] The Kabyle are a Berber-Arab people of North Africa.— (A.W.G.)

fessional group of the same order. One saw similar workers of different countries join directly, in associations more or less durable, more or less organized—in spite of national hostilities—and the drawing together of peoples resulted from this instead of being its initial cause. In succession there were established international societies of scholars, artists, industrials, workers, financiers, etc., which went on specializing further as they multiplied, and which, because of the increasing regularity of their functioning, soon became an important factor in European civilization. Whereas formerly it was peoples in their entirety who converged toward each other, now it is agencies similar to each other that tend to join directly and beyond frontiers. But this new internationalism does not have as its only characteristic the particular form of the groupings to which it gives rise. It is also distinguished by a force of resistance and expansion unknown until then. In fact, whatever resemblances neighboring peoples may have, they are on the whole small—at least in general—compared with the differences of tongue, customs, interests, which continue to separate them. As long as internationalism has no other basis, each nation runs little risk of losing its individuality in the midst of the vaster associations it enters, and hardly more than loose confederations can be formed, unless a war waged in common reinforces the unity. Now, however, professional sentiments and interests are endowed with a far greater universality. They are much less variable from country to country among like category of workers, whereas they are very different from one profession to another, within the same country. The result is that the corporative spirit sometimes tends to bind similar corporations of different European societies more tightly than different corporations in the same society. Thus national spirit encounters a formidable antagonist which it did not recognize until then, and as a result conditions are exceptionally favorable for the development of internationalism. These are precisely the two characteristics of the contemporary international movement which Saint-Simon places in relief, in the passages we just cited, at the same time that he endeavors to explain them. And as they were much less noticed then than they are today—they were scarcely born—

one can say that he anticipated and forecast them almost as much as he observed them. By the way he expresses himself at certain places, one might correctly say he prophesied the International.

Thus the realization of industrial society presupposed the establishment of a European concord and this concord was realized under the influence of the industrial spirit. Under these conditions, the attitude of the thinker and statesman is completely marked out. There can be no question of stopping a movement which is irresistible and which in addition is necessary so that industrialism can fulfill its destiny. It is only a matter of becoming aware of the degree of development it has spontaneously attained and then seeking the way to bring it to its final culmination. What is needed is to find an international European organization which makes possible the establishment, in each particular society, of the industrial system. It is evident, in the thinking of Saint-Simon, that this organization was not to remain enclosed within the limits of the European continent, but was destined to gradually extend itself so as to embrace all humanity. "The industrial regime," he says, "will be the ultimate organization of humankind." (VI, 81.) He glimpses in the future the formation of a society that would include all men and would undertake the systematic exploitation of the earth, which he calls the territorial property of human kind. (*N. Chr.*, VIII, 145 and 146-147.) This, however, is but a dream which is dear to him and which, from time to time, crosses his mind—but which he does not conceive as realizable for the present.

But in the European association which is now realizable, what will the position of the individual countries be? Saint-Simon does not go as far as to demand that they disappear; he conceives of a relative autonomy for them. But it is clear that in his thinking they should lose the great moral importance they have had until now. National particularism seems to him only a form of egoism, and consequently should have only a secondary role in the morality to come. "Moralists place themselves in a contradictory position when they defend egoism and approve of patriotism, for patriotism is nothing but national egoism; and this egoism causes the same injustices to be committed by nation to nation as personal egoism does among individuals." (*Lettres d'un habitant de Genève*, I, 43-44.) What caused the moral inferiority of the Greeks and Romans is precisely that they were not liberated from purely national sentiments. "The human heart was still not yet elevated to philanthropic feelings. The sentiment of patriotism was the commonest one experienced by the most generous of souls, and this feeling was extremely circumscribed, considering the small expanse of territories and the slight size of the populations in the nations of antiquity." (*N. Chr.*, VII, 145.) On the contrary, one of the great strides Christianity made in moral ideas was to subordinate patriotic affections to the broad love of humanity. "The best code of sensitive morality we have is Christian morality. In this code the reciprocal duties of members of the same family are much more frequently mentioned. It prescribes that all men regard themselves as brothers, but by no means does it urge men to patriotism." (*Catéchisme*, VIII, 200.) So too family feelings, according to him, are more founded in the nature of things than is attachment for one's native land. In fact, if, as Saint-Simon acknowledges, there are no social interests outside industrial interests—since industry is by nature essentially cosmopolitan—national loyalty is henceforth without reason, whereas love of family—in spite of its individualistic character—has at least the superiority of corresponding to a class of sentiments and interests *sui generis*, which industrialism does not eliminate. It is known how, starting from the same principle, economists reached the same conclusion. The cosmopolitanism of the masters of the (*laissez-faire*) School is no less insistent. However, here—as in all other cases where we have indicated the origin of the two systems—their agreement is not altogether complete. One divergence that we already noted should be described. According to economists, the internationalist rule does not require—in order to be established and function—that it be organized and administered according to a deliberate plan. There is need only to assert that there are no longer frontiers, and to permit industrials to come together freely in this universal market. For Saint-Simon, on the contrary, it is necessary to submit this regime to a systematic action; a definite organization is required, a body of institutions as common to European society as to each particular nation. "For every union of nations, as for every union of men, common institutions and organization is essential. Without that everything is decided by force." (I, 173.) What then will this international organization be?

This question absorbs Saint-Simon from his early writings; cosmopolitanism and industrialism are so closely joined in his mind that he has never separated the two problems. From the beginning of his studies he approaches them simultaneously. Already, in the *Lettres à un habitant de Genève* (1803) he expounds a plan by which the management of society would be given over to a supreme council of scholars, called the "Council of Newton," under whose authority national and even provincial councils, composed in the same fashion, would operate. But as Saint-Simon himself explains this project in the form of a dream, and as he does not return to it in any express manner in his other works, there is no need to dwell on it. Nonetheless one finds there on the whole—albeit in a conceptual, utopian, and mystical form— the fundamental ideas of the Saint-Simonian doctrine. In the essay on the *Réorganisation de la Société européene* (1814), a work written in collaboration with Augustin Thierry, he takes up the question again with more rigor and sobriety. At that time parliamentarianism impressed him as the solution to all political problems, and he demands that one start by establishing national Parliaments. Then, above these, a general Parliament, which will administer common affairs, coordinate all undertakings of general interest (and Saint-Simon gives as an example the construction of grand canals joining the Danube to the Rhine, the Rhine to the Baltic, etc.), establish a code of common morality for all peoples, and which above all will have the direction and surveillance of public instruction throughout Europe. In this fashion, gradually a European patriotism will be formed which will become as strong as national patriotism is today.

Since Saint-Simon quite quickly renounced parliamentarianism, one can be sure that he was not long in considering inadequate a parliamentarian constitution of European society. But he never abandoned the notion that it was possible to bind together, even in temporal affairs, the different peoples of Europe, for it is again very clearly asserted in the *Système Industriel*. (III, 53.) It is true that nowhere has he directly explained how his early plan was to be modified in order to harmonize with his new theory (on industrialism). But it is not difficult to recognize what these modifications were to consist of, and that, at bottom, they have no essential advantage. The basis on which the project of 1814 rested was certainly maintained, for it is profoundly Saint-Simonian. It is reformulated thus: Europe should be organized on the same foundations as individual societies. (I, 179-180.) The general and national governments should be homogenous. Consequently it was only a question of replacing the European Parliament by a system of councils recruited according to the rules indicated for the national councils, that is to say, composed of industrials, scholars, and artists, and administering the ordinary affairs of Europe in the same spirit, in order to place the constitution of the European Confederation in harmony with the principles of industrialism.

This project has occasionally been likened to that which the Abbé de Saint-Pierre had earlier expounded in his book *Paix perpétuelle*, and it has been concluded from the comparison that both were equally utopian. Saint-Simon, however, had taken care to indicate the difference which separated these two concepts. (I, 176 and f.) What the Abbé de Saint-Pierre demanded was simply that the sovereigns of Europe should agree to submit their differences to a permanent congress of plenipotentiaries nominated by themselves and whose decisions would be absolute. But each nation in the Confederation would retain its present organization. But, says Saint-Simon, it is naive to believe that national hatreds and rivalries, which the present political system necessarily supports, would be appeased, as if by magic, simply because a council of diplomats will have been established in which all antagonistic interests will be represented. An assembly which by definition includes only discordant elements has no other unity but that of the place where it meets, and agreement cannot be achieved by the single fact of a local meeting. Also, each will pull from his own side, will fight to have his own interests predominate, and assuming an equilibrium is finally artificially established, it could only be temporary. "There can be no agreement whatsoever without common attitudes, but can negotiating sovereigns—or plenipotentiaries named by the contractors and removable by them—have any but individualistic attitudes?" (I, 177.) Such is the fate he predicted in advance for the Congress of Vienna which had just begun and which, in part, was realizing the dream of the Abbé de Saint-Pierre. (I, 170 f.) Saint-Simon's thinking is altogether different. He does not believe that European accord can be realized by the stroke of a pen, with the help of a mock procedure which would amount, in short, to collecting a few signatures at the bottom of a piece of parchment. If he considers agreement not only desirable, but possible, it is because European societies strike him as now being motivated—although in unequal degree—by the same spirit, which tends to unite them, in other words, the industrial spirit. It is because there is now a community of attitudes and interests which the constitution he calls for, and whose details we just gave, serves to sanction, to organize, and to develop. But they could not be created if it (the community of thought) did not exist. His project therefore is far from having the same utopian character as that of the Abbé de Saint-Pierre. We have utopia, in the proper sense of the word, when a desirable ideal—although complex and of plainly difficult realization—is presented as executable by a turn of the hand or with the help of processes of child-like simplicity. Thus, one can label utopian an author who, not knowing how closely war is linked to the essential traits of our social organization, and seeing in it merely the effects of human folly, imagines he can relieve humanity with the assistance of a happy invention or well-built contrivance, or even simply with a few exhortations. On the contrary, Saint-Simon is entirely aware that war is grounded in the nature of feudal societies and that war cannot disappear unless feudalism is removed. So he is far from deceived about the gravity and difficulties of the undertaking. But as he believes these profound transformations of the social order to be imminent—and even partially realized—he sees nothing impossible in seeking and attaining a parallel transformation in international relations. His cosmopolitanism cannot be called utopian except to the degree that one would apply the same term to his industrialism.

And in addition, what gives his conception its real significance is that it was forced on him in large part by an historical fact, namely, the international character of papal power. "People made use of the lever without knowing how to explain what a lever was. . . . In politics—as in every type of learning—one did what was necessary before knowing why it was necessary, and after the practice came the theories, what one thought was often behind what one had done by chance. That is what occurred in this situation. The organization of Europe, such as it was in the sixteenth century, is infinitely superior to the plan of the Abbé de Saint-Pierre." (I, 179.) "We affect," he says a little farther on, "a superb scorn for the centuries called the Middle Ages. . . . We take no notice that they were the only time when the political system of Europe was founded on a real base. . . . While it lasted there were few wars in Europe, and those were of little importance." (I, 174.) He correctly notes that the Crusades were wars of the entire confederation and in which a European sentiment was asserted. It is not a question then of imagining an organization without precedent in history, but simply of recovering and pursuing an historic deed, by placing it in harmony with the changes occurring in the nature of societies. The modifications to be introduced are of two kinds. First, international interests could not today be of the same nature as under papal organization, for the very reason that the principle of the social system is changed. In addition, they should and can be complete. In the Middle Ages peoples were bound only to the spiritual—now they must be bound to both the spiritual and the temporal. "The tie will be more complete," he says, "in that it will at once be spiritual and temporal, whereas under the old system there was no bond among the different peoples of Europe except with respect to the spiritual." (*Syst, Industriel*, VI, 53.)

What we have just seen represents the temporal side of this organization. But as necessary as this complement of the papal system may be, it is not enough. "It should not be felt that the temporal bond—although very real and valuable —which exists among them [the States of Europe] to a certain degree, and which tends to tighten more and more, can dispense with a spiritual bond." (*Syst. Ind.,* I, 53.) Put another way, it is not enough to organize the economic life of European society; this organization requires a soul, that is to say, a body of doctrines, beliefs common to all Europeans, and which give it a moral unity. It is not enough that they co-operate industrially under the direction of a common administration; it is further necessary that a spiritual communion exist among them. And today, as in the Middle Ages, this communion cannot be assured except through a religion common to all humanity.

We are here entering upon a new part of the system, which one is at first surprised to meet. When one hears the adversary of the theological system, the founder of positive philosophy, call for the establishment of a new religion, one is tempted to believe that along the way some revolution has occurred in his thinking, and that he has become unfaithful to his principles. This supposition derives some likelihood from the fact that the *Nouveau christianisme,* the book in which his religious ideas are expounded (1824), is the last one he wrote. Death did not permit him to finish it. Some people have therefore attributed this work to an intellectual deterioration in Saint-Simon. Nothing, however, is less accurate than this interpretation. On the contrary, there is no doubt that religious preoccupations were very intense in Saint-Simon in all periods of his intellectual development. We have seen that, from the beginning, he broke with the irreligiosity of Condorcet and the writers of the eighteenth century, who saw in religion only a product of error, maintained by the guile and deceit of priests. At all times he had a very high regard for the role Christianity had played in the world. In a fragment preserved for us, and judged to be about 1818, he relates in beautiful language the birth of the Christian idea and the first phases of its evolution. As early as the *Science de l'homme* (1813) he was writing: "The religious institution—under whatever spirit one envisages it—is the principal political institution. . . . Neighboring peoples who have different beliefs are almost inevitably at war." (XI, 158.) Moreover the idea constantly recurs to him that the present crisis is analogous to that which the civilized world encountered when it passed from Greco-Latin polytheism to Christian monotheism. "The epoch which furnishes the closest analogy to our own is that in which the civilized portion of humankind passed from polytheism to monotheism, by the establishment of the Christian religion." (*Syst. Ind.*, VI, 61; cf. *Industriel,* III, 22.) Thus Saint-Simon never conceived positive and scientific philosophy as excluding all religious systems. On the contrary, it appears to him that one must naturally lead to the other.

But how are these two parts of the system integrated?

To answer this question we have only to compare his general concept of philosophy with the one he had of religion. Philosophy as he understands it consists of a synthesis of sciences which would systematize all our knowledge by seeking the fundamental and unique idea from which they are derived. To discover the unity of things by showing how all the particular laws are only corollaries of a primordial law which dominates the universe—that is the object of philosophy. And this law, which is the key to the system of the world, is, according to Saint-Simon, the law of gravity. "Universal gravity can be considered as the only law to which the universe is subject." (I, 94.) "It is possible to organize a general theory of the sciences, as much physical as moral, based on the idea of gravity." (XI, 304.) But the function of religion is of the same nature; it also has as its main objective to war against intellectual particularism. If it is necessary, it is because—since Christianity has lost its influence—men no longer have a common faith from whose breast they draw the feeling of solidarity. They have immersed themselves in specialized studies and individualistic research, and lost sight of the general principles which unify both things and people—they have even lost their taste for such unity. "Since the dissolution of spiritual power—the result of Luther's rebellion—the human mind has detached itself from the more general views. It has delivered itself to specialties. It has occupied itself with the analysis of individual facts, private interests of the different classes of society. And public opinion asserted that considerations of general facts, general principles, and the general interests of humankind, were only vague and metaphysical, unable to contribute effectively to the progress of intelligence and the perfecting of civilization." (VII, 183.) It is against this tendency toward dispersion that religion must react. It should again show men that the world—in spite of its diversity—is a phenomenon leading them back to God. Thus it has a role no different than that of philosophy. Religion does not require a celestial image opposed to the earthly ones. Its true mission is not to turn humankind away from temporal reality in order to bind it to some supra-experimental object, but simply to emphasize the unity of reality. And that is precisely what causes it to be summoned to furnish the spiritual bond which should unite the members of human society with one another. It is because it gives us consciousness of our unity. As long as humanity is conceived as springing from a plurality of beings and from distinct and heterogeneous principles, there must be many foreign and even hostile humankinds, among whom, in consequence, no regular co-operation, no durable association, can be established. History proves it. Ancient polytheism fragmented the human species into a diffuse multitude of small enemy societies. Each city, each village, considered those living outside its limits as outside humanity, for the reason that they were deemed to spring from other divine principles, derived from different origin. But what was basic in the Christian revolution is that it brought to the world one idea—the idea of monotheism—which could serve as a rallying point for all peoples. "The Christian religion had civilization take a long step forward by uniting all men through the belief in a single God, and through the dogma of universal brotherhood. By this means it was possible to organize a vaster society, and unite all peoples into a common family." (*Indus.*, III, 33-34.) That is the work which must be again taken up and pushed further, by putting it in harmony with the changes made in civilization since the founding of Christianity. That is the goal the new Christianity—whose establishment Saint-Simon believed necessary—must set for itself. And that is the source of the singular analogy between the present period and the one which followed the appearance of Christianity. It is the same problem which is posed in both cases—but under different conditions. It is a question of giving men a feeling of the world's unity, by taking account of the individual sciences whose studies have brought to light the whole treasure of the diversity of things. We will soon see what changes must be wrought in Christian concepts in order to elevate them to the eminence of their proper function.

If such is the nature of religion, it can be seen that by passing from philosophic and scientific speculations to religious, Saint-Simon did not renounce his early thinking. For religion, so understood, does not disown philosophy. It has its roots there; it is itself a philosophic thing. It would be easy, moreover, to demonstrate that philosophy, as he had always understood it, far from being inspired by an irreligious or even areligious spirit, tended quite naturally to take a religious form. For the single law which it strives to bring everything back to—the law of gravity—is from the beginning presented as being the law of God. "The idea of gravity is not at all in opposition to that of God, since it is nothing other than the idea of the immutable law by which God governs the Universe." (XI, 286.) It is possible, he says elsewhere, "to organize a general theory of the sciences . . . based on the idea of gravity, considered as the same law to which God has subjected the Universe and by which He rules it." (XI, 303.) Thus the idea of God and the idea of the fundamental law are only two aspects of the same idea— the idea of unity. Viewed from one side, this unity would appear under its more particularly abstract, scientific, metaphysical form; seen from the other, under its palpable and religious form. This manner of interpreting Saint-Simonian thinking has nothing hypothetical about it. It is Saint-Simon himself who presents his undertaking as plausible from either of these points of view. Speaking of "this general scientific theory, based on the idea of gravity" that he was in process of projecting, he says, "The result of these works will be the reorganization of European society, by means of a general, common institution for all the peoples who comprise it; an institution which according to the degree of intelligence of each, will appear scientific or religious, but which, in all events, will exercise positive political action—that of placing a check on the ambition of peoples and kings." (XI, 310.)

But even if no about-face occurred in his thinking, and although he never went from an irreligious or areligious rationalism to a mysticism scornful of science, there is nevertheless a difference between the early and later forms of this system. In the former, the scientific character of his doctrine is predominant, the religious character quite obliterated, whereas beginning with the *Système industriel,* and especially in the *Nouveau christianisme,* the idea of God—until then somewhat eclipsed by the idea of law—comes into the foreground. How does this change—which is interesting and unquestionable—come about? It is a result of what we noted above, namely that he was led to attribute a more and more important role to purely moral sentiments. As long as he believed egoism capable of insuring the progress of societies —provided that these were well organized—a unitarian but purely abstract theory of the world could legitimately seem sufficient to give men an adequate feeling of their unity. In fact, there was no need to specially urge individuals to play their social role, since their natural penchant towards egoism brought this about voluntarily. All that was required was to free minds of the false notions which prevented egoism from producing the social and useful consequences it naturally implied. And for that, it was enough to show people how by isolating themselves from one another, by dealing with each other as with so many distinct kinds of humanity, by refusing, consequently, to associate and co-operate, they were in contradiction with the nature of things, since not only human kind, but the entire universe, is one and subject to the action of a single law. Such a cold and purely scientific idea was then a sufficient rational basis for the co-operation of individuals. But this was no longer enough once Saint-Simon recognized that without charity, mutual obligation, and philanthropy, the social order—and still more the human order—was impossible. To influence individuals to aid one another, to have as their objective something other than themselves, it was not enough to give them a purely speculative picture of the logical unity of things. An abstract theory of universal gravity would not support the moral dogma of human fraternity. Such a notion might be adequate to stop men from misunderstanding their interests to the point of not co-operating among themselves; but it was inadequate to oblige each to forget his own interest and think of the interest of others. To have an active reason to fraternize, they had to feel a positive bond among them, a community of nature, a unique kinship which made them brothers. They had to feel it is the same life's blood which circulates in all bodies, the same spirit which animates all minds. And all this in such a way as to weaken the distinction between me and you, mine and yours, which is the stumbling block of philanthropic feelings. So it was indispensable that the unity of the world be shown as real and manifest; and that is how, through normal progress, the religious character of the system came to be accentuated.

As can be seen, religion did not occupy in this system the position of an added fragment, hastily joined, which could not be compatible with the rest. Quite the contrary—one can now discern that Saint-Simon's doctrine is profoundly consistent. One might even say that what characterizes it best is this sentiment of universal unity, which is its main point of departure and arrival. For Saint-Simon's thinking developed in one direction. It stems from the principle that it is necessary to find—through the synthesis of sciences—the unity of the world, in order to make it the foundation of a body of common beliefs. Then, to complete this synthesis, to establish the sciences that are missing: psychology, and especially what will later be called sociology. But after these special studies, he returns to his initial project, and, with the results obtained in the course of his research, undertakes to construct this unitarian synthesis that he never lost sight of. Thus his system opens and closes on the same question and remains in its entire compass inspired by the same thought.

*   *   *

We have seen that the industrial regime—as Saint-Simon understands it—cannot remain strictly national. It cannot be established in one European country except if at the same time this country enters—as an integral part and more or less autonomous province—into a vaster society formed of all European peoples all organized according to the same principles. In other words, industrialism is possible only by virtue of an international organization. This will be both temporal and spiritual. Temporally, it will consist of the institution of councils, analogous to those appointed for each particular society, but charged with the administration of the common affairs of Europe. Spiritually, it will consist of the establishment of a religion—new in part—common to all Europeans and open to all. This religion will be the soul of the whole industrial mechanism of this European society and will assure its harmonious functioning. Thus religion constitutes the principal part of the system, for it will render international association possible, and this is itself the necessary condition of industrialism.

We showed elsewhere that Saint-Simon was able to assign this essential function to religion without renouncing the principles of his doctrine, for the religious system, as he understands it, is only another face of the philosophic system, both expressing the same idea—the idea of universal unity —the one through its palpable and practical aspect, the other in its abstract and theoretical form.

But what will this religion consist of? This is what Saint-Simon was to explain in his *Nouveau christianisme;* but the incomplete state in which he left this book, interrupted by death, leaves the details of his religious concepts unknown (assuming that they had been clear in his own mind). But their principles can be determined with some exactitude.

In the first place, although the new religion was to have its creed and dogma, morality would be its central core. "The new Christianity," he says, "will have its morality, its creed and its dogma; it will have its clergy and its clergy will have its leaders. But . . . the doctrine of morality will be considered by the new Christians as the most important; creed and dogma will be envisaged by them only as accessories whose principal purpose is to fix the attention of the faithful of all classes upon morality." (VII, 116.) Under these conditions, theology, strictly speaking, loses all importance since at this point its practice become secondary. The best theologian will simply be the best moralist. "The best theologian is he who makes the most general applications of the fundamental principle of divine morality . . . he is the vicar of God on earth." (VII, 115.) In conformity with this method, Saint-Simon relies on history to demonstrate that it is clearly in this direction that religious evolution must move. With his sense of history, he had very clearly perceived the law—now axiomatic—that the more closely one approaches the origins of religious development, the more ritual and material practices surpass in importance purely moral beliefs and precepts, whereas the latter become more and more predominant in the religions of civilized peoples. "The material part of religion," he writes, "has played an important role to the extent that the institution was closest to its founding." "Religious practices—as well as reasoning on the advantages of these practices—were the portions of religion which most often occupied priests as well as the masses of the faithful." On the contrary, "the spiritual portion has always grown in the degree that the intelligence of man developed." (VII, 166.) What was "truly sublime, divine, in early Christianity, is the superiority of morality over all the rest of the law, that is, over creed and dogma." (VII, 103.) For he believes wholeheartedly in the maxim which "commands all men to act like brothers to each other." (VII, 120.) Unfortunately, the Catholic clergy did not remain faithful to the views of Christ. One has watched religious writings become obstructed with "mystical conceptions" without relation to "the principles of the sublime morality of Christ" (VII, 123), and vulgar rites of every sort offered to the faithful as the indispensable condition of salvation (VII, 153.) This is why Christianity cannot serve as the religion of humanity except on condition of its being changed and regenerated. The purpose of *Nouveau christianisme* will be to free the Christian idea, that is, the moral idea, of all alloys which debase it, to re-establish it in its original purity and make it the single basis of the religious system. It is indeed, as we have said, in order to give more effectiveness to moral sentiments, to charitable motives, that Saint-Simon was led to accentuate the religious character of his system, since the doctrine of philanthropy is for him the most essential element in religion. Elsewhere he himself tells us that his aim in writing the

Nouveau christianisme was "to refine morality, to perfect it, to extend its empire over all classes of society by conserving its religious character." (VII, 103.)

But in current conceptions the idea of religion is not separated from that of God. In fact, the only means of giving morality a religious character is evidently to attach it to some notion of the divinity which may be in harmony with it. So the *Nouveau christianisme* begins with these words: "I believe in God." How then was God to be presented in the new religion? What makes the answer to this question perplexing is that Saint-Simon has not explicitly dealt with it in his book. He speaks to us all the time of God, without telling us expressly how he conceives of Him. This is why most of his interpreters believed they should leave his ideas on this point in the same indeterminate state. It seems to us, however, that they can be specified—at least in essentials—particularly if it is admitted that his last writing is related without contradiction to his early works, and if, consequently, it is legitimate to make use of these earlier works to clarify his religious theory.

One principal proposition can be established with complete certainty, namely, that Saint-Simon never represented God as living and personal. He always formally rejected anything resembling an anthropomorphic conception. In the *Mémoire sur la science de l'homme*, addressing himself to the German philosophic school, he expresses himself in these terms: "You are indeed right to preach that a general theory is needed and that it is only in its philosophic bearing that science is useful to society . . . but you are very wrong when you want to provide as a foundation for your philosophy the idea of a living cause." And he adds: "It is no longer the idea of God which should unite the concepts of scholars—it is the idea of gravity considered as the law of God." (XI, 300.) This text explains the few passages of the same book in which Saint-Simon seems to radically reject the very idea of God, as when he says, "We will present this idea [that of gravity] as having to play the role of an absolute, general idea and to replace that of God." (XI, 276.) It is not every notion of God that he declares irreconcilable with his philosophical system, for some pages further (XI, 284) he shows there is no contradiction between the idea of God and of universal gravity considered as the law of God. (Cf. p. 300 and 309-310.) What seemed to him faulty in the old theories was only that God was presented as a personal will. "To impute life to the cause of all effects produced in the Universe," he says, "is to act like a child who, when he stumbles on a stone, gets angry at it." (XI, 163.) But how is universal gravity conceived as the law of God? Is such a God anything more than deified nature? Is not such a God one to whom it is logically necessary to attribute impersonality— failing which He would be in contradiction with the data of science?

A second proposition, which is clearly Saint-Simonian and which goes to confirm the preceding interpretation, could be formulated so: everything in nature participates in the divine. Physics and morality have equal dignity. Calling spiritualism "the tendency of moralists to subordinate moral man," and materialism the contrary tendency of naturalists, he says that neither should prevail over the other, that "the capacity of the human spirit for spiritualism and materialism is equal; that moralists and naturalists should hold a position of fundamental equality." The sensory is of no less an exalted nature than the intelligible. "It is no longer on abstract ideas that you should fix the attention of the faithful," he says to the priests, "It is by properly employing sensory ideas . . . that you will succeed in establishing Christianity as a general, universal, unique religion." (VII, 148.) Besides, there is nothing more in conformity with the fundamental principle of Saint-Simon, namely, that there are not two worlds in the world, but that the Universe is one. Therefore you must make a choice. If divinity is immanent, everything in the world is divine—the physical and moral, matter and spirit. But to be so it is obviously necessary that the principle of self be in things, that God be immanent in the world. For if He were outside it, there would necessarily exist in reality some beings who would be closer to Him, issued more directly from Him, who would share more of His nature, while others, on the contrary, would be more remote from Him and only receive weakened reflections. It is precisely because Christianity placed God outside of things that it could distinguish two types: those who are turned toward God, who express Him and who alone are truly real, and others, who are opposed to Him and consequently only represent more or less disguised forms of nothingness—on one side, the spiritual, the moral, the ideal, and on the other, matter, temporal interests, the passions they excite. The spirit reaches the first with the help of processes *sui generis* of a mystical nature; it is only religion that is qualified to understand and speak of this. The second type, on the contrary, are devoted to reason and the science of men: *Deus tradidit mundum disputationi hominum.* These two elements are so contradictory that their association is conceived by the Christian in the form of a struggle, a conflict of each moment, which—for this very reason—can only last for a limited time. The divine, bound and as if imprisoned in matter, tends to free itself in order to return to God, from Whom it came. When one separates God from the world, this duality is again found in the world itself, which is divided into two parts, according to whether it clings more or less closely to God. But such duality is as contrary as possible to the spirit of Saint-Simonianism, which is above all enamored of unity. For Saint-Simon, morality is an essentially earthly thing; these are its own utterances. It aims at no end beyond temporal interests. It is merely the law of their organization. Since all that is essential in religion is contained in morality, it too can have only an earthly objective. On this point Saint-Simon's thinking never varied. It is by seeking "to procure for humankind the greatest degree of happiness it can achieve during its worldly life that you will succeed in establishing Christianity." (VII, 154.) The true means of assuring its salvation is not to discipline it, to subdue its flesh, but to undertake great enterprises for the common good. The first Christian doctrine, thanks to the false axiom, render unto Caesar the things that are Caesar's, took no interest in anything temporal, precisely because such activity was not considered of divine order. The new Christian organization will draw from the principle that men should act toward one another like brothers, all the positive and temporal consequences it implies. "It will direct all institutions —whatever their nature—toward the improvement of the well-being of the poorest class." (VII, 113.) Thus the new religion has no proper goal outside this earth. It is itself an earthly thing. Its domain is of this world. It declares that God is not exterior to things, but is part of them, blends with them. Thus everything leads us to the conclusion that Saint-Simonian religion can be nothing other than a pantheism asserting the fundamental identity of all beings and deifying temporal reality as well as thought. For on the one hand, the God of such a religion, comprising all reality, is manifestly impersonal and so satisfies the first condition. On the other hand, since nothing is outside Him, everything has value and reality. The practical ceases to be excluded from the circle of things that serve as ends for the conduct of man. At the same time it is understandable how the Saint-Simonian doctrine presents—as we have noted—a kind of ambiguity. It can be—with no contradiction—scientific on the one side, religious on the other. This is so because in a general way, pantheism—or at least a certain kind of pantheism—also has two sides. For as the God, Whose existence is recognized, is at one with nature, it can be regarded sometimes as the nature studied by science, sometimes as the divinity adored by religion. On the other hand, it is not necessary to show how this manner of representing God can serve to rationally justify a morality of solidarity. For it is clear that if God is reality itself, if He is all things, we all communicate through Him and the principle of fraternity is founded in the nature of things.

Chapter 10

Saint-Simon—Critical Conclusions

A DOCTRINE OF PHILANTHROPY having a pantheistic conception of the universe as its basis—this is what the new Christianity must consist of. We have finally come to the highest point of the Saint-Simonian system. From there we can perceive all of its richness and unity. On one side, there is the greatest complexity, for in it are found the germs of all the great intellectual currents produced during the nineteenth century; the germs of the method with which Augustin Thierry, pupil of Saint-Simon, and all the great historians who followed were to revive the science of history; of the positivist philosophy to which Comte, another pupil of Saint-Simon, was to attach his name, and which is the greatest philosophical novelty of our time; of socialism, which is already found there in its most characteristic forms; finally, the germs of those aspirations for a religious revival which, in spite of periods of apathy, never remained completely foreign to the spirit of the century. When we follow the development of all these tendencies in the history of our era, and when we study them isolated from each other, they appear to be very different and to proceed in opposite directions. However, what proves that, in spite of their apparent diversity, they are not without unity and merely express the same social state in varied ways, is the fact that we find them all in Saint-Simon, founded on the same unified system. In fact they flow from the very principle that we must now specify in order to understand and examine it properly.

This is the principle Saint-Simon called industrialism. He expresses it so: Individuals and peoples should no longer pursue any but economic interests; or, in another form, the only useful functions are industrial functions. All others— military or theological—are of a parasitic nature; they are the vestiges of a past which should have already disappeared. Accept this idea and you must accept the system, for it is wholly implied in it.

If societies have only economic interests, then economic life is necessarily a social thing, totally or in part—unless it may be said there is no clearly social existence. For this reason, economic life should be subjected to collective and organized control. That is the economic principle of socialism. This organization will naturally assign the direction of society to representatives of industrial interests, since they alone have the competence necessary to administer common affairs. But just because they will have this character, their administration will not have to proceed according to ordinary methods of government, which imply that there are masters and subjects, inferior and superior beings, and that the first are obliged to obey the second. For, since social relationships will be essentially relationships of interest, the directors of society will have no function but to teach people, by virtue of their special ability, what is true or false, what is advantageous or not. Since it is unnecessary to repress humanity to make it pursue its interests, these directors will have no need for an authority which raises them above those they will direct. Governmental restraint will have no basis. That is the principle of socialist politics, that is the anarchistic creed. For the same reason, since nothing exists in the world except industrial interests, the only goal this collective administration can pursue will be to make the production of wealth as fruitful as possible, so that everyone can receive the most—particularly those whom fate has disinherited the most. That is socialist morality. Finally, as industrial interests are the same among all peoples, and as they tend naturally to coalesce in spite of frontiers, industrialism ends in internationalism as its logical conclusion. Even the pantheistic character of Saint-Simonian religion derives from this same source. If earthly interests are the only possible ends of human activity, they must have value and dignity, and this is not possible when the divine is conceived as outside the things of this world.

This explanation serves to clarify the profound difference which separates socialism from communism, since all the distinctive characteristics of socialism derive from a principle exactly contrary to that which serves as the basis of communism. In fact, the fundamental axiom of socialism is that there are no social interests outside economic interests, whereas the axiom of communism is that economic interests are anti-social, and that industrial life should be reduced to strict necessities to leave room for other forms of social activity—war, religion, morality, fine arts, etc. Thus these two theories are contradictory, not only at their origin, but also in every conceptual detail. Under socialism, the representatives of industry are the designated directors of society; under communism, these cannot acquit themselves of their functions unless freed from economic preoccupations, and often it is the rule that they must be chosen from outside industry. Thus Plato chose them from among warriors, and Campanella from metaphysicians. Whereas socialism has a tendency to anarchy, governmental restraint is necessary in communism; it is the only means of maintaining subordination of economic life which in itself is impatient of any limitation. Whereas the morality of one commands the increase and widest possible extension of the good things in life, the other, highly ascetic, tends to restrain this as far as possible—for such abundance is seen as a danger to morality. Finally, socialism, precisely because it seeks above all to intensify economic activity, urges men to form vaster and vaster groupings so that co-operation may be more fruitful by reason of greater numbers. Even the great European nations are too small, according to socialist thought—which is why it demands they leave their isolation and mix with one another so that their unified efforts may be more productive. We have even seen that it goes so far as to dream of a future when all humanity would constitute one workshop. Communism, on the contrary, tends to cut up society into the smallest groups possible, for fear that too broad a horizon may awaken desires, that a too active life may stimulate needs. Besides, the inevitable diversity implied in every great society, for the very reason that it embraces a great number of elements spread over a vast territory and placed in very different conditions of existence, is evidently incompatible with the absolute homogeneity, similitude of ideas and feelings, and the leveling that communism presupposes.

Moreover, if instead of studying these doctrines in themselves and their constitutive characteristics, one looks at their historic origins and interrelationships, it is impossible to believe that Saint-Simon ever fell under the influence of communist theories. Nowhere does he speak of them; neither Plato, Morus, Mably, not even Rousseau, engaged him. One might even wonder if he read them. On the contrary, it is certain that he studied the economists; he speaks often and with praise of Smith and J. B. Say; he acknowledges his dependence on them. Historically, socialism does not spring from economics, but is derived from a similar source. Born at almost the same time, the two systems should obviously correspond to the same social state they express differently. And as we have established, not only do they coincide in certain secondary characteristics, not only did we find in both the same tendency to cosmopolitanism, the same sensuous and utilitarian tendency, but further, the fundamental principle on which they rest is identical. Both are industrialist; both proclaim that economic interests are social interests. The difference is that Saint-Simon, and all subsequent socialists, conclude that since economic factors are the substance of common life, they must be organized socially, whereas the economists refuse to subject them to any collective control and believe they can be arranged and harmonized without prior reorganization.

Of these two ways of interpreting this principle, the second is inadmissible for it is self-contradictory. If everything social is economic, the economic domain must include the social, and on the other hand, what is social could not, without contradiction, be regarded and treated as a private thing. Economists cannot escape this objection by maintaining there is nothing basic which is truly collective, that society is only a sum of individuals juxtaposed, and that social interests are the sum of individual interests. But this concept no longer has many defenders, so irreconcilable is it with the facts. If therefore one regards as established the fundamental proposition on which the two doctrines rest, the socialist and Saint-Simonian theses are logically derived. If economic interests do have the supremacy attributed to them, if as a result, it is to these interests that human ends are reduced, the only goal society can set itself is to organize industry in such a way as to secure the maximum production possible, and finally, the only means to attain this goal and to cause individuals to apply themselves, is to apportion the products thus obtained so that everyone, from top to bottom of the ladder, has enough—or better still, as much as possible.

But what is the scientific value of this principle? Saint-Simon established it by demonstrating that the powers which had dominated industry until the present, were going into decline and that this decline was inevitable. From this he concluded that it (industry) did and should tend toward complete enfranchisement, toward absolute liberation, that it was no longer to be subordinated to anything which would surpass it, that henceforth it was to be its own end and draw from itself its own rule. But this conclusion was premature. To assume that the particular state of subjection in which industry had formerly been held could not be in agreement with the new conditions of collective life, does not imply that every other type of dependence would be devoid of reason. It can well be that the transformation now necessary does not consist in suppressing all subordination, but in changing its form—not in making industrial interests a kind of unlimited absolute beyond which there is nothing, but rather in limiting them in a different manner and spirit than formerly. Not only does this hypothesis deserve examination, but in fact it is easy to understand that in any social organization, however skillfully ordered, economic functions cannot co-operate harmoniously nor be maintained in a state of equilibrium unless subjected to moral forces which surpass, contain, and regulate them.

And in fact it is a general law of all living things that needs and appetites are normal only on condition of being controlled. Unlimited need contradicts itself. For need is defined by the goal it aims at, and if unlimited has no goal—since there is no limit. It is no true aim to seek constantly more than one has—to work in order to overtake the point one has reached, with a view only to exceeding the point at which one will have arrived. From another point of view, one might say that the persistence of a need or appetite in a living being can be explained only if it secures some satisfaction for the being who experiences it. But an appetite that nothing can appease can never be satisfied. Insatiable thirst can only be a source of suffering. Whatever one does, it is never slaked. Every being likes to act, to move, and movement is life. But he must feel his action serves some purpose—that by walking, he goes forward. But one does not advance when he proceeds without a goal—or what comes to the same thing—toward a goal situated in infinity. The distance is always the same, whatever the road, and no matter what the pace, one seems to be simply marking time. It is well known that insatiability is a sign of morbidity. Normal man ceases to be hungry when he has taken a certain amount of nourishment; it is the glutton who cannot be satisfied. Healthy people enjoy motion, but at the end of a period of exercise they like to rest. The deambulatory maniac experiences the need of perpetually moving about without stop or rest; nothing satisfies him. In its normal state sexual desire is aroused for a time, then is appeased. With the erotomaniac there are no limits.

Among animals this limitation comes of itself because the animal's life is essentially instinctive. Every instinct, in fact, is part of a chain of connected movements which unfolds its links under the impulse of a determinate stimulant, but which stops when it comes to its end. All instinct is bounded because it responds to purely organic needs and because these organic needs are rigorously defined. It is always a matter either of eliminating a definite quantity of useless or harmful substances which encumber the organism, or of introducing a definite quantity of substances which repair what the functioning of the organs has destroyed. The power of assimilation of a living body is limited and this limits the corresponding needs. This limitation is therefore built into the organism and controls its behavior. Moreover, the animal has no way of evading this pattern. The power of reflection is not yet developed enough to symbolize what is or what was and to set new goals for activity beyond those spontaneously achieved. This is why excesses are rare. When beasts have eaten enough to satisfy their hunger they seek no more. When sexual desire is met, they are in repose.

But it is not the same with man, precisely because instincts play a lesser role in him. Strictly speaking, the quantity of material nourishment absolutely necessary for the physical sustenance of human life could be considered definite and determinable, although its determination is less precise than in the preceding cases and there is more room for a free combination of desires. For beyond this indispensable minimum—which satisfies the need on the instinctive level—reflection, more alert, glimpses better conditions which appear as desirable ends and which invite activity. Yet it is clear that appetites of this kind sooner or later meet a boundary they cannot overstep. But how fix the quantity of well-being, comfort, luxury, that a human being ought not pass? Nothing is found either in the organic or psychological constitution of man which sets a limit to such needs. The functioning of an individual life requires only that he halt here rather than there, that he satisfy himself at little cost or otherwise. The proof is that such needs have continued to develop in the course of history, and have found increasingly complete satisfaction, and nevertheless the average state of health has improved and average happiness has not diminished. But as there is nothing within an individual which constrains these appetites, they must surely be contained by some force exterior to him, or else they would become insatiable—that is, morbid. Either, knowing no limits, they become a source of torment for man, exciting him to activity that nothing can satisfy, irritating and plaguing him in a pursuit without possible end, or there must be, outside the individual, some power capable of stopping them, disciplining them, fixing a limit that nature does not.

This is what seems to have escaped Saint-Simon. To him it appears that the way to realize social peace is to free economic appetites of all restraint on the one hand, and on the other to satisfy them by fulfilling them. But such an undertaking is contradictory. For such appetites cannot be appeased unless they are limited and they cannot be limited except by something other than themselves. They cannot be regarded as the only purpose of society since they must be subordinated to some end which surpasses them, and it is only on this condition that they are capable of being really satisfied. Picture the most productive economic organization possible and a distribution of wealth which assures abundance to even the humblest—perhaps such a transformation, at the very moment it was constituted, would produce an instant of gratification. But this gratification could only be temporary. For desires, though calmed for an instant, will quickly acquire new exigencies. Unless it is admitted that each individual is equally compensated—and such leveling, if it conforms to the communist ideal, is as opposed as possible to the Saint-Simonian doctrine, as to every socialist theory—there will always be some workers who will receive more and others less. So it is inevitable that at the end of a short time the latter find their share meager compared with what goes to the others, and as a result new demands arise, for all levels of the social scale. And besides, even apart from any feeling of envy, excited desires will tend naturally to keep outrunning their goals, for the very reason that there will be nothing before them which stops them. And they will call all the more imperiously for a new satisfaction, since those already secured will have given them more strength and vitality. This is why those at the very top of the hierarchy, who consequently would have nothing above them to stimulate their ambition, could nevertheless not be held at the point they had reached, but would continue to be plagued by the same restlessness that torments them today. What is needed if social order is to reign is that the mass of men be content with their lot. But what is needed for them to be content, is not that they have more or less but that they be convinced they have no right to more. And for this, it is absolutely essential that there be an authority whose superiority they acknowledge and which tells them what is right. For an individual committed only to the pressure of his needs will never admit he has reached the extreme limits of his rightful portion. If he is not conscious of a force above him which he respects, which stops him and tells him with authority that the compensation due him is fulfilled, then inevitably he will expect as due him all that his needs demand. And since in our hypothesis these needs are limitless, their exigency is necessarily without limit. For it to be otherwise, a moral power is required whose superiority he recognizes, and which cries out, "You must go no further."

This is precisely the role played in ancient society by the powers whose progressive dethronement Saint-Simon notes. Religion instructed the humble to be content with their situation, at the same time it taught them that the social order is providential, that it is God himself who has determined each one's share, and giving them glimpses beyond this earth of another world where everything will be balanced, whose prospect made inequalities less noticeable, it stopped them from feeling aggrieved. Secular power, too, precisely because it held economic functions under its domination, contained and limited them. But even *a priori*, it is impossible to suppose that for centuries it was in the nature of economic interests to be subordinated but that in the future the roles will become so completely reversed. This would be to admit that the nature of things could be completely transformed in the course of evolution. Undoubtedly one can be certain that this regulating function can no longer be fulfilled by the old forces, since nothing appears likely to arrest their decadence. Undoubtedly, too, this same function could not be exercised today in the same manner or spirit as formerly. The industrial organ, more developed, more essential than before to the social organism, can no longer be contained within the same narrow bounds, subjected to a system as heavily repressive, relegated to a position so subordinate. But it does not follow that it should be freed of all regulation, liberated from all checks.

The problem is to know, under the present conditions of social life, what moderating functions are necessary and what forces are capable of executing them. The past only helps us to pose the problem—it also indicates the direction in which the solution should be sought. What, in fact, were the temporal and spiritual powers that for so long moderated industrial activity? Collective forces. In addition they had the characteristic that individuals acknowledged their superiority, bowed voluntarily before them, did not deny them the right to command. Normally, they were imposed not through material violence, but through their moral ascendency. This is what accounted for the efficacy of their action. So, today, as formerly, there are social forces, moral authorities, which must exercise this regulating influence, and without which appetites become deranged and economic order disorganized. And, in fact, from the moment that this indispensable curb does not come from the inherent nature of individuals, it can come only from society. Society alone has the capacity to constrain and only it can do so without perpetually making use of physical restraint—because of the moral character in which it is clothed. In short, society, through the moral regulation it institutes and applies, plays, as far as supra-organic life is concerned, the same role that instinct fills with respect to physical existence. It determines, and it rules what is left undetermined. The system of instincts is the discipline of the organism, just as moral discipline is the instinctive system of social life.

Now it can be seen what, according to us, is Saint-Simon's mistake. He described perfectly the present situation and made a careful history of it. He showed: 1. That industry had been, up to the present, placed under subordination to powers which rose above it; 2. That these powers retrogressed irretrievably; 3. That this situation was unhealthy and is the cause of the crisis from which we suffer. It is no small accomplishment to have posed the question in these terms which, at least, make their unity clear. This time we are no longer in the presence of a simply critical study, such as we met in Sismondi and will find in Fourier, which consists of enumerating the merits and faults of the modern order and concluding the necessity for change—as if these defects were not compensated for by advantages, and as if a balance could be objectively established. We are in the presence of an historic law which dominates the whole development of our societies and—without comparing the advantages and drawbacks of the regime, which conclusion must necessarily depend on our personal feelings—it can of itself, if properly interpreted, tell us the secret of the future. The only question is: did Saint-Simon properly interpret it? Noting the progressive weakening of the old powers, he concluded that our modern uneasiness is due to the fact that, not yet having disappeared, they still disturb industrial activity. It followed that their downfall had only to be hastened in order to assure industry the supremacy it had a right to, and that industry should be organized without subordinating it to anything—as if such an organization were possible. In short, it seems to us that he was mistaken about what, in the present situation, is the cause of the uneasiness, and in having proposed, as a remedy, an aggravation of the evil.

In the end, Saint-Simon seems to have had some awareness of the inadequacy of the industrialist solution. For although the religion whose establishment he called for does not contradict his philosophical system, the former itself did not appeal to logic, but to religious faith. He assumes it rather artificially, because he felt the need of elevating something above the purely economic order, to limit it. Although in principle his philanthropic morality was purely industrial, he understood that to assure order morality had to be placed in a position of dominating industrial interests—and for that reason he gave it a religious character. In this there is something which is not completely harmonious with the industrialist principle and may even be its best refutation. Besides, this religion does not altogether correspond to the necessities we noted, for if it curbs the wealthy by assigning as their goal the well-being of the poor, it does not restrain the latter —and the desires of these should be no less regulated than the needs of the others. Moreover, even for the wealthy, the efficacy of the process is more than doubtful. The sentiment of cosmic unity, even expressed in a practical form, is insufficient to dominate egoism and to actively unify men.

But then one will ask where, today, are the moral forces capable of establishing, making acceptable, and maintaining the necessary discipline? This is not the place to treat the question. However, it can be said that among the institutions of the old regime there is one that Saint-Simon does not speak of but which perhaps, if transformed, could suit our present state. These are the professional groupings, or corporations. In all times they played the role of moderator, and moreover if one takes into account the fact that they were suddenly and violently destroyed, one has the right to ask whether this radical destruction was not one of the causes of the evil. In any event, the professional grouping could well fit all the conditions we have set. On the one hand, because it is industrial, it will not weight down industry with too burdensome a yoke; it is close enough to the interests it will have to regulate not to heavily repress them. In addition, like every group formed of individuals united by ties of interests, ideas, and feelings, it is capable of being a moral force over the members who compose it. Let it be made a definite agency of society, whereas it is now merely a private association. Transfer certain rights and duties to it which the State is less and less capable of exercising and assuring. Let it be the administrator of affairs, industries, arts, that the State cannot manage through its remoteness from material things. Grant it the power necessary to resolve certain conflicts, to apply the general laws of society according to the variety of labor, and gradually, through the influence it will exercise, through the rapprochement that it will produce in the work of all, it will acquire the moral authority which will permit it to play this role of restraint—without which there could be no economic stability.

But this is not the place to develop these theories. It is enough to have shown that, put this way, the social question would present itself in an entirely different manner. It no longer opposes the source of technic to that of power, as two antagonists who exclude each other in such a manner that the process of successive reorganization presupposes prior destruction. But one is only the continuation of the other. It does not awaken for everything that is or was a feeling of subversive hatred. It incites only to seek the new forms which the past should take today. It is not a matter of putting a completely new society in the place of the existing one, but of adapting the latter to the new social conditions. At least, it no longer stirs questions of classes; it no longer opposes rich to poor, employers to workers—as if the only possible solution consisted of diminishing the portion of one in order to augment that of the other. But it declares, in the interest of both, the necessity of a curb from above which checks appetites and so sets a limit on the state of disarrangement, excitiment, frenzied agitation, which do not spring from social activity and which even make it suffer. Put differently, the social question, posed this way, is not a question of money or force; it is a question of moral agents. What dominates it is not the state of our economy but, much more, the state of our morality.

Chapter 11

The Saint-Simonian School

SAINT-SIMON, WITH an extremely vital intellect and eager for knowledge, curious about everything new, gifted with a kind of intuitive empathy that made him sensitive to all the aspirations of his contemporaries, succeeded in making his work a kind of synthesis of all the tendencies of his time. On the other hand, he was always dominated by the same fixed idea, and across all the experiences and accidents of his career he had but one goal—to reconstitute on rational and temporal bases—that is, with the aid of science and industry —the social system which the old regime's ruin had disorganized. Thus the very different elements that successively entered into his doctrine grouped and crystallized themselves quite naturally around this main unifying thought. His system epitomizes the spirit of his time. And as it was the very spirit of the nineteenth century that was in the process of being elaborated, it is not surprising that we found the germs of all the great intellectual movements which simultaneously or successively occupied the thought of our epoch: the historic method, positivism in philosophy, socialist theories, and finally the aspirations for a religious regeneration. But despite their close relationship, these diverse currents could not co-exist in the same mind and work except by remaining unfinished. Certainly no marked differences among them strike the observer when he views them at a certain distance from their common source; deriving from the same collective state, they can only be different aspects of a similar social conscience. But as each was very complex in itself, they could develop only by dividing. The material was too rich. This is why none of his successors continued his thinking in full but divided it among themselves. Even in Saint-Simon's lifetime, Augustin Thierry first, and then Auguste Comte, had separated from their teacher and had undertaken, one his historical work and the other his philosophic labor, apart from the master and his influence. As for the social and religious theories, after Saint-Simon's death they became the appendage of the school, which, because it consisted mainly of the friends of his last hours, assumed and retained in history the name of the "Saint-Simonian School." We will examine it because, following Saint-Simon, it has played a part that has much interest for our study. But it is important to indicate that it was formed by a kind of dismemberment of the system—and consequently is its successor only in part.

Strictly speaking, Saint-Simon did not leave a school when he died. But he had succeeded in uniting around him a number of faithful friends, of whom the principal ones were Olinde Rodrigues, the jurist Duveyrier, the poet Halévy and the physician Bailly. Rodrigues especially was very active and devoted and set to work immediately and enthusiastically to realize one of the dearest of Saint-Simon's projects: to found a journal of Saint-Simonian propaganda. He applied himself first to recruiting new adherents to the doctrine. In particular, he searched for a group of writers whose talents could serve the cause—and we can note that he was successful. In fact it was he who discovered Bazard, Enfantin, and Buchez. The first two were shortly to become the heads of the school. They founded the *Producteur*, a weekly journal. The tone was Saint-Simonian but it also printed articles of varied inspiration—on technology and industrial statistics. Among the collaborators we find Auguste Comte, who had not yet broken completely with Saint-Simonianism; Armand Carrel, Adolphe Blanqui, Adolphe Garnier, etc. Though such collaboration seemed to promise success, the existence of the *Producteur* was of short duration. Only four volumes and one book of the fifth appeared. Lacking 8,000 francs which it could not secure, the publication was suspended.

One might imagine that this would be a mortal blow to Saint-Simonianism, and in fact the philosophic press of the time declared confidently that the new doctrine was finished. But just the opposite occurred. The *Producteur* had had time to stimulate lively curiosity—and indeed burning sympathies —among its limited but elite circle. The proof is that, although its disappearance dissolved all contact between representatives of the new ideas and readers whose interest had been awakened, the latter—distressed and anxious to be informed more thoroughly about this new doctrine—themselves initiated personal relationships with the former editors. "Truly apostolic correspondence opened up with the initiates." The reason was that at the time a very special state of mind existed among cultivated circles which facilitated the task of the new apostles. They were tired of the present, disgusted with the past, weary of old theories, curious and disturbed about the future. There was a general feeling of confusion along with an intense hope to get out of it. "We were," one of the contemporaries, Hippolyte Carnot, says, "on watch for any philosophic manifestations which seemed to have a religious tendency." The book by Ballanche, a neo-religious writer, was highly esteemed. Moreover, it was the moment (1824) that Jouffroy was writing his famous article, *Comment les dogmes finissent*, "How Dogmas End," in which he shows how religions die in order to come to life again under new forms. This thirst for the new and the unknown on the part of many young men destined to play an important role in the history of the century, such as Hippolyte Carnot, DeLas Cases, the Roulleaux brothers, Dugage, Louis de Montebello, Michel Chevallier, Mantalivet —to cite only the principal ones—led them to enroll in the Order of the Templars, in the vague hope—soon disappointed—of finding in it the doctrine they so strongly felt the need for. In 1821 a group called *Société de Morale chrétienne* was founded, which specifically had as its objective the extrication of Christian morality from its ultramundane and clerical spirit. It had among its members the Duke de Broglie, Casimir and Augustin Thierry, Perrier, Laffitte, Benjamin Constant, Guizot, Lamartine, de Remusat, Montalivet. A state of general hope existed which naturally availed itself of the first system to be established which had some coherency.

This is why the material defeat of the *Producteur* had the effect of heightening curiosity and sympathy—rather than weakening it. When through failure of publication the gospel was prevented from reaching the public, it was the public itself who requested it from those who had been in charge. Direct and personal action replaced the abstract influence of the journal. They wrote, they visited, and "gradually gatherings formed . . . centers of diffusion were established at various points." They met at Enfantin's, Comte's, at Carnot's. (It was at that time that Carnot became affiliated with the school, like Michel Chevalier, Fournel, Barault, the two Pereires, Charloes Dunoyer.) Soon—in 1829—they had to look for larger quarters, and regular verbal instruction began in a hall on Rue Taranne. Bazard undertook a complete exposition of Saint-Simonian theory in a long series of lectures which was very successful and attracted numerous adherents, notably among former and present students of the École Polytechnique.

This instruction at the Rue Taranne was an important event in the history of Saint-Simonianism. For the doctrine we have been speaking of was presented there for the first time in a systematic and integrated form. Instead of the multitude of diffuse writings over which Saint-Simon had spread his thinking, there was finally a synoptic representation of the principal theories in cogent form. But Bazard's role was not reduced to the work of coordination. At the same time that he arranged them in logical order, he changed them at more than one point and so gave the system a new aspect. He made no additions to the principles postulated by the master, but developed them, elucidated them, carried them to their logical conclusions, and at the same time distinguished more radically the purely rationalist and scientific elements, which later served to supply Comte's theories. Since it is in the form that he gave them that Saint-Simonian ideas became general, extended their influence and finally became one of the factors in our intellectual evolution, the lectures at Rue Taranne deserve noting. Besides, that was the moment when the system reached its maturity. In Saint-Simon it had been somewhat in a state of confusion and incomplete organization. Later, when the Enfantin's influence predominated, it became disorganized and entered into decadence. But with Bazard it attained its maximum logical consistency and flowering. Besides, in itself his discussion is most remarkable. In addition to its very fine form—although a little too continuously oratorical—Saint-Simonian thinking is expressed and developed with a fullness which makes its consequences and significance better understood. We will give a brief account of it, emphasizing particularly the innovations it contains, according to the version published in volumes XLI and XLII of the general edition of the work of Saint-Simon and Enfantin.

The method Bazard used should in itself serve notice of a change in the orientation of the system, for the tone became more idealistic and less scientific. Saint-Simon started from the past with the observation of feudal societies, and had demonstrated the need for industrialism, how industrialism, in its turn—and as a condition of existence—required cosmopolitanism, and how, finally, the latter found its success and guaranty in the dogma of universal unity. Thus he went progressively from the past to the future. But it was a reverse process—or nearly so—that Bazard followed. He takes as his point of departure what was for his master the point of arrival, and the whole series of ideas unfolds in inverse order to the one in which they had been logically linked in the mind of their founder. He begins by postulating the fundamental unity of everything, deduces internationalism, and from that, industrial organization. That is to say he has his eyes fixed on the future much more than on the past; he is less concerned with the laws of history than with determining the conditions under which a previously chosen ideal should be realized.

The world is one. Order and harmony are the normal state of all things; discordance and conflict are contrary to nature. This is the axiom from which he starts. By reading him (Bazard) one understands better what Saint-Simon meant in asserting that all the laws of the universe were only particular forms of the laws of gravity. In fact the molecular attraction that gives birth to inorganic bodies, the cellular attraction from which organisms result, the social attraction by which societies are born, are phenomena no different in nature than the attraction of astronomical bodies which the law of gravity expresses. (XLI, 91.) It is also probable that in addition to the logical unity resulting from the reduction of all laws to a single one, Bazard saw in this universal conspiracy of things which tended more and more to approach and meet, a manifestation of the need for unity and equilibrium which he made the fundamental quality of all reality. It is a remarkable fact that this purely cosmic law has so frequently been invoked by theoreticians of socialism as the scientific principle of their doctrine. Fourier had it play a no less important role in his system than did Saint-Simon, but without there being any suspicion that he had borrowed the idea from Saint-Simon. The reason for this peculiarity is that this law is in fact the physical and material reflection of solidarity. It has the additional advantage of connecting this last fact—which in appearance is entirely human—with the rest of nature, and emphasizing its irresistibility, since instead of presenting it as a privilege of our species, it demonstrates its necessity in the biological realm and even, still lower, in the world of minerals. By placing the center of the universe beyond the planet, and consequently beyond man, it inclines us to admit more readily that the center of the social system is found outside the individual.

If this is so, the natural state of humanity is unity, that is, the grouping of all men in the same universal association, the combination of all human forces in only one and the same direction, which as a result could only be peaceful. And in fact if humankind has not yet reached this idea, history shows that this is the goal it tends toward, and approaches more and more. There is a contrary condition that retards unity but which it always dominates more completely and always moves further away from. This is the state of antagonism that separates men instead of uniting them, which arms them against one another instead of making them collaborators in the same work. At the beginning, antagonism is preponderant while association is only rudimentary. "The more one goes back into the past," Bazard says, "the narrower one finds the sphere of association, and therefore the more incomplete the association." (p. 183.) Humanity was then fragmented into many hostile groups among whom war was the chronic state. Then, little by little families united into cities, cities into nations, nations into confederations. The last result of this progressive series is the formation of "the great Catholic alliance" which, at the height of its power, held a notable portion of humanity under the authority of a similar faith. At the same time as the circle of association enlarged, the principle of order, union, harmony, struck deeper roots in the midst of each group. Not only does the field of peaceful relations gain in extent, but the peaceful character of these relations continue to be accentuated. "Conflicting elements within each association are weakened to the degree that several associations unite into one." (190.) When society does not extend beyond the family, struggle is constant between sexes, age groups, between brothers and sisters, seniors and juniors. When the city appears, marriage serves to pacify sexual relations, but then the antagonisms of masters and slaves, plebeians and patricians arise; then both these grow weaker. The patrician and plebeian disappear completely, while the slave system is replaced by the milder antagonism of serf and seigneur, which itself is more and more attenuated. What determines this progressive pacification is the diminishing role of force in social relationships. In the beginning, force is the basis of all social organization; the society involves the subjugation and exploitation of the weaker by the stronger. But more and more this arrangement loses ground, to the degree man perceives that the exploitation of things is more profitable to him than the exploitation of those like himself—that is, to the degree industry appears more productive than war.

"The exploitation of man by man—that is the state of human relations in the past. The exploitation of nature by man associated with man—this is the picture the future offers." (206.)

The end that humanity should and does pursue is therefore not in doubt. It must strive towards a state in which all its members, co-operating harmoniously, unite in order to exploit the globe together. It is all too plain that we are far from this goal. Struggles between peoples are far from extinguished and, within each, what conflicts of every type!

In spite of the progress already realized, there is much more to do before human society can be considered established. Still, as indisputable as this declaration may be, it is of itself insufficient to demonstrate the necessity for an immediate change in civilized societies. In fact it could well be that though still far from the goal, nevertheless they had neither the means nor the desire to approach it more closely. For there are moments in the history of every people when it arrives at the maximum harmony of order and peace it is then capable of. This is what Bazard calls the organic epochs or periods. This is due to the fact that there is a body of doctrines, of common beliefs, sufficiently broad and generally respected to neutralize the effect of the antagonisms and hostilities that persist, to check the dispersive tendencies which result—that is to say, to dominate selfishness and make all individualistic activities converge toward a common end. What characterizes these periods outwardly is the establishment of a dogma recognized by everyone, and under which—in whatever way—are spontaneously grouped the particular theories that are only divisions of it and which assure a unity of minds, and consequently of wills. As an example of an organic epoch, one can cite, in the history of Christian societies, the period extending from the eleventh to about the sixteenth century—that is, almost to the Reformation. In the history of ancient cities, we find the period during which Greco-Latin polity was at its height and which ended at Rome with Augustus, and in Greece with Pericles. From the time that a society has reached the phase of maturity which Bazard calls organic, it is neither desirable nor possible to seek to change it. It is not possible, as it would be necessary to destroy the system of beliefs on which the social order rests, and these beliefs are too alive, too strongly-rooted then to be annihilated in an instant. Nor is it desirable, for one should not overthrow what he cannot replace, and centuries are required to elaborate a new dogma and have it penetrate the mind.

Therefore, if our epoch were organic, one might well strive to evoke new progress but not to demand radical change. But in reality, far from having attained its maximum of stability, it is in ruin. Far from being everything it can be, today it does not even have the beneficent effects it formerly had. The advance of societies toward universal confederacy is not, in fact, an absolute continuity. There are moments when a kind of recoil is produced, when there is less order and harmony than before. These are the critical periods that stand in the way of organic periods. What characterizes them is that the body of ideas that until then rallied minds is, beneath the blow of new forces, disputed and shaken. To the degree this process of destruction advances, antagonisms, being less contained, develop more and more, and anarchy appears. Individual activities, ceasing to be organized in groups, go in divergent or contrary directions, and as a result comes to blows. Selfishness is unleashed for the very reason that the force that held it in check is weakened. "The mark of critical eras, like that of great debacles, is egoism." (113.) And egoism brings war in its train. Another exterior sign by which these periods are recognized is that individual philosophies, personal opinions, hold the position occupied until then by established religions. Without doubt they are far from useless and, if in one sense they constitute a backward movement, in reality they are the indispensable condition of all progress. For, once arrived at the organic period, societies would be immobilized there forever if criticism did not do its work, if it did not examine and reveal the inadequacy of those ideas which, until then, are secure from criticism. It is essential that critics vex the state of equilibrium so that it does not fix itself once for all in the form it happens to have taken at a given moment. But on the other hand, these critical phases—even less than the organic phases—cannot be considered the last stage in evolution. For destruction is death, and death is not a goal for life. One should destroy only to build. Critical periods are therefore useful only insofar as they render new organic periods possible. And, in fact, in the history of antiquity the critical period is the one which began with Socrates, with the great development of Greek philosophy, and ended with the establishment of Christianity. In the history of Christian societies it begins with the Reformation, with the shaking of Christian dogma, and it is not over. On the contrary, everything indicates it has reached its maximum of activity. For never has anarchistic individualism attained such a degree of development. In the intellectual order, everyone has his own system and all these contrary systems struggle unfruitfully with one another. The so-called scholars are sunk, as if in quicksand, in their special studies—which are unrelated—and have lost all feeling of their unity. "They pile up experiences, they dissect the whole of nature . . . they add more or less curious facts to facts previously observed. . . . But who are the scholars who classify and coordinate these treasures heaped in disorder? Where are those who put the ears of corn from this abundant harvest in place? A few sheaves are seen here and there. But they are sparse in the vast field of science, and for more than a century no great theoretical vision has been produced." (91.) In industry the conflict of individualistic interests has become the fundamental rule—in the name of the famous principle of unlimited competition. And finally, the arts no longer express any but anti-social sentiments. "The poet is no longer the divine singer placed at the head of society to serve as interpreter to men, to give him laws, to repress his backward tendencies, to reveal to him the joys of the future. . . . No, the poet no longer finds any but somber chants. Now he arms himself with the whip of satire, his fire is exhaled in bitter words, he unleashes himself against the whole of humanity. . . . Now, with enfeebled voice he sings to it in elegiac verse the charms of solitude; he abandons himself to the emptiness of reveries; he paints the happiness of seclusion. And yet if man, seduced by these sad accents, fled his fellow-creatures, apart from them he would find only despair." (113, 114.) "Let us say it— fine arts no longer have voice when society no longer has love. So that the true artist may be revealed, a chorus is needed to repeat his songs and receive his soul when it pours itself out." (115.) Thus, reorganization of society is not only possible, it is vital. For the work of criticism has reached its last stop—everything is destroyed and must be reconstructed, and since destruction has been caused by the advent of new needs, reconstruction cannot consist of a simple restoration of the ancient edifice. It must be built on new foundations.

This distinction between critical and organic periods was already indicated in Saint-Simon, but it is Bazard who developed it into a distinct theory. And it constitutes an important advance in the philosophy of history. To the philosophers of the eighteenth century, ancient peoples, because they were infinitely distant from what seemed the true goal of human societies, constituted so many monsters, anomalous creatures, whose persistence and generality were consequently explicable only with difficulty. Thus it was said of the institutions of those peoples who most offended the modern ideal, that they had been able to maintain themselves only by artificial means—cunning and violence. On the contrary, Bazard, by perceiving (apart from the ultimate perfection that he allows as the final aim of humanity) relative states of health, with the conditions of equilibrium varying at different moments in history, was not obliged to represent humanity as if it had perpetually lived outside of nature. He could recognize that in the history of each society there were times when it had been all it could be. Moreover, the law so formulated is incontestable—at least on the whole. Everywhere one sees successive systems of beliefs elaborated, reaching a maximum of consistency and authority, only to succumb progressively under criticism. What escaped Bazard is that the further one advances in history, the more one sees the traits of the critical period prolonged into the midst of the organic period. In fact, the more cultivated a people the less does the dogma which unifies it bar free examination. Reflection, criticism, exist next to faith, pierce that very faith without destroying it, and occupy an always larger place in it. So Christianity, even in its organic period, admitted reason more than did Greco-Latin polytheism at its corresponding period, and the Christianity of tomorrow should be still more rationalist than that of today. Saint-Simon, much more than his disciples, considered this rationalism to be increasing under the influence of collective beliefs.

Whatever the process, since we are at the extreme limit

of a critical phase, we must get out of it. And for that we need: 1. To so change secular institutions as to harmonize them with the new needs that developed and destroyed the old system; and 2. To establish a system of common ideas to serve as a moral basis for these institutions. But, what is new about the present needs of humanity is the growth in feelings of sympathy, brotherhood, and solidarity. This makes extremely intolerable to us the last survivals of the old regime—which strength and power preserve—and all remnants of old institutions that allow man to exploit man. We have reached the point when it can no longer satisfy us to seek simple palliatives for the old system, such as those which until now have been the only improvements sought by societies. For now we know the final ideal humanity is aiming at, and as soon as it revealed itself we clung to it and were unable to tear ourselves away. This is why the temporary aims men were once content with are without appeal now and cannot satisfy us. Christianity was the last effort in this progressive revelation of the human ideal. It had taught us to know and love one single humanity, completely unified spiritually, but now we are elevated to the loftier idea of a human solidarity, both spiritual and temporal, both in action and in thought, and as a result we can no longer set ourselves other ends. Undoubtedly such a goal cannot be achieved with one stroke. On the contrary, it is too exalted ever to be entirely attained so there is no need to fear that progress ever arrives at its limit or that human activity lacks material. But what one must do is to have it before his eyes—it, and nothing else that conceals it—to act in terms of it, to strive to represent it in all its wholeness, by rejecting all temporary forces whose hour has passed, and to labor to fit the social organization to it.

To reach this result many reforms would now be required and possible. But there is one which seemed to impress Saint-Simonians more urgently than others. It is the change in the rights of ownership.

In fact the characteristic of property as now constituted is that it is transmissible outside of any social competency, by virtue of the right of inheritance. The result is that some men are born with the privilege of doing nothing, that is, they live at the expense of others. Thus, the exploitation of man remains, in this form, the basis of our social system, for the latter rests entirely on the organization of property. Therefore if this exploitation must disappear, it is also necessary that the institution perpetuating it disappear in its turn. "It is alleged," says Bazard, "that the property owner does not live at the cost of others, for what the worker returns only represents productive services of the instruments lent him." "But," he answers, "it is not a question of knowing whether these services should be recompensed, but to whom this remuneration should revert, and whether by assigning it to the property owner—who has no other claim to it except through the accident of birth—one is not consecrating a privilege of material force. But for the single reason that by birth he is a property owner, a man can exercise over the ordinary workers he has transactions with, a superiority that allows him to impose his wishes and does not differ in nature from that which places the vanquished in the hands of the victor. For the worker—forced to depend for daily food on his labor of the day before—is obliged to accept, at the risk of life, the conditions imposed on him. Moreover, inheritance of wealth implies as its counterpart the inheritance of misery. Thus in society there are men who, by the single fact of their birth, are prevented from developing their faculties—which offends all our sensibilities." (227.)

In conformity with Saint-Simon's method Bazard attempts to demonstrate that this in fact is the path historic evolution spontaneously travels, that of themselves societies have noticeably approached the goal he proposes. In fact, in a general way, "the moral dogma that no man should be stamped with incompetence through birth has for long penetrated the thinking, and political constitutions of our day have expressly sanctioned it." (p. 225.) Well, there is no reason not to extend it to the economic world. The owner has a social function, which is to distribute the instruments workers require to produce. (247.) Why should this function be inherited rather than others? More than that, not only is the right of the capitalist in contradiction with the core of our social system, but it is already losing importance—so strong is the feeling that it should disappear. What made for its importance "is the privilege of levying a premium on the labor of others. But this bonus—represented today by interest and rent—is constantly decreasing. The conditions under which relations between owner or capitalist and workers are regulated are more and more advantageous to the latter—in other words the privilege of living in idleness has become more difficult to acquire and conserve." (p. 235, 236.) So, far from maintaining—with so many theoreticians of socialism—that property rights have steadily become more excessive, thus justifying the claims of the working classes, Bazard, on the contrary, recognizes that the supremacy of capital is constantly diminishing. And in view of this progressive diminution, he concludes that to demand its radical suppression is to propose nothing unsuited to the natural and spontaneous course of societies. For he sees proof in the course of events that this measure is more and more required by the feeling of humanity.

To achieve this result one final change is sufficient. It is necessary "that the State—and no longer the family—inherit accumulated wealth since it constitutes what economists called the basis of production." (p. 236.) There must be a social institution, single and perpetual, which is the repository of all instruments of production and which presides over all material exploitation. (p. 252.) Under these conditions there will actually no longer exist in society any superiorities that do not correspond to greater intellectual and moral capacity. The material strength with which capital arms the owner will be definitely abolished. Moreover economic interest itself, as well as moral feeling, demands this transformation. In order that industrial labor may reach its highest possible degree of perfection, the following are necessary: 1. That instruments of production be allotted proportionately to each branch of industry and each locality; 2. That they be placed in the most capable hands in order to produce all the benefits possible; 3. That production be so organized as to accurately meet the needs of consumption—in other words, in such a way as to minimize the risks of scarcity and glutting. But in the present state of things, who originates this distribution of the instruments of work? It is the capitalists and owners, for such a way as to minimize the risks of scarcity and glutting. But isolated individuals are not in a position adequately to understand men, nor the requirements of industry, nor their means of satisfaction, and hence to properly discharge their functions. Inevitably each sees only a small portion of the social world and does not know what happens beyond. Thus, at the time he is establishing his enterprise, he does not know whether others are not already engaged in answering the need he proposes to fill, and if, as a result, all his trouble and expense run the risk of failure. It is even more difficult for him correctly to assess the extent of these needs; how can he know the importance of the demand in the whole country, or the portion which will come to him? From this come the trials and the blunders that manifest themselves in periodic crises. Finally, what has prepared capitalists for their sensitive function of choosing those most adept in using the instruments of production in the common interest? How could their birth, of itself, place them in the position of correctly judging the value of industrial capacities? And still, since they lend their capital only to those they wish, it is they (finally) who authoritatively designate who should be the functionaries of industry.

Let us transport ourselves now to a world where this triple mission no longer belongs to separate individuals, but to a social institution. The latter, being in contact through its ramifications with all localities and all types of industry, sees all parts of the industrial scene. Thus it can take into account general and particular requirements, can carry hands and equipment where they are needed, and at the same time it is better situated to understand true capabilities and judge them in their relationship to the public interest.

What should this institution consist of?

Bazard, and Saint-Simon before him, were struck by the considerable role played by banking in modern societies.

They saw in it a beginning of the voluntary organization of industrial life. Actually the function of bankers is to serve as intermediary between workers, who need instruments of production, and the owners of these instruments, who do not wish to use them themselves. Thus banks are substituted for capitalists and owners in the job of distributing means of production to producers, and can acquit themselves with much greater competence than separate individuals. Placed at a much more central viewpoint, in contact with various sections of the land and different branches of industry, they can better appreciate the relative extent of the various industrial requirements. They are already public institutions in the sense that they embrace far vaster portions of the economic domain than a simple capitalist could do. At the same time, since it is the very profession of a banker to discover the skills that the funds of production can advantageously be entrusted to, the capital that passes through his hands has much more chance of being placed with those most likely to extract profit from it. One can see that a simple development of the system of banks might furnish the sought-for institution.

The present organization would not do, first, because its centralization is very imperfect. If bankers are in a better position than owners to judge the needs of industry, nevertheless there is no bank which is the center where all industrial operations end up and unite, and which consequently can take hold of the whole and with full awareness regulate the reapportionment of capital. Further, each banker remains a private entrepreneur who has his personal point of view and is concerned with levying the highest possible tithe on the products of labor—just as the owner who turns over his funds to him seeks to obtain the greatest advantage he can. The privilege of inherited capital is therefore not suppressed. To free this institution from its disadvantages and place it definitively on a par with its functions, three measures are necessary and sufficient: 1. Subject all banks to the authority of a centralized managing bank which controls them; 2 Give this bank administration of all production funds; 3. Differentiate the subordinate banks. This is how the system would function; inheritance being abolished, all real and personal wealth would go to the central establishment, which in this way would have at its command all instruments of production. Under the jurisdiction of this bank, there would be banks of a secondary order assigned to special branches of industry. They would spread into each locality through other institutions of the same—but more limited—kind, and so be in direct contact with the workers. Through these channels the former would be aware of the requirements and productive power of industry in its entirety. It would decide, as a result, how capital should be apportioned among the various categories of undertakings; that is, it would open up for each a fixed amount of credit, proportionate to its needs and to society's means. Every special bank then would have the function of distributing among the workers of each category—through the intermediary of the local agencies—the share of credit granted the branch of industry it is charged with managing. Each producer is no more than the manager of the shop or of the instruments he uses. For this he receives a fixed salary, but the revenue of his business does not belong to him. It reverts to the local bank, and through it to the central bank. He has free use of his pay, has full ownership of it, but is accountable for the rest. On his death the capital he has administered is transmitted to the person who seems most worthy, by way of administrative advancement. Thus establishment of a unified system of banks which centralize and distribute the means of production, allocation of the latter to managers who receive compensation in line with their services—such are the foundations of the system conceived by Bazard. Thanks to this well-informed hierarchy, the condition of each individual in society is determined by his capacity, in harmony with the Saint-Simonian axiom: "To each according to his ability, to each ability according to its work."

Undoubtedly, Saint-Simon would have been astonished at the extreme conclusions drawn from his principles; in truth the path taken in only a few years (1825-1828) by the ideas which he first formulated, is surprising. But this exposition of Bazard is interesting in another way. We see a complete plan of economic reorganization whose socialist character is unmistakable. We have just met formulae that foretell those of Marx. We have just been told of the possibility that economic life can be completely centralized.

But it happens that neither in his criticism of the present order, nor in his program of reorganization, does Bazard refer to large-scale industry. He does not rely on its pattern or invoke the special behavior attributed to it, either to justify the changes demanded nor to confirm the practical character of his proposed reforms. These two facts are remarkable, as the organization of large industry—especially its centralized character—was, it would seem, a very natural argument to demonstrate that industrial functions can and should be centralized. And yet he did not make the point. Evidently, then, he did not have this in mind when he raised his voice against the present system, or even when he constructed his own. But this same remark could be made about Saint-Simon. In fact we saw that the only serious economic reform he demanded concerned landed property. He saw no objection to leaving the capital employed in industry, manufacturing, or commerce under the existing order of things. And we may likewise see in Fourier that the concept of large industry is not at all clear. In other words it did not play the part often attributed to it in the genesis of socialism. At the same time, it is certainly a secondary and concurrent factor. These two phenomena developed side by side, rather than having a cause and effect connection. Perhaps it could even be said that both socialism and large industry are the product of the same social state. In any case, we see that if socialism was not established alone, at least it was established first.

*　　　　*　　　　*

We have seen how, according to Bazard, when modern societies reached the extreme limit of their critical period, a profound change in secular institutions was required in order to satisfy new needs that arose. Above all the property system had to be reformed for it, more than any other thing, contributes to antagonism and war by allowing the owner through birth to exploit those of his fellow men who possess nothing. Thus it becomes necessary, through suppression of the right of inheritance, to remove from these privileged persons the material force with which the mere fact of birth arms them, and which assures them unfair superiority. At the same time the function of distributing the instruments of production among producers will no longer be surrendered to private individuals, incompetent and selfish, but be vested in a social institution. But this reform is not the only one sought by Bazard. He proposes others touching education, legislation, courts. But as all these are placed under the jurisdiction of the first, it is not necessary to explain them in detail.

Moreover—whatever the importance of all these measures —they do not have the central position in the work of reorganization. For these civil institutions have authority—without which they could not function normally—only by virtue of the support of the system of common beliefs rooted in the individual conscience. In short, a system of institutions must express a system of ideas. So it is of great importance to strive to establish these ideas, and as long as they are missing, the most skillfully administered civil organization can have only an artificial existence. It is the letter of which the other is the spirit. It is vital that the ideas give birth finally to an institution *sui generis* in which they will be concretely embodied and dominate all else. Thus, without beliefs which inspire it, not only is the body of social institutions without a soul, but it is not even complete. The head is lacking. Therefore the problem that remains to be dealt with is by far the major one. The second volume of the *Exposition* is devoted to its solution.

It can be formulated in this way: Given the new needs and feelings appearing in the human heart, what should be the beliefs which can henceforth serve as a bond among men?

In the first place, they should have a religious character. In fact, what distinguishes organic from critical periods is the religiosity of the former and the irreligiosity of the latter. Humanity has never succeeded in passing from the anarchistic and riotous egoism of the one to the ordered equilibrium of the other except through the establishment of a new doctrine. It is only when a new religion has replaced one which criticism had definitively and properly destroyed that confusion has come to an end and that social forces were again grouped and planned harmoniously. So there is no basis for believing that there is another way for us to escape the present crisis, that some different path exists that men have ignored until now.

Besides, how could this be possible? A people cannot be organized except by synthesizing its concepts. For it is these that determine action and as long as they are uncoordinated there can be no order in movement. A society whose ideas are not systematized in such a way as to make an organic and unified whole is necessarily a prey to anarchy. But in order for the ideas we have of the world to receive this unification, the world must be one—or at least we must believe it is. However, we can conceive of it in this way only if we view it as derived from one and the same principle—which is God. The idea of God is the foundation of all social order, because it is the only logical guarantee of universal order. If irreligion, if atheism, are the characteristic traits of periods of crisis, it is because the disorganized state of ideas in these moments in history has caused all feeling of unity to vanish. When everything seems discordant one has no reason to relate everything to one being. "The idea of God," says Bazard, "is for man merely a way of conceiving unity, order, harmony, of being conscious of a destination and of accounting for it." But "in periods of crises man no longer has either unity, harmony, order, or destination." (XLII, 123.) Inversely then, you cannot pass into an organic phase except by restoring the fundamental idea, which is the condition of all systematization. In other words, religion is nothing other than the expression of the collective thinking peculiar to a people or to humanity. On the other hand, all collective thought necessarily has a religious character.

This thesis clashed with both the rationalist critiques of

the eighteenth century, which still had adherents, and with
the famous law of three stages, which Comte had just formulated in his "positive politics." As for the rationalists, who
tended to see every idea of God as irreconcilable with science, Bazard is easily right. He establishes without difficulty
that science—in order to proceed with explanation—is obliged to postulate order in things, since its only objective
is to seek it, and order without God is unintelligible. The
other objection was more embarrassing, all the more as it
appeared to enjoy the very authority of Saint-Simon. Had
not the master proclaimed that humanity had passed successively from the theological to the metaphysical age, and
finally from the latter to the rule of science, the positive
age? And from then on did it not seem that the era of
religions was ended, unless cilivization turned back?

Bazard extricates himself by an ingenious distinction which,
however, is not without some truth. One speaks of these
three stages, he says, as if they corresponded to three ages
of humanity taken as a whole, and one concludes that men,
having reached the second, can no longer return to the
first, nor to the second once they have attained the third,
the same as an individual—once adult—cannot proceed towards infancy, nor from maturity to youth. But actually this
law expresses only the series of transitions through which a
specific people passes from the organic to the critical phase.
The theological age is the period of equilibrium; the positive
age, the age of disintegration; the metaphysical age is intermediate, when dogma begins to waver. But one knows that
the cycle formed by these periods recommences all the time,
that new organic states succeed critical states. So it is false
to say that religious beliefs are no more than remnants of
a past destined to disappear. The truth is that they alter-
nately die and are reborn, without anyone having the right
to fix an end to these series that so succeed each other.
Auguste Comte's law correctly describes the way modern
societies have developed from the tenth to the nineteenth
century—but it does not at all apply to the entire course
of human evolution. That is why it could not be used to
foretell the future. But just as the theological age—repre-

sented by the societies of the Middle Ages—followed the epoch of atheism—to which the fall of the ancient cities corresponds—so it may be assumed that the irreligiosity of the present does not constitute the last term in history.

These alternations are in truth incontestable and are therefore a very strong objection to Comte's theory. But it did not satisfy Bazard—and it could not—to have demonstrated that religion is subject to rebirth. He still had to show that on each return, far from losing ground, it gains it; otherwise his fundamental thesis could not be regarded as established. Since, according to him, humanity tends toward a more perfect state of harmony and peace, and since on the other hand social harmony develops like religion—which is its basis—collective organization as it becomes more harmonious also becomes more impregnated with religiosity, and as a result societies become more and more religious. Does history confirm this hypothesis? Bazard attempts to prove it but his argument on this point is very weak. He is content to distinguish three phases in religious evolution: fetishism, polytheism, monotheism, and to show that in each, religion is practiced by the broadest societies. Under fetishism the cult is confined to the family, with polytheism it becomes an institution of the city, while in Christian monotheism it extends to the whole of humanity. From this he concludes—not without sophistry—that the social character of religion always becomes more evident. But how did he not see that the social importance of religion is not in the number of individuals adhering to it but in the number of institutions of which it is the foundation and which it marks with its imprint? So a miniscule society can be more thoroughly religious than an immense association, since it can very well be that every detail of social relationships in the small society is regulated by religion while in the great nation, on the contrary, there is very little of it. It matters little that all humanity has the same faith. This faith will have merely a secondary social role if it does not extend beyond one small segment of collective life, if the latter is in major part secular. But in fact, as one advances in history, from inferior societies to the city, from the city to

Christian peoples, one observes consistently that religion withdraws more and more from public life. If, then, it is true that until now it was regenerated after every period of decline, it must be added that at each rebirth it has always lost importance as a social institution. So history is far from favorable to Bazard's proposition, far from showing a constant parallel between the advance of religiosity and the progress of collective harmony. As a result it does not authorize us to expect in the future a social system more essentially religious than those of the past.

But let us assume this proposition to be demonstrated. The conclusion is that the peaceful society towards which we should and do strive will only be possible if a new religion is founded. On the other hand, as each stage of progress is and can be merely the perfecting of the preceding one, this new religion itself could not be other than a perfected Christianity. What then are the changes Christian religion must undergo to be equal to the mission that must fall to it in the future?

The great error of Christianity is to have hurled anathema on matter and everything material. Not only did the Church place the physical outside of religion, not only did it refuse it any sacred nature, but it went so far as make it the very principle of evil. Certainly it asumes that through original sin man had fallen both in body and soul, but in the elaboration of its dogma it left the downfall of the spirit in shadow in order to highlight—almost exclusively—that of the flesh, which ended by being considered the unique source of sin. Thus, most of its moral tenets have as their objective the repression of materials needs and everything related to them. It sanctifies marriage, but regards it as an inferior state and prescribes abstinence and mortification. But what best indicates this aversion for anything physical is that the Christian God is conceived as pure spirit. The result was that all modes of secular activity developed outside the Church and its influence. Industry has always remained foreign to it—it even removed all reason for its existence by placing poverty and physical privation foremost among virtues. And if it likened work to prayer it is simply because it regarded work as penitence, as expiation. Also, although science had its birth in monasteries, it remained stationary while there and only started to develop when it freed itself from this milieu—which was not its own—and became secularized. And finally, art—as far as it expresses life—has always been treated as suspect and even as an enemy by representatives of Christian thought. These social forces, organized outside of the Church and its law, turned quite naturally against it once they became mature. And precisely because they had developed in spite of dogma, as they acquired importance they revolted against this dogma which had renounced them, and in turn renounced it. Because by scorning the world the Church had abandoned it, the world gradually escaped the Church and ended up rebelling against it. But in a struggle such as this the Church could not but be defeated since all the human civilization it had cast from its bosom was against it. In this way the antagonism between the secular and religious order brought on the ruin of the latter.

For the new religion to be exempt from this constitutional vice and be sure of the future, it is indispensable that in principle it renounce this duality and this exclusiveness, that it extend itself to all reality, that it consecrate equally the material and the spiritual, the physical and the intellectual. In a word, it must make this world its domain. "The most striking, the most novel . . . aspect of the general progress humanity is called upon to make today consists of the rehabilitation of matter." (282.) Instead of proscribing the research of scholars, the enterprises of industry, the work of artists, instead of according them at most a disdainful tolerance, it must declare they are holy things, pious works, and make them the very substance of cult and faith. Only on this condition can it escape the duel in which—as Christianity—it will sooner or later succumb. Moreover, by proclaiming this homogeneity of all things, it will merely be conforming to the fundamental principle of unity and universal harmony, and because Christian antinomy was a violation of it, it is only by changing that Christianity can maintain itself.

There is only one way of rehabilitating matter—have it re-enter God Himself. (p. 301.) So that all things may have the same value, either everything or nothing must be divine. The second hypothesis discarded—since it is the negation of all religion—the first remains. But for all beings to equally share in the divine, God must be in everything. This in effect is the conception Bazard arrives at and which gives us the following definition of God: "God is one. God is all that is; everything is in Him. God, the infinite universal Being, expressed in His living and active unity, is infinite love, which manifests itself to us in two main aspects, as spirit and as matter, or—what is merely another expression of this double view—as intelligence and force, as wisdom and beauty." (293-294.) So the seeds of pantheism we found before in Saint-Simon have now arrived at their full development. It is true that Bazard did not accept the label of pantheist without reticence, but that was for reasons of tact. It was to avoid confusing the new concept with old doctrines discredited elsewhere. But he recognized that "if the word had no meaning other than that of its etymology" there would be "no reason to reject it." And he added, "To consider only abstractly the religious progress of man toward unity, and allowing for the new progress we are indicating, one might properly say that the general terms it compromises are polytheism, monotheism, and pantheism." (306.)

Serious practical consequences grow out of these abstract and philosophical speculations. If religion extends to everything, then everything in society must rise from religion. It is not for society to determine. "Every political order is, before all else, a religious order." (299.) This proposition does not indicate that society should be subordinated to religion, that it should pursue transcendental ends, foreign to its secular aims. Such subordination is impossible since, in the doctrine, religion has no sway outside the spiritual order. Bazard merely understands it to mean that everything social is religious for that reason, and inversely, that theological and political matters are identical "and present, strictly speaking, only two different facades on which facts of the same nature can be envisaged" (298), just as God and the world are only two aspects of a single and identical reality. Since science is the study of the universe, it is the understanding of God, and can perhaps be called theology. Since industry's purpose is to act upon the world, through it man enters into an exterior and material relationship with God. It becomes religion. It also follows that, just as God is the highest expression of the world, the representative of God —the priest—should be the highest agent of the social order. This, according to Bazard, is substantially how the preceding principles should be translated into the political system.

As no function in society is more vital than insuring unity, and since the idea of God alone must serve as the nub of the social system, the priest will be in the best position to so direct the common life as to hold the deepest feeling of God. "It follows that the heads of society can be none other than the repositories of religion, and can only be priests." (335.) To them will belong the task of making all individual activities converge toward one end; it is the sacerdotal group which will serve as a link between men and social functions. Every detail of its duties will flow from this. Since there are two major social functions, science and industry, theory and practice, the priest will have to— above everything—link industry and science in general and watch over their harmonious development so that theory concerns itself with practical requirements and practice understands its need of theory. This will be the role of the most eminent priest in the hierarchy.

In their turn, science on the one hand and industry on the other embrace an infinity of separate branches. Science resolves itself into a multitude of special studies, industry into a plurality of different enterprises. To make these particular pieces of work, whether of a scientific or intellectual order, proceed in agreement, other intermediaries will be required. This task will go to other priests, lower and subordinated to the first. Some will have the various sciences cooperate so as to make use of one another, exchanging services, constantly feeling their relationship, in order that the unity of intellectual work may be maintained. Others will do the same for the various kinds of industry so that each may have its proper degree of development and all will aim at the same goal. In short, all religion will lend itself to perpetually recalling workers to a feeling of their unity. To fulfill this task priests will be chosen from among the most compassionate of men, for sympathy is the unifying faculty *par excellence*. It is the most capable of joining one to another, the most able to unite the largest possible number in a like feeling of love, since its spirit embraces a greater part of the universe and is therefore closest to God.

Thus it was quite correct to say that this social system cannot be understood without the religious system, which gives it unity since it is the sacerdotal function that dominates and unifies all others. It is through the priest that industry and science are united and co-operate; it is the priest who shows the place suitable for each, that is to say, who distributes tasks according to capacity and compensates capacities according to accomplishment. Only in taking a theocratic form does industrial society find equilibrium.

At first such a concept seems very remote from those we found in Saint-Simon. Thus it has been said that the Saint-Simonian school had more affinity with the theories of Joseph de Maistre than with those of the liberal school. (Janet, III.) But this is to misunderstand the original character of this theocracy that has as its main purpose the development of science and industrial affairs. It is to forget that its *raison d'être* is not to confine temporal interests, but to sanction them. While religious, its aims are exclusively earthly—like those of the old literal rationalism. Actually, Bazard's doctrine contains no other ideas than his master's. Only, these ideas are magnified, which permits them to be better understood and, even more, it makes their fundamental defect more noticeable. This theocratic organization, which in one sense seems artificially superimposed on the industrial socialism of Saint-Simon, shows, on the contrary and with greater evidence, its exact character at the same time that it conspicuously exposes its inadequacy.

As a matter of fact we know that Saint-Simon's error consisted in wishing to construct a stable society on a purely economic foundation. As he began by postulating in principle that there are only industrial interests, he was obliged to grant that they could be balanced through skillful management, but without the intervention of any factor of a different nature. It was sufficient to organize industry in such a way that, by producing as much as possible, it could satisfy the various requirements as completely as possible. But we have seen that such an undertaking is unrealizable. For it assumes that men's desires can be satisfied by a certain quantity of comfort, that in themselves they have a limit and are appeased once it is reached. But in reality all needs exceeding simple physical necessities are unlimited, for there is nothing within the organism that imposes a boundary. Therefore in order for them not to be without end—that is, so that they are not forever unsatisfied—there must be forces outside of the individual, in society, which hold them in check, and—with authority acknowledged by all—indicate what is the proper standard. And in order to thus contain and regulate economic forces, forces of another nature are required. It is indispensable that there exist in society powers other than those deriving from industrial capacity. These are moral forces. We saw elsewhere that Saint-Simon, toward the end of his life, had become aware of the inadequacy of his system on this point and had accentuated its religious character. The considerable development of religion in Bazard's system demonstrates that the School understood more and more the need to complete purely industrial organization by another which would rise above it. Actually, one of the functions of religion has always been to place a rein on economic appetites. We just noted that with Bazard, the priest, elevated far above the professional councils which Saint-Simon made the supreme power of society, has become the sovereign regulator of all economic life. So it might appear that the indicated lack is now supplied. But in reality, precisely because this very religion has a strictly economic base, we will see that it is purely nominal and in no position to fulfill the role it was to be assigned, that this system is theocratic only in appearance and that, if Bazard succeeded in giving the industrial doctrine a mystical varnish, he did not add the ingredient that is wanting. Industrialism cannot go beyond itself—however it may need to.

What, in fact, is this religion? It has science for theology and industry for creed, according to Bazard's statements. And since science has no reason to exist except if useful to industry, it is the latter, finally, which constitutes the highest aim of society. Thus, ultimately, men have no other end but to prosper industrially, and the priest's role is reduced to having the various scientific and industrial function cooperate so as to assure this prosperity. In all this, where is the bridle that curbs passions? Everywhere one merely sees direct or indirect economic interests without seeing how from any one of them a force would evolve which dominates them. Will it be said that an idea of God exists, and that the priest is invested with an authority *sui generis* which puts him above producers of all kinds, because he is nearer than they to divinity, because he embodies it to a higher degree? But this is to forget that God in this system is the world, that it is a simple name given to the totality of reality. Consequently, to conceive God more nobly than does the mass is simply to understand the world, to grasp better its unity in the diversity and relationships of things, thanks to a more developed awareness. So the priest is not stamped with any unusual character that places him above others; he is nothing more than a cultivated person, a finer intelligence endowed with a broader sympathy. The supreme high priest of such a religion is the worker in the best position—through his understanding of men and things—to advance public interest and the studies needed for it. This is why one could very justly call him the pope of industry. If Christianity has been able to fulfill its social role, it is because—quite the reverse of Saint-Simonian theology—it set God beyond things. Ever since then, there has been a moral force—illusory or not is of no moment—outside of and above men, their desires, their interests—a force, consequently, capable of controlling them, at least through the mediation of those regarded as accredited representatives—that is, priests. But if God is one with the world, and as we dominate the world as much as it dominates us, and since of itself it is not a moral force, we are thus on a par with divinity—so the indispensable dicipline cannot come from there. If, as Christian dogma asserts, material concerns are inferior to spiritual and should be subordinated to them, then the former find a very natural check in the latter. But if they are on the same level, if they have the same value and there are no others, how could any control be established that could be imposed either on one or the other? Any regulating authority is rendered impossible by such leveling.

Undoubtedly Bazard did not sense this difficulty because for him the origin of social conflicts is principally in the unfair distribution of functions and products, so that the position of individuals has no relation to their capacity. Consequently harmony would be assured as soon as a regime were established which would classify workers exactly according to their value and compensate them according to their services. But he is of the opinion that the priest-group—recruited according to the rules he has set—would be in a position to proceed to this classification and apportionment as well as could be done. Obviously, however, we must acknowledge that objections are easy. One must be able to dry up the source of struggle and discontent. For the very principle invoked to demand this reform will just as quickly and properly be invoked on behalf of others that are actually implied. You start in fact with the idea that it is neither good nor just that individuals have superiority by birth. Yet intelligence, taste, scientific, artistic, literary, industrial worth —are they not also aptitudes which each of us receive through birth and which in great measure we are not the cause of, just as the property owner is not the creator of the capital he received at birth? Thus the proposition that inherited prerogatives should be suppressed has a corollary, which is that everyone should be rewarded in the same manner, that sharing should be equal and independent of worth. He does not assume, for his argument, that this would affect actively or passively the inherent dispositions of individuals, whether good or bad. The tendency exists right now. It inclines us more and more to lighten the hardship we inflict on criminals. This conscious indulgence is but an application of the principle in whose name Bazard demands the suppression of inheritance. So if social war is really caused by the existence of congenital inequalities, peace cannot be re-established except by virtue of a strictly equalitarian and communist organization. Will one go as far as this extreme conclusion? You strike real difficulties; social life could not exist if there were no premium on capability. Would you limit the application of this moral principle in the name of its collective advantage? Or refuse to extend it to the innate aptitudes of individuals so as not to injure social interests too seriously? But then is it so certain that inheritance itself also cannot be defended for the same reason? Is it certain that hereditary transmission of wealth is without economic advantages; if it were, would it be maintained so generally? If the family inherits, then instruments of work surely do not go to the most capable; but if it is the State, what waste! From a purely economic point of view it is difficult to strike a balance.

Besides, when, contrary to moral principle, an institution defends itself only for utilitarian reasons, it is condemned and cannot long endure. It is not by considerations of this kind that one will ever be able to halt and limit the aspirations of the public conscience—for these calculations have no influence on it. Thus, if it is admitted that the most essential thing is to refuse all social sanction to hereditary inequalities, that this should be the basis of social reorganization, then needs are unleashed which cannot be satisfied and new dissatisfactions created at the very moment when everything was believed pacified. We do not intend, however, to draw the conclusion that there is no need to mitigate the effects of these inequalities. On the contrary, it is clear that feelings of human sympathy—which are always becoming deeper—push us toward alleviating the results of this unequal apportioning of gifts and things in their most grievous and shocking aspects. We even consider it certain that this aspiration for a more just and generous morality will progessively affect the right of inheritance. But I say that such a principle cannot serve as the basis for a social system and can have only a secondary influence on the organization of society. It cannot be its foundation because in itself it is not a principle of order and peace. It does not carry with it the moderate contentment with fortune which is the condition of social stability. Assuredly it has its significance, which keeps on growing, but if it can and if it should minutely correct and mitigate the force of social institutions, then it could not be the basis on which they rest. This basis should be sought elsewhere, in the establishment of moral powers capable of disciplining individuals.

Bazard's system thus confirms the criticism we directed at Saint-Simon's and better demonstrates its generality. It is a very forceful attempt on the part of industrialism to succeed in rising above itself—but it will be aborted. For when one starts with the maxim that there are none but economic interests, one is their prisoner and cannot rise above them. Bazard tried in vain to subject them to a dogma which dominates them. But this dogma merely expresses them in another tongue. It is only another aspect of its subject. For the one religion possible in such a doctrine is a materialist pantheism, since the physical and the spiritual must be placed on the same plane. The God of this pantheism was only another name for the universe and could not constitute a moral power whose purpose man may recognize. Even in developing the religious character of industrialism, Bazard only makes its shortcomings and dangers more conspicuous. For in Saint-Simon's system, a rationalist appeal gave it an air of correctness that concealed the consequences it implied. But when passions are overtly sanctioned, how can there be a question of limiting them? If they are hallowed they should be permitted to exist. So the only incentive Bazard appeals to is love, which according to him, is increasingly acquiring a leading position. It is the spontaneity of love that ought to take the place of authority. Likewise, when matter and material needs are defied, what right is there to impose a curb or law upon them? In impregnating industrial life with religiosity, Bazard put nothing above it—on the contrary, he has placed it above everything. He has strengthened industrialism instead of subordinating it. Such a doctrine could only end in a mystical sensualism, in an apotheosis of comfort, in the sanction of excess. In fact this is what happened and what destroyed it. Its history, starting with this period, is an experimental verification of the preceding discussion.

However, these results did not manifest themselves immediately. Bazard's rigid logic was enough, for some time, to prevent these germs of disorder and decomposition from developing. The period immediately following the instruction at the Rue Taranne marks the apogee of success of the school. Two journals were founded in succession to spread Saint-Simonian ideas; the *Globe* and the *Producteur* (1831). A lively burst of proselytism ensued. This period marks the initiation of Clapeyron, of Bureau, Minister of Finance under Napoleon III, of Adolphe Jullien, since Director of the P.-L.-M., of Avril, Director of the École des Pons et Chaussées, of Lambert, later called Lambert-bey. Whole families were drawn in, such as the Rodrigues, Péreires, Gueroults, the Chevalliers, Fournel, Director of Creusot and his wife, Charles Lemonnier and his wife, Jules Renouvier, the brother of Charton, the historian, the d'Eichthal family, LaMoricière who brought along several of his army colleagues, etc. But the movement was not confined to cultivated groups. "The abundance of converts," H. Carnot says, "men and women of every class and profession—was so considerable that in France they could be numbered in the thousands. It was no longer a school—it was a population, devoted to its government." Indeed the school had given itself an official organization. It had assumed the name of "sacred college" and recognized as heads—that is, as supreme high-priests—Bazard and Enfantin. When the initiated became too numerous, preparatory schools of second and third grade, on the order of seminaries, were established, forming a kind of nursery from which the sacred college was recruited. Its seat was set up in a house on Rue de Monsigny. Bazard and Enfantin lived there. Saint-Simonians from abroad very often took their meals there. Soirées were held and the salons much sought after, especially by scholars and artists, such as Liszt, Adolphe Nourrit, Dr. Guépin, E. Souvestre, Félicien David, Raymond Bonheur. Later, propaganda and instruction centers multiplied in Paris and all of France.

But in spite of this brilliant exterior the school was approaching its decline. If Bazard—a cool and moderate intellect—resisted the germs of sensualist mysticism that we observed in the system, on the contrary Enfantin, a tumultuous and impassioned genius, relying more on heart than mind—

had little inclination to share this leaning. Differences ensued which ended by breaking out into the open. The schism came over the question of women and marriage. Bazard, along with the rest of the school, demanded that women be treated as the equal of man in marriage. But Enfantin went much further and his theory was hardly more than a sanction of free love—almost of sacred prostitution. He granted that marriage is the state best suited to men and women of constant and faithful temperament but held that other dispositions, because of their instability, are resistant to it. Therefore it is important to accommodate conjugal society— or as Enfantin puts it, the religion of love—to the needs of that group by giving it the necessary flexibility and mobility. Since God endowed certain beings with inconstancy as a boon, why not make use of it? It will be profitably employed by authorizing these volatile hearts to change their conjugal situation at will. So the absence of regulation in the foundation of the doctrine produced the expected results. When Enfantin dared express these ideas for the first time, there was a great stir in the sacred college. Discussions —so emotional they were beyond belief—were pursued for days on end. Minds were so over-stimulated that frenzied spells occurred among those present. At the end of these intellectual battles, Bazard's mind was injured. In one controversy he was struck with a cerebral congestion. When he recovered he separated from Enfantin and the break in ranks began.

Enfantin remained at the head of the institution on Rue Monsigny, and under his influence the Saint-Simonian creed fell into increasing disorder. "The body was solemnly reinstated; work was hallowed, food was hallowed, voluptuous appetites were hallowed. . . . The winter of 1832 was one long celebration on Rue Monsigny. Religion was crowned with roses; it appeared in the aroma of punch and in noisy harmonies of the orchestra . . . At these gatherings a number of young, elegant women appeared . . . who danced for the sake of dancing . . . without perceiving the religious side of these dances and pleasures." (Reybaud, *Et s.l. Réformateurs*, 107.) Expenditures like these brought financial trouble. At the same time the police forbade the continuation of Saint-Simonian instruction on Rue Taitbout. Differences arose between Enfantin and Olinde Rodrigues who accused him of religious promiscuity and parted company with him. Through lack of funds the *Globe* stopped appearing and finally Enfantin was obliged to abandon the house on Rue Monsigny. He set himself up at Ménilmontant in an estate he owned. That was the end. It is needless to relate the final convulsions of the school, which have a bearing on anecdotal history, but not on the history of thought. A lawsuit instituted against Enfantin in 1832 ended in his being sentenced to prison. That was the signal for the final dispersion. But Saint-Simonian ideas did not die so quickly. They had made a deep impression on these generations and for a long time continued to challenge minds. Discriminating, distinguished men who had been adherents of Saint-Simonianism brought the ideas to the various professions they represented and only very slowly did they come to mistrust them. And their influence would probably have been still more lasting if not for the ridicule that Enfantin's sect brought upon itself and which discredited the whole movement.

Chapter 12

Conclusions

WE HAVE LINGERED for a long time over the study of Saint-Simonianism The reason is that aside from the fact that there are few doctrines richer in fertile observations, the school in certain respects has a very immediate interest. Its study is valuable for a better comprehension of the circumstances we find ourselves in today. In fact there are striking analogies between the period we have just been studying and the one in which we now live. From an intellectual point of view what characterizes the former is that the three following ideas were simultaneously produced: 1. The idea of extending to social sciences the method of the positive sciences (out of which sociology has come) and the historical method (an indispensable auxiliary of sociology); 2. The idea of a religious regeneration; and, 3. The socialist idea. There is no question that in about ten years [written in 1896], we have seen these three currents reform themselves simultaneously and assume more and more intensity. The sociological idea, which had been neglected to the point that the world itself was unrecognized, once more spread with extreme rapidity; a neo-religious school was founded and, however vague its concepts, one cannot deny that it is gaining more ground than it is losing; and the progress made in these last years by socialist thought is well-known. When these three currents are viewed from the outside they seem to repel one another, and those most actively involved only see antagonism among them. The religious movement is presented as a protest against the ambitions of practical science; the socialist movement—because it carries with it more or less definite solution of the social problems that concern us—cannot accept sociology unless it becomes subordinate and renounces itself, that is, as an independent science. It would therefore seem that there is only contradiction and opposition in these different tendencies of contemporary thought. Here the retrospective study we just made becomes instructive.

The fact that twice in the course of the century these tendencies were spontaneously produced and developed cannot be due to a simple accident—especially since all of them uniformly disappeared from about 1848 to 1870. So there must be connections between them that are not readily perceived. This hypothesis is further confirmed by the connected state in which we saw them at the core of Saint-Simon's system. We begin to wonder whether these theses appear and are regarded as contradictory simply because each expresses only one aspect of social reality, and, unaware of its fragmentary nature, believes itself the only one—and is consequently irreconcilable with any other. Actually what does the development of sociology signify? How does it happen that we experience the need to reflect on social matters, if not because our social state is abnormal, because the unsettled collective organization no longer functions with the authority of instinct—for that is always what determines the rousing of scientific thought and its extension to a new order of things. And on the other hand, what do the neo-religious and socialist movements indicate? It is that if science is a means, it is not an end, and as the goal to be achieved is distant, science cannot reach it except slowly and laboriously, whereas emotional and zealous beings attempt to lay hold of it instantly. Without waiting for scholars to sufficiently advance their research, they undertake to discover the remedy by instinct, and nothing would be more natural than to convert this method into a unique procedure and exaggerate its importance by denying science. Besides, the latter has much to learn from this two-sided movement which expresses two different aspects of our present state, one considering things from a moral view, the other, in their economic aspect. What gives strength to the first movement is the feeling that we must believe in an authority which controls passions, makes egoism bend to its domination, and which will require a religion—without its being seen just how it can be constituted. And what gives power to the second is that the condition of moral disorder has economic results which it places in relief. For if the objective causes of suffering are not more severe than formerly, the moral state makes individuals more aware and consequently more impatient with them. No longer curbed, needs are more urgent and increasing exigencies do not permit man to be satisfied with his former lot. There is no longer any reason to accept it, submit to it, or resign himself to it. Our conclusion therefore is that if you wish to have all these practical theories (which have not advanced much since the beginning of the century) go forward a step, you must force yourself habitually to take account of their different tendencies and discover their unity. That is what Saint-Simon attempted. His undertaking must be renewed and in the same direction. His history can serve to show us the way. What caused the failure of Saint-Simonianism is that Saint-Simon and his disciples wanted to get the most from the least, the superior from the inferior, moral rule from economic matter. This is impossible. The problem must be put this way: to discover through science the moral restraint which can regulate economic life, and by this regulation control selfishness and thus gratify needs.

In summing up we can say that the [opposition of all these schools] . . . stems from this two-fold cause: the effort of some to regulate, and of others to free, economic life. These diverse currents are united in their search for the element that is the cause of disturbance. For economists and Saint-Simonians, the trouble comes from the fact that the [pure in spirit?] are not [understood by all?] and the remedy can consist only in organizing economic life in and by itself —some believing this organization can be spontaneously established, others that it should more and more be consciously directed. With regard to this solution, there is another which consists of finding, through rational processes, moral forces which can be [superimposed?] on those that are not. In addition to the various paths on which we [expend] our energies, there is another that can be tried. It is sufficient to have indicated it.[1]

[1] The entire end of the course is scarcely legible. We have not attempted to reconstruct it completely; we indicate by dots what we could not decipher and what is doubtful by brackets. It is clear that Durkheim was alluding to his theory of the professional group, conjointly inspired by social science and socialism, and laying the foundation for a system of morality.—M.M.)

Bibliographical Note

The relevant literature is enormous and I will suggest only a few of the more interesting materials available in English.

Concerning Durkheim: the footnotes to the preceding introduction indicate his major works. One can profit also from Harry Alpert's, *Emile Durkheim and his Sociology*, Columbia University Press, 1939, which, among other things, contains the most complete biography of Durkheim in English. See, also, Alpert's, "France's First University Course in Sociology," *American Sociological Review*, June, 1937, and Robert Marjolin, "French Sociology, Comte and Durkheim," *American Journal of Sociology*, March, 1937. Despite my occasional disagreements with it, by far the most profound analytic treatment of Durkheim's sociology is to be found in Talcott Parsons, *The Structure of Social Action*, McGraw-Hill Co., 1937.

Concerning Saint-Simon and Early French Positivism: In the following text, Durkheim himself indicates Saint-Simon's original works. Publishers may take note that there are few translations of Saint-Simon's work in English. A recent translation of sections of Saint-Simon's writings, along with a first-rate summary of his ideas, is to be found in F. M. H. Markham, *Henri Comte de Saint-Simon: Selected Writings*, Basil Blackwell, 1952. To my mind, the best biography of Saint-Simon is Frank E. Manuel, *The New World of Henri Saint-Simon*, Harvard University Press, 1956. The biography by Mathurin Dondo, *The French Faust: Henri de Saint-Simon*, Philosophical Library, 1955, provides useful supplementary material, especially on the disciples. A. J. Booth's *Saint-Simon and Saint-Simonism*, Longmans, Green, Reader, and Dyer, 1871, is still enlightening both as a summary of Saint-Simon's major writings and for study of the social circle which succeeded him. There are few better summary statements of Saint-Simon's work than that to be found in that classic of French scholarship by Charles Gide and

Charles Rist, *A History of Economic Doctrines*, tr, R. Richards, D. C. Heath and Co., ed. of 1913. Two recent works, both deeply hostile, and to my mind often erroneously so, are those by Hayek and Salomon. Hayek's study is commendable for the sociological penetration of its analysis of the institutional sources of Saint-Simonism, as well as for his cogent history of the reverberating consequences which this school had on European history. See, F. A. Hayek, *The Counter-Revolution of Science*, Free Press, 1952, and Albert Salomon, *The Tyranny of Progress*, Noonday Press, 1955.

For a lively account of French politics and the political thought of this period see Roger Saltau, *French Political Thought in the 19th Century*, Ernest Benn, Ltd., 1931. For a careful historical study of the diffusion of Saint-Simonian ideas to Germany see, E. M. Butler, *The Saint-Simonian Religion in Germany*, Cambridge University Press, 1926. Valuable historical analyses by American sociologists may be found in Robert A. Nisbet, "Conservation and Sociology," *American Journal of Sociology*, Sept., 1952, and R. A. Nisbet, "De Bonald and the Concept of the Group," *Journal of the History of Ideas*, June, 1944, and, Frank E. Hartung, "The Social Function of Positivism," *Philosophy of Science*, April, 1945.

34114